Negro Mecca

NEGRO MECCA

A HISTORY OF THE NEGRO
IN NEW YORK CITY, 1865–1920

by SETH M. SCHEINER

NEW YORK UNIVERSITY PRESS 1965

The author wishes to thank Harper & Row, Publishers for permission to quote from Gunnar Myrdal, *An American Dilemma: The Negro Problem and Modern Democracy,* © 1940, 1962 by Harper & Row, Publishers; Holt, Rinehart and Winston, Inc., for permission to quote from Charles S. Johnson, *The Negro in American Civilization,* © 1930, 1958 by Holt, Rinehart and Winston, Inc.; Mrs. James Weldon Johnson for permission to quote from James Weldon Johnson, *Black Manhattan,* © 1930 by James Weldon Johnson; and Twayne Publishers, Inc., for permission to quote from the *Selected Poems of Claude McKay,* © 1953 by Twayne Publishers, Inc.

To ELAYNE

Preface

IN THE 1960s American whites have become increasingly aware of the Negro's existence, if not his plight. Their knowledge of the Negro world, however, has too often been drawn from limited contacts with the Negro or from reading works that look at the Negro only in relation to white society. Through an exhaustive examination of the social, economic, and political life of the Negro of New York City, this work will attempt to fill this void. For a complete picture of the American Negro, and the New York Negro in particular, can only be achieved by studying the institutions and thought of the Negro community as well as the relations between Negroes and whites.

In the course of doing research for and writing this work I have accumulated many scholarly debts. My research was facilitated by the staffs of the New York Historical Society, the Library of Congress, the New York Public Library, and the New York University Library. To Ernest Kaiser, Mrs. Jean Blackwell Hutson, and other members of the staff of the Schomburg Collection, I wish to express the gratitude that every historian owes to dedicated and patient librarians.

I am especially indebted to Professor Bayrd Still of New York

University. His discerning suggestions and meticulous reading of major portions of the manuscript at various stages of its development was of invaluable assistance. Professors James A. Barnes and S. M. Chiu, both of Temple University, found time in their busy schedules to make many helpful suggestions. A summer research grant from Temple University made possible the early completion of this work. I also wish to thank *New York History* and the *Negro History Bulletin,* published by the Association for the Study of Negro Life and History, Inc., for permission to reprint in chapters one and seven material that appeared in somewhat different form in the pages of those journals.

My deepest debt of gratitude goes to my wife. Her critical reading of the manuscript prevented many errors and her moral support assured its completion.

Contents

Contents

Introduction

FROM SLAVE TO FREEDMAN, 1626–1827

In 1623 Dutch settlers established their short-lived colony on Manhattan Island. Three years after these pioneers arrived in what they called New Amsterdam, the Dutch West India Company transported 11 Negro men to the settlement. These men were joined by three Negro women in 1628. In the next twenty-seven years fewer than 100 Negroes arrived in New Amsterdam. Although some of the Dutch settlers, like Peter Stuyvesant, wanted the Dutch West India Company to supply the colony with additional Negro laborers, others opposed any increase in the Negro population. But the demand for Negro labor increased when the settlement assumed more of an agricultural nature in 1655. In the next nine years some 600 Negroes were brought to New Amsterdam by the Dutch West India Company and sold at public auction. This was a departure from the Company's previous policy, for in the past it had retained ownership of the slaves while renting their services to interested New Amsterdam settlers. As a result of this somewhat wider use of slaves, there were approximately 700 in New Amsterdam when Peter Stuyvesant surrendered to the English in 1664.[1]

1

The English not only changed the name of the colony from New Amsterdam to New York, but they altered the status of the Negro slave. In time they were to prove harsher masters than their Dutch predecessors. Under the Dutch, the Negro slave was closer in status to an indentured servant than a slave. He could marry, own property, and, in some cases, obtain his freedom — in 1644 some 11 slaves were freed. But unlike the indentured servant, his term of service was determined by the wishes of his master not a contract. Beginning in 1702, however, the English settlers proceeded to abolish the more "humane features" of the New Amsterdam slave code. One reason for this change was the growth of New York's Negro population — in 1703 approximately 1,500 Negroes were living in Manhattan, Brooklyn, and the surrounding areas that were later to become part of New York City. The frequency with which New York slaves fled to Canada and the slave revolt of 1712 attested to the severity of the New York slave code.[2]

In 1712 a small group of discontented slaves set fire to a number of houses. When the white citizens came to extinguish the conflagration, the rebels fired upon them. In the ensuing battle the insurgent slaves fled into the woods. In the days that followed, all of the insurrectionists either were captured or killed. The trial that followed was conducted in an atmosphere of mass hysteria. England at this time was at war with France, and New Yorkers feared both Indian and French attacks. The slave revolt served to augment their sense of insecurity. Against this background of fear, more slaves were sentenced to death than were involved in the plot. So great was the fear of another slave revolt that many New Yorkers demanded the closing of the school for Negroes in the city. It was of no matter that only one of the accused plotters attended the school established by the Society for the Propagation of the Gospel.[3]

As a result of the plot, the New York State Legislature adopted a rigid slave code that was to remain in force until the end of the eighteenth century. According to one study of Negro slavery in New York, this system "equalled the severity of the codes in operation below the Potomac."[4] Negro slaves, for example, were not permitted to enter into contracts, to bear witness against a freeman, to marry, or to hold property. A slave was forbidden to purchase goods without his master's approval. Fearing a recurrence of slave revolts, a limit was placed on the number of slaves who could attend a funeral. And, as in many a southern state, a master was compensated for the loss of a slave who was executed for the commission of a crime. Enforcement of these laws and the enactment of new provisions varied with the white community's sense of security. Rigid enforcement, for instance, followed an alleged slave plot in 1741. It is very doubtful if any plot had existed, but an hysterical white community proceeded to convict more than 150 Negroes on the basis of insufficient evidence.[5]

The process of manumission as well as the activities of slaves were regulated by law. Even those masters who contemplated manumitting their slaves found it difficult to achieve. Until 1712 a master could free a slave at will, but the effects of the plot of that year caused the state legislature to enact a law making manumission virtually impossible. Under the law of 1712, a master who freed a slave was required to post a surety that would guarantee the slave an annuity. This attempt to prevent the emergence of an unregulated and impoverished free Negro class brought a virtual halt to manumission. Slight modifications in this law failed to increase the number of manumissions. Consequently, most Negroes in New York City remained slaves before the American Revolution. Still a sizable community of Negro slaves emerged. Between 1703 and 1771 Negroes accounted for 14 to 18 per cent of those persons living on Manhattan Island.[6]

Movements to abolish slavery in New York State began in 1767 when a group of Quakers urged fellow members of their church to free their slaves. Some Quakers failed to adhere to this request; therefore, in 1776 the Society of Friends resolved that it would not accept contributions from slaveholders. Abolitionist sentiment soon was advocated by other elements of New York's white community. When a state constitution was being drafted in 1777, John Jay, who was later to hold among other offices the governorship of New York, called for the inclusion of a provision abolishing slavery. This proposition failed, but those slaves who served in the Revolutionary Army for three years and received an honorable discharge were freed. In 1785 advocates of manumission received assistance when the Society for Promoting the Manumission of Slaves was formed with Jay as president and Alexander Hamilton as secretary. Jay in petitioning the state legislature to abolish slavery asserted that it was inconsistent for his fellow whites "to contend for our own liberty and to deny that blessing to others." [7] Although Jay's request for complete manumission was not enacted, the legislature did adopt a modification of the earlier law. By virtue of the act of 1785, manumission of slaves under the age of fifty was permitted if masters obtained a certificate that future freedmen were capable of providing for themselves. In addition, a manumitting master was relieved of the obligation to provide a surety for the freedman. The act also attempted to halt the selling of slaves in New York — any slave brought into the state after June 1, 1785, for the purpose of sale was to be freed. Except for a few minor measures preventing the extension of slavery in the state, no further action toward abolishing slavery was taken until 1799.[8]

In 1795 the election of John Jay as Governor of New York augured well for the abolitionist cause. Through Jay's hard work a gradual abolition act was passed in 1799. The law provided that all offspring of slaves were to be freed upon reaching age twenty-five for males and twenty-eight for females. Until their day of freedom, the future freedmen were to remain the bonded servants of their mothers' masters.[9] For those slaves not covered under the law of 1799, legislation was enacted that made voluntary manumission easier. In 1809 a slave was granted the right to obtain real and personal property and to enter a marriage having the force of legality behind it. No doubt the prospect of a large free Negro population prompted New Yorkers to prevent the development of a propertyless, shiftless, and immoral class in their midst. In line with this thinking, a law of 1810 provided that the children of slaves would be freed at the age of twenty-one if the master failed to teach him to read the Scriptures.[10]

Following the passage of these laws, Negro slavery began to disappear from New York City. In 1790 only 15 per cent of the Negroes living in Brooklyn and Manhattan were classified as free. But this proportion climbed to 37 per cent in 1800 and 84 per cent in 1820. By 1830, after slavery had come to its final demise in New York, there were approximately 16,000 Negroes in Brooklyn and Manhattan.[11]

With their new-won freedom, Negroes were entitled to the same rights enjoyed by whites. Voting qualifications for white and black were identical. In casting their ballots, according to the historian Dixon Ryan Fox, most Negro voters supported the Federalist party for they "had been reared in Federalist households; their cause had been advocated by distinguished Federalists, and now under the auspices of that party freedom was provided." The former slave "became in politics a client of his former master." [12] Although the Federalists appreciated this loyalty, it soon angered Republicans. The party of Jefferson emerged as the leading advocate of Negro disfranchisement in New York State. At first, Republicans challenged prospective Negro voters who failed to furnish certificates of freedom. An act of 1811 provided the force of law for this practice. The law did establish procedures whereby a Negro could obtain the needed certificate; however, they were cumbersome and expensive.[13] Nevertheless, many Negroes still voted the Federalist ticket. In order to correct this situation, the Republican delegation to the state constitutional convention of 1821 introduced a proposal to disfranchise the Negro. One member of the party maintained that "a few hundred Negroes in the city of New York virtually gave law to the state." Another Republican asserted that Negroes were "peculiar people" who exercised the franchise without "discretion, prudence, or independence." Still other Republicans charged that Negro voters were the lackeys of their former Federalist masters. The Federalists came to the defense of the Negro voter. Peter A. Jay, the son of John Jay, and Chancellor James Kent condemned any provision that would deny the Negro the vote. They were successful in defeating a clause that would have restricted the franchise to whites, but they failed to block a provision that required Negroes to meet a higher property qualification than whites.[14]

By 1827 the New York Negro was no longer the white man's slave, but he was not the white man's political equal. Negro leaders in the years that followed petitioned the state for equal suffrage rights. All these attempts ended in failure. Even the voters of the state rejected proposals to extend the vote to all citizens regardless of race. It was not until the state legislature approved the Fifteenth Amendment that the New York Negro was accorded voting equality. Nor was all discrimination in the pre-Civil War period limited to the voting booth. Separate school and public transportation facilities were provided, certain restaurants and neighborhoods barred Negro entrance, and economic and social equality were unheard of. Relatively speaking, slavery died a quick death. Political, legal, economic, and social discrimination persisted.[15]

POPULATION GROWTH, 1820–1920

At the close of the Civil War, 14,804 Negroes were living in New York City. Although this number increased steadily in the next fifty-five years, it was the smallest group of New York Negroes since 1840 when there were 19,204 members of the race residing in the city.[16] This decline resulted in part from the severe restrictions placed upon slaves by southern states in the thirty-five years preceding emancipation. These constraints made freedom almost impossible to attain, thereby reducing the number of free Negroes and diminishing the size of the northward migration. Many Negroes also avoided New York City because of the hostility shown by many whites of the city toward anti-slavery groups. New York at this time could not be regarded as a refuge for Negroes. Following the federal Fugitive Slave Act of 1850, which made the position of runaway slaves precarious, many Negroes fled to Canada. With the closing of the southern source of New York's Negro population, the high death rate of the city's nonwhite population reduced further the size of the Negro community.[17] Not only did the actual number of New York Negroes decline in these years, but as the city's population increased more numerously from other sources, the proportion of Negroes in New York City's total population also decreased. It fell from 9.4 per cent in 1820 to 5.3 per cent in 1840 and to 1.6 per cent of the total in the year before the outbreak of the Civil War. The horrible days of the draft riots of 1863 furthered the proportionate decline; by 1865 New York's Negro citizenry was only 1.4 per cent of the city's total population. In the next four and one-half decades, the Negro element never exceeded 1.9 per cent of Gotham's populace.[18]

After World War I the Negro proportion of Gotham's residents increased. In 1920 it climbed to 2.7 per cent of the total. This increase continued during the next forty years. By 1960 Negroes accounted for 13.9 per cent of New York City's population. The increase between 1910 and 1960 can be attributed to the migration of Negroes to New York City during World War I and the decline in European emigration to the United States because of the war years and the immigration restriction laws enacted in the 1920s.[19]

Despite its lack of size, relatively speaking, New York City's Negro population grew continuously between 1860 and 1920. Each decade saw an increase over the previous ten-year period. In the half-decade between 1865 and 1870, the city's Negro citizenry rose 26.7 per cent. Between 1870 and 1880 it increased by 53.6 per cent. The decade of the 1880s witnessed a less spectacular growth, when the number of Negroes living in New York was enlarged by only 17.6 per cent; but in the decade between 1890 and 1900, the Negro influx into the city once again rose — a 79 per cent increase for the decade. For the period from 1900 to 1910, the increase dropped to 51.2 per cent. With the northward migration of Negroes during World War I, the city's Negro population increased by 66.2 per cent between 1910 and 1920.[20]

The growth in the Negro population of New York City from 1870 to 1920 can be explained in part by natural increase. Figures for the sources of the city's Negro populace are not available; therefore, calculations must be made on data given for the state. The Census of 1870 counted 38,504 Negroes born in New York State; the number at the Census of 1920 was 62,369 — an increase of 23,865. However, at the same time, the number of New York-born Negroes declined in proportion to the total Negro population of the Empire State. In 1870 New York-born Negroes constituted 74 per cent of the state's Negro inhabitants; by 1920 the percentage had declined to 31.4 per cent of the total. The huge growth in New York City's Negro population, therefore, cannot be explained by natural increase alone. Migration into the state was also a factor in the enlargement of New York's Negro population in these years. The number of New York Negroes born in other parts of the United States and in foreign lands rose from 13,577 in 1870 to 136,114 in 1920 — an increase of almost 900 per cent. This growth is even more striking when compared to the 62 per cent increase in New York-born Negroes between 1870 and 1920.[21]

The South Atlantic states were the major source of Negroes migrating to the Empire State. Some 7,649 Negroes born in these states were living in New York State in 1870, and they accounted for 15 per cent of the state's Negro population. By 1920 this number expanded to 77,859, some 39.2 per cent of the total number of Negroes living in the state. The migration of Negroes from the South Atlantic states to New York began in the 1870s.[22] Although this group was smaller than the massive number of Negroes moving in these years to the Middle West, it was sufficiently large to merit attention, something that contemporary historians have sometimes overlooked. This oversight appears to be the result of not differentiating between the Negro migrants who resided along the South Atlantic coast and those of the interior South.[23] For example, of the almost 20,000 Negroes who migrated to Kansas between 1870 and 1880, only 1,982 were born in the South Atlantic states. On the other hand, New York received 6,084 Negroes from the southern states that bordered the Atlantic Ocean in the same period. Although the size of the Negro migration to New York State was not as great as the movement to Kansas and other states of the Middle West, it was still significant enough to mark the beginning of a southern migration to the Empire State.[24]

In the decade between 1880 and 1890, some 6,634 Negroes born in the South Atlantic states moved to New York State. A greater influx of South Atlantic Negroes, however, came in the decade of the 1890s with the arrival of some 20,361 Negroes born in those states. Another 16,557 from this source moved to New York between 1900 and 1910. From 1910 to 1920 this section added another 20,274 Negroes to New York's population. Other sections made relatively minor contributions to New York State's Negro citizenry. About 5,500 Negroes moved from New Jersey and Pennsylvania to New York between 1870 and 1920. New England added some 2,200 persons and the East North Central states contributed approximately 1,800 Negroes to the Empire State's population. Almost 2,000 came from the West South Central section. Smaller contributions were made by the West North Central, Mountain, and Pacific states to New York's Negro population.[25]

New York State received its largest contingent of adopted Negro citizens from Virginia. Almost 28,000 Virginia-born Negroes moved to New York between 1870 and 1920. In the same period 37,223 Negroes born in North Carolina, South Carolina, Georgia, and Florida came to the Empire State. In 1920 some 2,506 Negro residents of New York State gave the nation's capital as their place of birth, an increase of 2,117 persons over 1870. In addition, Kentucky, Tennessee, and Alabama provided 3,890 Negroes in the fifty-year period. A sizable number of Negroes also came from states that bordered New York. Thus, New York State drew the bulk of its Negro population from the states on the Atlantic seaboard.[26]

A large proportion of Negroes migrating to the Empire State selected New York City as the place to make their new home. During the period 1870 to 1920 the portion of New York State's Negro population living in New York City increased. In 1870 only 35.4 per cent of the Negroes in the Empire State gave New York City as their place of residence. This proportion rose to 43.2 per cent in 1880. By 1890 almost half of the state's Negro residents — 49.5 per cent — made their homes in New York City. At the turn of the century — no doubt reflecting the great migration of Negroes to the Empire State — some 63.4 per cent of the state's Negro citizenry resided in Greater New York. In 1910 this proportion rose to 75.6 per cent and to 77 per cent in 1920. It appears that New York City was receiving a sizable portion of those Negroes who had moved from other states of the Union to New York State.[27]

Negro migration to New York was not limited to residents of the continental United States. After 1900 Negroes from Puerto Rico and other Caribbean islands came to New York in large numbers. Between 1900 and 1920 at least 28,000 foreign-born Negroes, mainly from the West Indies, migrated to the Empire State.[28] West Indians left their native land because of impoverished living conditions, limited educational facilities, disenchantment with British rule, and the opportunities they believed New York offered. Skilled as well as unskilled rushed to the city. By 1917 the *New York Times* estimated that these newcomers accounted for one-quarter of the Negro population of Harlem.[29]

The factors that motivated the mass migration of West Indian Negroes were similar to the forces that caused southern Negroes to come north. As the census statistics have indicated, there was a constant migration of Negroes to New York City between 1870 and 1920. It ebbed and flowed as the tide — rising in the 1870s, receding in the 1880s, rising once again in the 1890s where it remained at a level until the flood crest of World War I. The migration of the 1870s was part of a mass exodus of Negroes

from the South. Most of these Negroes went to the West; however, a large number also came to New York. In the South,
economic discontent was rising because of the partial crop failure
of 1878 and the debtor condition the Negro endured under the
crop-lien system. The attraction of opportunities in the agricultural West as well as in the growing cities of the Northeast drew
the Negro northward. In addition, the return of the Democratic
party to power in the South left the Negro with a sense of insecurity.[30]

After the somewhat smaller migration of the 1880s, the flow
of Negroes northward resumed in the 1890s. In the next thirty
years some 63,124 southern-born Negroes were to seek refuge in
New York State. More and more Negroes deserted the South because of their debtor position, their low standard of living and
their generally depressed condition in this period.[31] A period of
severe economic hardship, such as that between 1914 and 1918,
would swell this steady flow northward. In 1914 and 1915 the
South suffered an economic decline that made more insecure the
southern Negro's already precarious economic position. If this
was not enough, beginning in 1915 sections of the South were
struck by a series of floods and a boll weevil plague. This accounted, in part, for the large migration of Georgia and Alabama
Negroes to New York State in the 1910s. Unemployment for
southern Negroes increased; those who were fortunate enough to
obtain jobs discovered that wages had declined. But it was not
only economic hardships that caused Negroes to move north, the
injustice that permeated the southern segregation system — which
had become part of its legal system in the 1890s — gave further
impetus to the exodus.[32] Although these inequities were only
"secondary and contributing causes" of the northward movement,
it seemed "probable that like discrimination, mob violence" ex-
erted a "strengthening and accompanying cause." [33] Any predilection to desert the South was reinforced by such wrongs as the
unequal justice dispensed by many southern law enforcement
agencies, the inadequate educational facilities of a segregated
school system, and the prevalence of lynchings.[34] So many Negroes were deserting the South that it caused one student of the
exodus to remark in 1920 that Negroes were leaving the area "as
though they were fleeing some curse." [35] Songs and verse ex-

pressed the feelings of Negroes abandoning the South. One Negro was purported to have gone north singing:

> Boll-weevil in de cotton
> Cut wurn in de cotton,
> Debil in de white man,
> Wah's goin' on.[36]

But more was needed to bring the Negro to the North than the economic hardships and social and political injustices in the South. Alternatives to these conditions had to be offered. Like those early pioneers who moved west, attracting and propelling forces encouraged Negroes to migrate north. An economic attraction was offered the Negro in employment when World War I stopped the flow of immigrants to America. Where 1,218,480 Europeans had come to the United States in 1914, only 326,700 came in 1915.[37] Losing this source of labor, northern industry turned toward the southern Negro to fulfill its needs. In addition, those enterprises that were meeting the wartime requirements of European nations offered the Negro employment. Many northern companies sent labor agents southward to inform Negroes of the opportunities awaiting them in the North. Once the stream of Negroes northward had begun, agents were no longer needed to lure the Negro above the Mason-Dixon Line.[38] Stories of new horizons in the North spread from Negro community to Negro community. Letters from friends and articles in the northern Negro press, which had a large reading public in the South, told of this land of milk and honey to the north.[39] The Negro *New York Age* carried such headlines as "Unrest In South Grows. . . . Labor Wanted In N.Y. State." It told of employment opportunities in the state as well as the greater degree of freedom enjoyed by New York Negroes in comparison to their southern kinsmen.[40] Such descriptions of the city were not new; Negro commentators had noted their prevalence in the early 1900s. One Negro minister returning from a trip to the South in 1901 told of the southern Negro who had "his heart . . . wrapped up in a desire" to come north.[41] These stories could not be dismissed as fiction. The northern Negro enjoyed higher wages, a shorter workday, and less political and legal segregation.[42]

The lure of the northern city, especially New York, with its glamour and excitement attracted the mistreated, impoverished, frustrated, and bored southern Negro. It was of little importance that housing conditions were far from adequate; it was the opportunity that the North appeared to offer that counted. Nor did southern criticisms of the North have any appreciable effect on the Negro migrant. It was next to impossible to counteract the glowing descriptions of northern cities contained in letters from friends who had moved north. Negro leaders in New York and throughout the North were flooded with letters asking them to obtain a job for the writer. To the unskilled Negro, who constituted the bulk of the northward migration, New York was the city of refuge.[43]

Notes

[1] Leo H. Hirsch, Jr., "The Negro and New York, 1783 to 1865," *Journal of Negro History*, XVI (October, 1931), 383; Edwin Olson, "Negro Slavery in New York, 1626–1827," unpublished Ph.D. dissertation, New York University, 1938, pp. 4–6, 14–17, 20–21, 24–26; Aaron H. Payne, "The Negro in New York Prior to 1860," *Howard Review*, I (June, 1923), 11.

[2] Hirsch, "The Negro and New York," pp. 383–84; Payne, "The Negro in New York Prior to 1860," pp. 11–12, 20–26; James Weldon Johnson, *Black Manhattan* (New York, 1930), p. 5.

[3] Olson, "Negro Slavery in New York," pp. 81–83, 107–15; Payne, "The Negro in New York Prior to 1860," pp. 13–14, 20–26, 38–39.

[4] Olson, "Negro Slavery in New York," p. 82.

[5] *Ibid.*, pp. 86–91, 415–23; Payne, "The Negro in New York Prior to 1860," pp. 18–20.

[6] Olson, "Negro Slavery in New York," pp. 34, 150–64.

[7] Hirsch, "The Negro and New York," pp. 385–88.

[8] *Ibid.*, pp. 388–89.

[9] *Ibid.*, pp. 390–91.

[10] *Ibid.*, pp. 392–94. In 1817 the age was reduced to eighteen.

[11] *New York State Census of 1875* (Albany, 1877), p. 151; *Ninth Census of the United States, 1870, Statistics of the Population of the United States* (Washington, D.C., 1874), p. 51.

[12] Dixon Ryan Fox, "The Negro Vote in Old New York," *Political Science Quarterly*, XXXII (June, 1917), 254–55.

[13] Charles H. Wesley, "Negro Suffrage in the Period of Constitution-Making, 1787–1865," *Journal of Negro History*, XXXII (April, 1947), 143–68.

[14] *Ibid.*, pp. 158–60; Fox, "The Negro Vote in Old New York," pp. 256–57, 259–64.

[15] Wesley, "Negro Suffrage in the Period of Constitution-Making," pp. 93–102; Hirsch, "The Negro and New York," pp. 420, 423; Leon F. Litwack, *North of Slavery: the Negro in the Free States, 1790–1860* (Chicago, 1961), pp. 87–91, 111–12, 132–33, 168.

[16] See table 1.

[17] Robert Ernst, "The Economic Status of New York City Negroes, 1850–1863," *Negro History Bulletin*, XII (March, 1949), 131–32; Hirsch, "The Negro and New York," pp.

397–411; Clement Eaton, *The Growth of Southern Civilization* (New York, 1961), p. 93.

[18] See table 3.

[19] *Fourteenth Census, 1920, New York* (Washington, D.C., 1923), p. 62; *Eighteenth Census, 1960, Population of New York, Detailed Characteristics* (Washington, D.C., 1961), p. 420; Oscar Handlin, *The Newcomers: Negroes and Puerto Ricans in a Changing Metropolis* (Cambridge, 1959), pp. 42, 45–46, 48–50.

[20] See table 2.

[21] See table 4.

[22] See *ibid.*

[23] Handlin, *Newcomers*, p. 49; Arthur M. Schlesinger, *The Rise of the City, 1878–1898* (New York, 1933), pp. 375–77.

[24] See table 4.

[25] See *ibid.*

[26] See table 5.

[27] See tables 1 and 4.

[28] See table 4.

[29] *New York Times*, September 2, 1917; *New York Tribune*, April 1, 1900; "The Negro in the Cities of the North," *Charities*, XV (October 7, 1905), 2; W. A. Domingo, "The Tropics in New York," *Survey Graphic*, LIII (March 1, 1925), 648–50; Rollin L. Hartt, "I'd Like to Show You Harlem," *Independent*, CV (April 2, 1921), 335; Helen A. Tucker, "Negro Craftsmen in New York," *Southern Workman*, XXXVI (October, 1907), 550.

[30] John G. Van Deusen, "Negro Exodus of 1879," *Journal of Negro History*, XXI (April, 1936), 111–29; Carter G. Woodson, *A Century of Negro Migration* (Washington, D.C., 1918), pp. 126–46.

[31] George E. Haynes, "Negroes Move North: Their Departure from the South," *Survey*, XL (May 4, 1918), 117; Carl Kelsey, "Causes of Negro Emigration: the Men," *Charities*, XV (October 7, 1905), 15;

R. R. Wright, Jr., "The Negro in Unskilled Labor," *Annals of the American Academy of Political and Social Science*, XLIX (September, 1913), 21, 24; Woodson, *Century of Negro Migration*, pp. 126–92; *New York Age*, November 21, 1912.

[32] Henderson Donald, "The Negro Migration, 1916–1918," *Journal of Negro History*, VI (October, 1921), 410–20; Louise P. Kennedy, *The Negro Peasant Turns Cityward* (New York, 1930), pp. 49–52, 106, 186–87, 206; Emmett J. Scott, *Negro Migration During the War* (New York, 1920), pp. 13–25; United States Department of Labor, Division of Negro Economics, *Negro Migration in 1916–1917* (Washington, D.C., 1919), pp. 11–12, 21–22, 58–66; Haynes, "Negroes Move North: Their Departure," pp. 117–20; *Living Age*, CCXCV (October 6, 1917), 158–59; *Survey*, XXXVIII (June 2, 1917), 226–27, and (August 11, 1917), 428; *New York Age*, February 8, 1917.

[33] Kennedy, *Negro Peasant Turns Cityward*, pp. 50, 52. Miss Kennedy has pointed out that the Negro population in those districts with the highest incidence of lynching increased and those counties which showed a decrease in their Negro element recorded a similar decline in their white citizenry. *Ibid.*, p. 49.

[34] *Ibid.*, pp. 49–52; Scott, *Negro Migration*, pp. 16–25.

[35] Scott, *Negro Migration*, p. 45.

[36] Haynes, "Negroes Move North: Their Departure," p. 120.

[37] Kennedy, *Negro Peasant Turns Cityward*, p. 43; "The Negro Migration," *New Republic*, VII (July 1, 1916), 213–14.

[38] *New York Times*, September 5, 1916; Kennedy, *Negro Peasant Turns Cityward*, p. 53; Donald, "The Negro Migration," pp. 27–28; *Survey*, XXXVIII (July 14, 1917), 340.

[39] Emmett Scott, ed., "Letters of Negro Migrants, 1916–1918," *Journal of Negro History*, IV (July, 1919), 290–340, and (October, 1919), 412–65; Kennedy, *Negro Peasant Turns Cityward*, p. 53; *Crisis*, XIX (January, 1920), 105; *New York Age*, February 22, 1917.

[40] *New York Age*, February 8, 15, 22, 1917.

[41] *New York Times*, March 11, 1901. Also see Kelsey, "Causes of Negro Emigration," pp. 16–17; Tucker, "Negro Craftsmen in New York," pp. 545–54.

[42] *Survey*, XXXVIII (April 7, 1917), 27; Kennedy, *Negro Peasant Turns Cityward*, p. 206; United States Department of Labor, *Negro Migration*, pp. 21–22.

[43] Haynes, "Negroes Move North: Their Arrival in the North," *Survey*, LXI (January 4, 1919), 455–61; Kennedy, *Negro Peasant Turns Cityward*, pp. 53–54. For southern use of propaganda in attempts to halt northward migration, see *New York Age*, February 15, 1917; *Living Age*, CCXCV (October 6, 1917), 50–57; Scott, *Negro Migration*, pp. 72–85.

· 1 ·

A Place to Live

MOVEMENT WITHIN THE CITY

Once in New York, the Negro became part of the city's constantly moving population. Each decade between 1860 and 1920 witnessed some change in the Negro's place of residence, whether he was moving from the Greenwich Village area of Manhattan northward or from the Borough Hall neighborhood of Brooklyn southeastward. Negroes, though, were not limited to one area of the city. As early as 1860, Negro colonies existed in Greenwich Village, the west Twenties and east Eighties. By 1920, however, Negroes tended to move to a single area — in Manhattan, Harlem, and in Brooklyn, Bedford-Stuyvesant.

Before 1860, Negro settlement in Manhattan was limited to the lower part of the city. In 1800 two-thirds of the Negro populace lived in an area bounded on the north by Canal Street and on the south by Cedar Street. Between 1820 and 1840 the center of the Negro population shifted uptown — extending north and west from the infamous Five Points. In 1835 reference was made to a small Negro settlement in the Greenwich Village area. Some fifteen years later the majority of the city's Negroes were living in the southern portion of Greenwich Village and the area immediately south of it. They filled such blocks as West Broadway, Greene, Leonard, Mercer, and Mulberry streets. In addition, a small colony of Negroes had taken shape in the east Eighties. Between 1850 and 1860 Negroes began to leave the southern portion of Greenwich Village and the area east and south of it for MacDougal, Bleecker, Carmine, Sullivan, and Thompson streets and Minetta Lane of the upper Village. At the same time, other Negroes found homes in the west Teens and west Twenties.[1]

By 1860 the city's Negro population could be said to be living in segregated areas, even though Negroes were not limited to a single area, nor did they constitute more than 8 per cent of any ward's population. The ghetto may have been limited to a few blocks, but it was still a ghetto. Thus, in the 1860s the Board of Education could refer to a "scattered" and yet "colonizing" Negro population. In recognition of the Negro's "colonizing" nature, the schools "for their use" had been "located in the immediate neighborhood, if not directly in the midst of the communities," the Board reported in 1868.[2] Segregated housing, with a few exceptions, was a condition that the Negro faced throughout the period from 1860 to 1920.[3] The Negro's segregated position varied in size from a few blocks to a community of over a dozen streets. The hostility of white landlords and tenants restricted the Negro to specific districts. Occasionally he broke out of the ghetto and moved to another section of the city; however, it was not long before that section became segregated. To say that the Negro's "colonizing" nature in itself explained his segregated state is unfounded. No doubt many Negroes preferred to live with members of their own race; the security that the Negro ghetto offered was a compelling attraction. Like other immigrant groups, many a Negro newcomer discovered that the adjustment to his new home was made somewhat easier by living near members of his race. Within the Negro ghetto a separate society was developed that somewhat insulated its denizens from the prejudices of the wider community. But living within a segregated community was not always a matter of choice, for Negroes were not offered the luxury of choosing between colonization and integration. Segregation was not created by the Negro; it was the white man's creature.[4]

During the decade of the 1860s, Negroes continued their movement uptown. Where a majority of the city's Negro population — 55.2 per cent — made its home south of Houston Street in

1860, by 1870 this proportion had fallen to 41.5 per cent since the Negro community north of Houston Street contained more than half of the city's Negroes. Of this number, 17.3 per cent lived between Houston and Fourteenth streets and 36 per cent between Fourteenth and Eighty-sixth streets. The greatest growth occurred in the upper Teens and lower Thirties on the West Side of Manhattan. Negro colonies in the lower part of the city, therefore, were on the wane. Despite the increase in size of the Greenwich Village Negro community for the decade of the 1860s, its share of the city's Negro population had declined.[5]

This shift in the Negro population was reflected in the closing of the "colored" schools. In 1867 such a school in lower Manhattan, on Franklin Street, was terminated. Three other "colored" schools were closed in the 1870s. Number Six at Allen Street was discontinued in 1875 because of the Negro exodus from the district. The school located in the upper East Side, which served the small Negro community of the area, was closed in 1872 and the children of the neighborhood were transported to a "colored" school farther downtown. In 1878 the students of the "colored" school on South Fifth Avenue were transferred to a similar school in one of the newer Negro neighborhoods. Even when the city abolished separate schools for Negroes in 1884, those schools in Negro neighborhoods remained predominantly Negro. Thus, districts which had lost their Negro citizens, lost their "colored" schools. In those wards in which "colored" schools were closed, but in which Negroes continued to reside, segregated schools were maintained for the Negro child.[6]

Negro migration and segregation within the city persisted throughout the 1870s and 1880s. The northward movement continued as new neighborhoods were entered. By 1890 almost 80 per cent of Manhattan's Negro citizens lived above Fourteenth Street. The area south of Fourteenth Street contained only 20.7 per cent of the city's Negro inhabitants — a decrease of 38.5 per cent from the 59.2 per cent of 1870. In addition, the portion of Manhattan north of Eighty-sixth Street had expanded from 631 Negroes in 1870 — 4.8 per cent of the city's total — to 3,951 persons — 17.3 per cent — in 1890.[7]

When Negroes deserted the Greenwich Village district in increasing numbers during the 1870s and 1880s, their place was taken by the Italians. An article in the New York Age for Decem-

ber 20, 1890 attested to the declining Negro population in the
Greenwich Village area when it asserted: "This section is largely
losing its distinctive features as an Afro-American district, and
many portions of it have become flooded by the sons of sunny
Italy." Two symptomatic features, observed the Negro paper,
were Garibaldi's statue in Washington Square and the replacement of a Negro church by an Italian house of worship. Jacob
Riis, the famed social reformer, noted that the Italian was moving
into the run-down buildings formerly occupied by the Negro.[8]
Because of this inrush of Italians, Negroes moved to the west
Twenties and Thirties of the notorious Tenderloin district with a
vanguard moving directly north into the Forties and Fifties and
an advance colony expanding along the East Side from the
Eighties into the Nineties and One-hundreds.[9] A Captain Reilly,
of a Tenderloin police precinct, remarked in 1889 that Negroes
had "taken up every street from Twenty-Fourth to Thirty-Third,
between Sixth and Seventh aves." [10] Reporting some six years
later, the New York Tribune noted that this area had "snatched
away the long held preeminence of Thompson and Sullivan sts.,
famed in verse and story throughout the country." Within the
Tenderloin neighborhood, Negro quarters gradually shifted west-
ward and, in some cases, went as far west as Tenth Avenue. At
the same time other Negroes relocated farther uptown. Limited
in moving eastward by the exclusive nature of the areas surrounding Fifth Avenue, less resistance was found in the Irish neighborhoods west and north of Eighth Avenue and Thirty-fifth Street,
respectively.[11]

Although the Negro moved to new quarters, most of his
churches remained in the older areas. A few churches, such as the
Bethel African Methodist Episcopal Church and the lone Negro
Catholic church in the city, St. Benedict the Moor, followed their
congregations. New churches were established to minister to the
area that extended from the west Twenties to Fifties; however,
on the whole, the older houses of worship were slow in following
their flocks. A religious dislocation — which will be discussed in
chapter four — was one result of the Negro's movement within
the city.[12]

Throughout the 1890s the Negro continued to move farther
uptown. In 1900 only 10.2 per cent of Manhattan's Negro citizens
made their homes below Fourteenth Street. The Tribune, in the

same year, recognized the disappearance of Greenwich Village's Negro community when it wrote that the Negro of that district no longer existed "save in the imagination of the comic paper." While the Negro population of the Village was declining, the area from Fourteenth to Eighty-sixth Street saw an expansion of its Negro population. This area had contained 36 per cent of Manhattan's Negro residents in 1870; by 1890 its share had soared to 62 per cent and to 65.5 per cent in 1900. But the greatest increases for 1900 were in the neighborhoods north of Eighty-sixth Street. The proportion of the county's Negro population in this area rose from 4.8 per cent in 1870 to 24.3 per cent in 1900.[13]

Although the Tenderloin district — extending from the west Twenties to the west Fifties — continued to attract a large number of Negroes, it was now experiencing competition from the San Juan Hill area of the west Sixties and the Harlem community of the One-hundreds. Between 1900 and 1910 the San Juan Hill neighborhood grew so rapidly that it became the largest Negro community in Manhattan. Negroes continued to crowd into the Tenderloin district, especially southern and West Indian newcomers, but not however at a pace which could compare to the rapid growth of San Juan Hill. Almost as soon as the Negro community in San Juan Hill emerged as the leading black district in the city, Harlem showed signs of becoming the future home of the Manhattan Negro. The Negro population in the Tenderloin had declined and the growth of the San Juan Hill area did not equal the growth taking place in Harlem. During the 1900s Negroes moved in ever increasing numbers to Harlem. They had moved into small sections of the area as far back as the late 1880s. A better class of apartment houses had been made available to them on 122nd Street, between Fifth and Lenox avenues, and from 124th to 126th streets, extending between Eighth and Tenth avenues.[14] In the years that followed, other blocks in Harlem were slowly filled by Negroes. In 1901 the *New York Times* could refer to 130th Street, between Amsterdam Avenue and Broadway, as "Darktown."[15] With the end of a Harlem real estate boom in 1902, the Negro movement to Harlem advanced from a trickle to a flood. Writing in 1906, a *Tribune* reporter commented on the "general exodus of negroes from all other neighborhoods to Harlem." Attempts by white property owners to restrict the Negro ingress ended in failure. Many whites because of their prejudice against the Negro fled areas populated by the race.[16] By 1911 the National Association for the Advancement of Colored People estimated that at least 20,000 Negroes lived in the area bounded by Eighth Avenue on the west, Fifth Avenue on the east, and 132nd to 137th streets on the south and north. With 135th Street and Lenox Avenue as the focal point, this Negro community proceeded to expand in all directions. So great was the growth of Negro Harlem that 70 per cent of the Negroes living in Manhattan in 1920 resided between 118th and 144th streets, from the Harlem to Hudson rivers. This increase is attested to by the fact that in 1910 only 50 per cent of Manhattan's Negroes resided in the entire area north of Eighty-sixth Street. The greatest concentration of Negroes in Harlem was between 130th and 144th streets, extending from Park Avenue on the east to Eighth Avenue on the west.[17] Here was what writers were to refer to as the "greatest Negro city in the world." [18]

Negro movement within the city cannot be explained by any single theory. An answer can only be found in the interrelationship of many different forces. On the one hand, there were factors that compelled the Negro to find new living quarters. On the other hand, certain incidents attracted the Negro to new areas. Nor was the internal migration limited to Manhattan; it extended to other parts of the metropolitan region. Many Negroes deserted Manhattan in the 1860s for Brooklyn because of the draft riots of 1863.[19] Throughout the years that followed, Negroes continued to leave Manhattan for the Bronx, Brooklyn, and Queens. These areas usually attracted the more affluent Negro. On occasion, some of these people found it possible to secure a home in a white neighborhood. Others found living conditions better and prejudice less marked in Brooklyn and the Bronx. In 1895 the *Times* declared that as soon as Negroes "amass a comfortable fortune they move from the city across the East River" to Brooklyn. "Cultured and comfortable" Negroes had established a community in the Bronx on Brook and Morris avenues, near 161st Street, by the 1890s. Many of the more prosperous Negroes, however, would not desert Manhattan. To avoid the high incidence of congestion and poor housing in Negro neighborhoods, they would move, on occasion, to areas within the county that offered healthier living conditions. When, because of prejudice, whites deserted these neighborhoods, a general influx of Negroes followed. The affluent Negro found that he was again living among all classes of his people — the rich and indigent, the refined and vulgar, the honest and criminal.[20]

It was not merely the dilapidated conditions of the older Negro neighborhoods that drove the Negro to new areas. Beginning in the 1880s Negroes discovered that new immigrant groups were moving into or around their community.[21] It is difficult to determine whether the Negro was driven from his old home by the immigrant or whether he left of his own volition. As noted earlier, Jacob Riis reported in 1892 that the Italians had taken possession of the poor housing facilities of the Greenwich Village Negro.[22] Census figures indicate that districts with the greatest Negro concentration had a foreign-born population below the city average. Of the six wards which were composed of at least a 2 per cent Negro population in 1870, three had a foreign-born population smaller than their Manhattan average. By 1890 only the Eighth Ward had both a Negro population of over 2 per cent and a foreign-born element above its county average of 42.3 per cent. It is important to note that the Eighth Ward contained Greenwich Village, which was losing its Negro residents. The Census of 1910 showed that the Negro and the foreigner continued to live apart. Of the fourteen assembly districts that contained at least a 2 per cent Negro population, only one had a foreign-born element greater than the borough average. In 1920 almost the identical pattern was discovered. In addition, the Irish were the largest foreign-born group in the areas with a large number of Negroes.[23]

Negroes, therefore, appear to have avoided the non-English speaking foreigners, which explains their association with the Irish more than other foreign elements. Mary White Ovington, a white social worker in the Negro community, wrote that the Negro shunned neighborhoods populated by the "chattering foreigner." "The ambitious Negro," being "scornful of the gibberish-speaking Italians," she declared, deserted lower Manhattan; thus reluctantly surrendering his home in that part of the city to the alien.[24] The coming of the foreigner gave the Negro competition for an already limited housing market; however, the Negro preferred to make his home apart from the European newcomer.[25]

Negro movement to new neighborhoods also was made possible by real estate depressions. Such was the case when Negroes moved in large numbers to Harlem between 1902 and 1905. The real estate boom in Harlem, which had been stimulated by speculators, came to an end in 1902. To offset severe economic losses, landlords were forced to rent apartments in this neighborhood to Negroes. Many whites in the area of Negro settlement left in panic. This opened Harlem to more extensive Negro inhabitation. Since higher rentals could be secured from Negroes than whites, a number of landlords rented apartments to Negroes. Negro real estate agents now found it possible to secure housing for their Negro clients. Some of these agents purchased houses for Negro occupancy; others entered into agreements to fill the buildings of white landlords with Negro tenants. White proprietors experienced not only an increase in income from Negro occupancy, but a decline in the number of vacant apartments.[26]

In addition, the erection of model apartment houses was an indirect aid to Negroes. White persons left houses that were in fairly habitable condition for the model apartment houses, thereby making available to the Negro the older buildings. Transportation developments also opened sections of the city to Negro settlement. When elevated lines were constructed on certain streets, whites deserted these avenues because of the resultant noise and loss of sunlight. White residents of West Fifty-third Street, for example, left after the Sixth and Ninth Avenue Railroad Companies constructed an elevated railway on that street to connect their uptown and downtown routes. Negroes, who were given little choice in their selection of housing accommodations, replaced the whites. Similarly, the Negro's entry into Harlem was facilitated by the surface railways that traversed that neighborhood. Negroes were not only drawn to new areas by changes in the face of the city, but such innovations forced them out of older neighborhoods. The construction of Pennsylvania Station compelled many Negroes to leave the west Thirties during the 1890s.[27] Still another factor accounting for the race's movement within the city was the ever increasing Negro population of New York. Newcomers from the South, needing a place to live, contributed to the expansion of Negro districts.[28]

Across the East River, in Brooklyn, the Negro's internal migration followed a pattern similar to that of his Manhattan brother. Throughout the period from 1865 to 1920, the Brooklyn Negro moved into new neighborhoods. The communities that existed at the close of the Civil War declined in size and new ones took their place. Two major differences did exist between the Manhattan and the Brooklyn Negro's population pattern. First, the more affluent Negro did not find segregation as rigid in Brooklyn as in Manhattan; and second, Brooklyn's housing for Negroes, throughout most of the period, was superior to that of Manhattan.

In 1860 two Negro communities contained 84.6 per cent of Brooklyn's Negro population. One area was the Borough Hall-Fort Greene Park section, which contained 53.3 per cent of Brooklyn's Negro citizens. It extended southward and eastward from the Brooklyn Navy Yard to and along Atlantic Avenue until it reached the western border of the Bedford-Stuyvesant area. On its western side, a small portion of the community was in the northwestern section of the Brooklyn Heights neighborhood. The second Negro community was centered in the southern portion of Williamsburg and the northern extension of Stuyvesant Heights. This neighborhood accounted for 30.7 per cent of Brooklyn's Negro residents. By 1870 the Negro settlement in the eastern section of Borough Hall had declined; however, its western and southern portions witnessed an increase. The Borough Hall-Fort Greene Park community had extended by 1870 into the Crown Heights district and the western portion of Bedford-Stuyvesant. It then contained 57.3 per cent of the county's Negro population. At the same time, Negroes were deserting the Williamsburg section. A large number were moving through the Stuyvesant Heights neighborhood into the northern portion of the Bedford-Stuyvesant area. This section contained only 13.4 per cent of Brooklyn's Negro citizenry in 1870, and though it fell to 11.1 per cent of the total by 1890, its actual size almost doubled.[29]

In 1890 there were two Negro communities in Brooklyn. One was a small community in Stuyvesant Heights. A second, which contained the large majority of the city's Negro population, went south and east along Atlantic Avenue from the Fort Greene Park district. The second district contained the Bedford-Stuyvesant neighborhood. This community was referred to as "New Brooklyn" in 1890. It contained two Colored Republican Leagues, a building association, and various educational societies. Within this and other Negro sections of Brooklyn, the Negro was limited to specific streets. This fact is attested to by the protests of white residents near the Fort Greene Park area when a Negro in 1894 attempted to buy a house in their community. Though a few Negroes were able to buy expensive houses in white neighborhoods, as a group the race was as segregated as it was in Manhattan.[30]

During the 1890s the Brooklyn Negro continued to move in increasing numbers to the Crown Heights and Bedford-Stuyvesant districts. The Negro was leaving the western part of Brooklyn. The Census of 1900 reported that except for the Tenth and Eleventh wards, all wards containing more than 1,000 Negroes were west of Fort Greene Park. In addition, Negroes began to move into Flatbush, Brownsville, and East New York. This eastward and southward movement of the Negro continued during the 1900s. By 1910 only about 38 per cent of the borough's Negro citizens resided in the area extending from the Borough Hall and Fort Greene Park districts. However, a change in the method of census reporting makes it impossible to locate the Negro population with any degree of accuracy. For instance, the Twenty-third Assembly District extended from the Bedford-Stuyvesant area to Jamaica Bay. It is impossible to determine where in that vast district its 3,973 Negroes resided. A similar problem exists in using the 1920 Census. According to its method of reporting, there was one great Negro neighborhood extending from the Fort Greene-Borough Hall area to Bedford-Stuyvesant and two small colonies in Crown Heights and Brownsville. The largest Negro community, though, appeared to be in the Bedford-Stuyvesant district.[31]

The Brooklyn Negro was impelled to change his address for reasons similar to those of the Manhattanite. More well-to-do Negroes were constantly in the vanguard of the movement, always looking for a better place to live. Building deterioration, the low standard of living, and the industrial rebuilding program of the Borough Hall-Fort Greene Park area drove the Negro to new sections. The growing population increased the necessity to expand. Manhattan Negroes after making a little money would often look to the better areas of Brooklyn for a home. And, as in Manhattan, Brooklyn Negroes avoided, whenever possible, living among the non-English speaking immigrants.[32]

HOUSING CONDITIONS

Wherever the average Negro made his home in New York City, he was offered inferior quarters. Whether rich or poor, he was limited by prejudice in his choice of location. Houses with "unsavory" reputations were left for the Negro, as were houses "which the police had cleared and for which decent white tenants could not have been found." According to a report in the *New York Times,* in 1889, Negroes, in most cases, were "hedged in by prejudice" in the "meanest tenement districts" and buildings which had "outgrown their availability for any other class of occupants." From 1865 until the late 1880s, the Negro's living conditions were at their worst. Squalor and poverty continued to dominate Negro housing after 1890; however, a number of more healthful apartments were opened to the Negro.[33]

In 1869 the *Times* wrote that Greenwich Village Negroes lived like "sardines in a box in rickety-old houses." It found that these conditions made "decent" living impossible. Two years later the New York Colored Mission, seeing horror wherever it turned, called the tenement house system a "source of evil." It complained that a "majority of our colored people inhabit these structures." About a decade later a Negro newspaper, the *New York Globe,* angrily wrote that the localities offered the Negro were "always the meanest in the city." In 1889 both the *Times* and the First Colored Catholic Congress condemned housing conditions which the Negro was forced to accept. The Negro was limited to the "meanest tenement districts," wrote the *Times,* and buildings were opened to him only after they had "outgrown their availability for any other class of occupants." Negro Catholics rebuked the "poorly lighted, poorly ventilated" tenements that were "hot-beds of vice." [34] The "ramshackle tenements" of the Thompson-Sullivan Street district, wrote Jacob Riis in the 1890s, were "falling into hopeless decay." One such building, 17 Sullivan Street, according to the Board of Health in 1894, was "occupied by the lowest white and negroes . . . the filthiest . . . we have seen." Riis believed that the worst housing for Negroes was found in the "black-and-tan" districts that bordered Negro and white communities.[35]

The squalor and decay of the west Twenties and Thirties in the Tenderloin district was second only to that of the Sullivan Street region. The *Tribune* in 1889 described a typical building, the "Florida Flats," on West Thirty-second Street:

It is situated in the rear of the lot, and is entered from an alley-way. Its only safety, from a sanitary point of view, is in the ventilation which it obtains from the court-yard running through the centre and the open space running all around. The western wall is practically barricaded from the light, with the exception of small windows sufficient to give air to the sleeping rooms. The front rooms in the courts are almost pitch dark. Yet, with all this, the class of people . . . were very respectable — in dress, demeanor, and in appearance of their homes.[36]

Despite some improvement in housing noted by the late 1880s and early 1890s,[37] the Negro's opportunity to acquire adequate housing was limited by the deterioration of Negro communities. For example, living conditions in the Tenderloin district continued to deteriorate. Negro poverty, squalor, and crime centered in this community during the 1890s and the early 1900s. Conflicts arose between whites and Negroes that culminated in the race riot of 1900. The New York *Post* in that year described the Tenderloin as the focal point of white and Negro vice. It was a "wide open" district, where prostitution, gambling, and thievery were rampant, wrote the newspaper. The law-abiding Negro, who was in the majority, deserted the area. A Negro social critic, George E. Haynes, described the Tenderloin ten years later as of the "lowest grade of social condition." Even the most necessary sanitary appliances, reported the *Age* in 1916, were lacking. The paper charged that it was next to impossible to get landlords to correct these conditions. Negroes sought better homes in the northern portion of the Tenderloin, the Sixties of the San Juan Hill neighborhood, and the Hundreds — both east and west — of Harlem. But it was not long before the upper Tenderloin and San Juan Hill fell victim to the deteriorating conditions that had brought lawlessness to the Tenderloin.[38]

A race riot in 1905 appeared to mark the decline of the San Juan Hill community.[39] It had been the refuge of those who fled the deplorable conditions of the Tenderloin. Now it contained not merely the refugees of the Tenderloin, but the conditions that had made the exodus necessary. Negroes and whites commented on these changes. Helena Titus Emerson, a social commentator writing in 1905, saw San Juan Hill as "one of the largest and worst colored settlements in the city." In an article in the *Outlook* for the same year, a white reporter, G. L. Collins, agreed that the area between Fifty-ninth Street and Sixty-fifth Street was one of the most run-down in the city. Mary Ovington described the unventilated nature of the apartments in 1903, where air shafts were as small as "culture tubes." [40] In the same year the anti-Negro New York *Sun* claimed that San Juan Hill was a community "of slovenliness," which the "appearance of the negroes themselves" matched. A policeman told the newspaper that there had been "good" Negroes in the area, "but there ain't a good one in the whole lot" now. [41] Mary Ovington, while not proceeding from the *Sun*'s bias, portrayed the "rough behavior . . . readiness to fight . . . coarse talk" of a large number of Negroes living on the Hill in 1910. The Free Kindergarten Association, which served the Negro community, bemoaned the "poverty and evil influences" that dominated the west Sixties. Sixtieth, Sixty-first, and Sixty-second streets were the worst examples of dilapidation, deprivation, and crime in the San Juan Hill community. As early as 1897 a church survey reported that there were buildings in the three-block area without "access to the outer air." Three years later the New York *World* asserted that these were the most populous blocks in the city. Sixtieth Street, wrote Helena Emerson, was "the heart" of decay in San Juan Hill. [42]

Like other Negro sections of the city Harlem could not avoid its share of poor housing. Restricted in their choice of a home, Negroes were forced to accept housing accommodations made available to them regardless of condition. Moreover, Negroes who had moved to Harlem to avoid the lawless element of their race found themselves once again entangled by all the housing evils that went with the Negro ghetto. Mary White Ovington, writing in 1910, summarized this condition when she asserted that the best and worst Negro elements in the city lived side by side in Harlem. A decade earlier, J. Gilmer Speed, a white journalist, wrote that "virtuous and vicious" Negroes live in such close proximity that they "elbow each other." "It has long been a problem," the *Age* commented in 1908, "to separate the hoodlum element from the respectable class of colored people." [43] In 1903 the *Times* described the problems Negro parents faced in raising children in neighborhoods composed of "desperadoes, gamblers," and "moral lepers." But the paper placed the blame for such conditions at the door of the Negro. It charged "respectable negroes, prompted by the instinct of self-protection," with harboring and protecting the criminal "among them." The respectable Negro, the paper concluded, must place the "worthless" Negro under the "ban of his own people." But Mary Ovington saw the problem in a different light. Writing in 1905, she asserted that the landlord's failure to make "any attempt to discriminate among his applicants," forced "the colored people to dwell good and bad together."[44] Hence, the prejudice of many whites — both tenants and landlords — compelled Negroes of different educational and social backgrounds to live virtually side by side. It forced the rich and poor, the moral and immoral to rub shoulders.

It was not merely the squalor of most houses or the dilapidation of the neighborhood that threatened morality, but the necessity to seek boarders to mitigate the high rental costs. The lodging system was not unique to the Negro; however, it was more prevalent than among other groups. In a canvass of the Nineteenth Assembly District in 1897 the Federation of Churches found that 40 per cent of the Negro families in the district had boarders. Only one group — the Austrians — had a higher percentage. In almost half of these Negro rentals, the boarders were not related to the family.[45] An investigation by the National League on Urban Conditions Among Negroes in 1915 found similar conditions in an area of Harlem. According to the study, lodgers constituted 32 per cent of the area's Negro population. Only 30 per cent of the boarders were related to the families in whose house they lived. The League's investigation also indicated that 88 per cent of those apartments occupied by women without husbands contained boarders.[46] Negro leaders considered the high incidence of lodging a threat to morality. W. E. B. Du Bois, Negro educator, sociologist, historian, and social critic, observed in 1901 that "unknown strangers are thus admitted to the very heart of homes in order that rent may be paid."[47]

In addition to breeding crime and immorality, tenement houses contributed to the death rate. Mary Ovington blamed the "hot, crowded tenements" for the high rate of infant mortality among Negroes. Hot and damp living conditions were made worse by Negro mothers who were driven to convert their living quarters into a laundry to help support their families. The Charity Organization, which campaigned against the evils of the tenement house system, believed that the conditions under which the Negro was compelled to live were responsible for his "peculiar susceptibility" to tuberculosis. It reported in 1905 that the Negro mortality rate was almost twice that of any other group.[48] Circumstances other than poor housing conditions also accounted for the high infant mortality among Negroes. A large percentage of Negro mothers, many of whom were recent immigrants from the South, had not had the opportunity to acquire adequate health habits. To offset these conditions, day nurseries were established to remove children for at least part of the day from the unhealthy conditions of the tenement. Governmental and private agencies conducted schools, lectures, and campaigns to instruct New York Negroes in proper health habits. Mothers, for example, were encouraged to breast-feed their infants — "Babies need mother's milk; cow's milk is a mighty poor substitute." [49]

Negroes also were limited in the selection of a home by the prejudices of tenants and landlords. In 1869 a Negro resident of Greenwich Village asserted:

> We find it so difficult to persuade anyone to rent us a decent place on account of our color. Hundreds of us would gladly pay twice the rent to live in some more respectable neighborhoods; but the landlords will not accept us as tenants on any terms, declaring that should they rent a couple of rooms to a colored man, all their white lodgers would immediately give them notice to leave.[50]

In 1889 a Negro clergyman, R. F. Hurley, pastor of the Bethel Methodist Episcopal Church, reported that "only after a house" had gained "a bad name" would the owners allow "it to be rented to colored tenants." Hutchens C. Bishop, pastor of the most affluent Negro church in the city, St. Philip's Protestant Episcopal Church, also declared in 1889 that "so strong" was this prejudice on the part of landlords and tenants "that many of our best people" had left "the city entirely." [51] Social commentators seconded the protests of the Negro clergymen. Jacob Riis, writing in the 1890s, reported that a Negro was admitted to an apartment house only after it had received an "unsavory reputation." Prejudiced whites, proclaimed the New York *Post* in 1900, were responsible for the "miserable abodes" which Negroes were forced "to call their homes." William H. Baldwin, president of the Long Island Railroad, speaking at the Plymouth Church of Brooklyn in 1903, said that a landlord will only lease a house to a Negro after he "gets as much use as possible out of his property from the Irish, when he can no longer rent his tenement house to the Italians." One year earlier a Negro woman writer argued that her people were left "without any choice" in their selection of a home. "A rattlesnake would be more quickly accommodated," a Negro journal reported in 1905, than the Negro "by some landlords in certain sections of the city." E. F. Dyckoff, a white writer, maintained that those whites who fear "the encroachment of a Negro slum have done their best to thwart the growth and the progress of New York Negroes in obtaining better housing and living conditions." [52]

Negroes, therefore, usually had to wait until there was no demand from other groups for a building before it was opened to their patronage. On occasion, however, they did secure residences against the wishes of the whites of a neighborhood, but this appears to have been only when the people replaced were an underprivileged group and usually Irish. On rare occasions, Negroes did move into a white neighborhood to the chagrin of its older residents. In 1901 the residents of Central Park West were annoyed by a Negro renting an apartment near the Park. Though the Negro colony of the area was only one block west of Central Park, whites did not want it seeping farther eastward. When Negroes moved into the neighborhood extending from West 90th Street to West 110th Street in the early 1900s, a series of white protests culminated in the formation of the West Side Improvement Association. This group's idea of improvement was to evict Negroes from the area. The Association, which the *Age* reported as being "composed in the main of Jews," explained that it had no prejudice against the race; "still the fact" existed that "their presence in a neighborhood" caused the "value of property to deteriorate." [53]

Similar protests greeted the Negro's entrance into Harlem. At first, property owners called meetings and passed resolutions opposing the Negro invasion. When the Negro community continued to grow despite these protestations, white property owners resorted to more drastic action. In 1913 they organized the Property Owners' Protective Association. The Association asserted that Negroes were dangerous, poor tenants, and destructive of property values. To implement their feelings, the members urged white property owners to enter into agreements not to rent or sell to Negroes. They also attempted to buy property of whites who claimed they could find only Negro purchasers. A similar group, the Committee of Thirty of the Property Owners' Improvement Corporation of Harlem, announced in 1914 that it had the "enthusiastic support of many of the largest owners of real estate in this district." It also beseeched Negro leaders to organize a committee to buy and erect homes in an area that would be exclusively Negro. Although some Negro real estate brokers approved the plan, others denounced it as anti-Negro and a cruel joke. The Negro leadership also dissented from the claim that the influx of Negroes to a neighborhood reduced property values. John Royall, a Negro real estate agent, declared that depreciation was attributable to the prejudice of whites, not to Negro residents. Reduced property values were a matter of attitude, not any rigid law of economics. For after World War I, the increased demand for apartments in Harlem caused a rise in the real estate values of the area.[54]

These attempts at restricting the extension of the Harlem Negro community ended in failure. Negro churches and real estate firms continued to buy houses for Negro habitation. Many landlords owning partially occupied apartment houses discovered that when they rented to Negroes their vacancy rate decreased and their rental rates increased. Negroes now spread farther into Harlem, and, once again, whites because of prejudice fled those streets where Negroes made their homes. Harlem was no different than those areas of the city that Negroes had occupied in the past — housing segregation was as strong as ever.[55]

In addition to suffering under inferior living conditions, Negroes were forced to pay higher rents than whites. The *Globe* in 1883 bemoaned "exaggerated" and "usurious" rental charges. Real estate agents realized a greater profit when renting to Negroes. In 1889 one landlord had been receiving $127 a month from white tenants. When he leased the same building to Negroes, the rental rose to $144.[56] In 1871 Negroes paid on the average of $12 a month for three- or four-room apartments. By the mid-1880s rentals had advanced to between $11 and $16 for three rooms, with a slightly higher figure for homes in the Forties and Fifties. These sums were greater than the rentals paid by whites for apartments near Negro neighborhoods. A white person paid from $7 to $11 for a three-room apartment. A similar disparity existed for larger flats. Whites paid as high as $14 for a four-room dwelling, whereas Negroes as much as $20.[57]

During the 1890s and the 1900s, rental rates increased for

all persons; however, one factor remained constant — the Negro still paid a higher rent than the white man. "The old robbery still goes on," wrote Jacob Riis in 1900, where "the Negro pitches his tent, he pays more rent than his white neighbor."[58] It was estimated that the Negro sometimes had to pay from $1 a month to twice what the white man's rent would be for a comparable apartment.[59] In the area below the west Seventies, the Negro paid from $11 to $17 for three- and four-room apartments, whereas in Harlem rent varied between $13 and $23. In addition, Harlem apartments offered more conveniences — baths, hot water, carpeted halls, and tiled bathrooms. Apartments in the San Juan Hill and Tenderloin districts provided, at most, baths and hot water.[60]

While landlords agreed that the Negro paid higher rentals, they were not unanimous in their opinion of the Negro as a tenant. In 1889 one proprietor remarked that the Negro was careless of property and contended that the lower class of Negroes moved too often. However, another real estate agent said that Negroes pay "their rent more promptly than the poorer class of whites and keep their apartments in better condition." Landlords preferred the Negro tenant, observed a *Tribune* reporter in 1889, "to the lower grade of white people." The poorer European immigrant was considered less desirable than the Negro. In 1890 a landlord remarked that he "would rather have negro tenants" in his "poorest class of tenements than the lower grades of foreign white people." Negroes are "cleaner" and "do not destroy the property so much," the proprietor concluded. Another *Tribune* reporter, writing in 1895, was surprised by the "cosiness" and well-furnished nature of Negro apartments.[61]

During the first two decades of the twentieth century, many observers continued to express the view that Negroes were, in general, good tenants. Jack Thorne, a Negro, writing in a letter to the *Times* in 1900, claimed that landlords had learned that there were good Negro tenants. A Negro social commentator, Helen Tucker, asserted seven years later that Negro apartments were "clean and well kept, some very prettily furnished." "Given the same income or lack of income," wrote Mary Ovington in 1910, "the colored do not allow their surroundings to become so cheerless or so filthy as the white." An Englishman visiting the city in 1910 noted that even in the poorest Negro sections apart-

ments were "clean, wholesome, and attractive as compared to
the dwellings of many respectable Londoners." Such comments
were seconded by members of the National League on Urban
Conditions Among Negroes and the New York Tenement House
Commission. *"The money-mad white owners and business men,"*
claimed John T. Clark of the Urban League in 1913, were the
greatest problem facing Negro tenants. The Negro's preservation
of property and prompt payment of rent earned the praise of
Lawson Purdy of the Tenement House Commission in 1919.[62]
The Negro, therefore, was limited in his choice of an apartment
by an illusion created by most whites. It was not because the
Negro destroyed apartments; it was because the white man
convinced himself that the Negro reduced the value of buildings. Furthermore, most white tenants were averse to living with
the man of the darker skin; therefore, they created a picture of
corrupt, dishonest, adulterous, and murderous Negroes. Let one
Negro fit any one of these categories and the white man believed
his fantasy proved.

Although most Negroes were compelled to reside in inferior
living quarters, improved housing for at least some became available between the late 1880s and 1910. In the late 1880s the better
buildings for Negro tenants were located in the west Fifties, Sixties, and One-hundreds. The "Dolly Mount," 211 West Sixtieth
Street, had carpeting, steam heat, and various furnishings. The
"Sumner" and the "Garrison" — located on 126th Street — offered
marble fire hearths guarded by iron grates, gas illumination, hot
and cold water, toilets on each floor, and embellishments such as
walnut mantels, mirror glasses, and washtubs. In 1889 Florence
Williams, a Negro columnist, praised the building of decent homes
for Negroes. "It has enabled them to enjoy a little of the blessings
of living respectably, with conveniences that they were deprived
of even upon paying large rents," she wrote. Advertisements of
buildings containing the "choicest apartments in the city for select
colored families" were carried by the *Age* in 1889. The prospectus
referred to the absence of "dark rooms" and the existence of
clothes and dish closets, washtubs, marble mantels, two toilet
closets on every floor, and electric bells. "The Adele," on 122nd
Street, publicized features similar to those of the other buildings
as well as separate bathrooms, ranges, stationary ice chests, and
"halls heated in winter." The "Beaufort," at Fiftieth Street, of-

fered dumbwaiters, decorations, set tubs, and ranges. A building on West 124th Street claimed carpeted halls and two water closets on each floor. In the Tenderloin district it was claimed that "completely renovated" buildings were available. The "Chelsea," 124–130 West Twenty-seventh Street, proclaimed its electric vestibule bells, speaking tubes, private letter boxes, coal and ash elevators.[63] Along with the poverty-ridden and dilapidated nature of certain Negro districts, decent housing had emerged in some areas. The *Age* summarized this change for the better in 1890: "We are not now restricted so much to unpleasant localities and there has been a marked improvement in the grade of houses offered us and reduction in the rental demanded." [64]

Better housing conditions also were offered the Negro in Brooklyn. In 1889 Hutchens C. Bishop asserted that many Negroes left Manhattan because of the better housing conditions of Brooklyn.[65] In a letter to the *Age* in 1887 a person calling himself the "Observer" wrote:

> Here [Brooklyn] a family may be reared with healthful surroundings and without contamination by those gaudy viceful influences, which seem to keep with Negro colonization in New York city [*sic*]. . . . Here, also, is an entire absence of the great tenement system.[66]

Among the dwellings of Brooklyn were a greater number of private homes. The Census for 1890 reported 71 homes owned by Brooklyn Negroes as opposed to 21 for Manhattan Negroes.[67] But it was not long before the Brooklyn Negro fell victim to inferior housing. Whereas Brooklyn had been a refuge for Negroes seeking better living conditions before the 1890s, between 1890 and 1920 it came to contain a large number of below standard houses. Its decent homes usually were limited to private houses. "The houses are squatty and unfit for human habitation," declared a white clergyman in 1910, and "women and children are huddled in small rooms." Houses that Negroes were compelled to inhabit, read a report of the Brooklyn Urban League in 1919, were "totally unsatisfactory as homes in which to bring up healthy, moral families." [68]

In the 1900s with the help of realty companies, largely Negro, a greater number of Negroes obtained better apartments. Improved housing conditions were found in a few areas of the deteriorated San Juan Hill neighborhood. Decent homes were made available between Sixty and Sixty third streets one of the most crowded areas in the city. These buildings featured hot water, steam heat, and baths. A reporter for the New York *Sun* commented on the incongruity of these buildings in the midst of squalor. This illustrated the difficulty Negroes had in obtaining apartments in better neighborhoods. Even adequate housing, when it could be had, was in dilapidated communities.[69]

The best housing facilities provided Manhattan Negroes were located in Harlem. Although Harlem contained its share of poor housing, it was the "home of the best-housed Negroes in the world." According to the Urban League, in 1915 many of Harlem's Negroes occupied houses that were "substantially built" and "with regard for sanitation and convenience." Harlem provided houses, wrote Mary Ovington in 1910, where Negroes can "live in privacy, and with the comforts of steam heat and a private bath." The area itself, with its wide avenues and tree-lined streets, was more attractive than any section open to Negroes in Manhattan.[70] From 133rd to 136th streets and 141st to 142nd streets were to be found the largest number of better apartment houses for Negroes. In 1920 the purchase of the so-called Astor Houses on 130th Street added another group to the growing class of decent apartment houses. The buildings on 141st and 142nd streets, which were purchased by a Negro real estate firm, offered gas, electricity, mail chutes, and hardwood trim. In general, the better buildings in Harlem boasted steam heat, hot water, tile bathrooms, and various ostentatious decorations. These features were far superior to the mere offering of "improvements" made available in other Negro neighborhoods.[71]

A large part of the credit for these steps forward — and they were only steps, as the average Negro lived in below standard housing — must go to Negro realty companies. Although a few white groups, such as the City and Suburban Homes Company, erected decent homes for Negroes, the major burden was carried by Negro groups. The outstanding Negro realty firm was the Afro-American Realty Company. This Company was incorporated in 1904 with capital of $500,000. Its purpose was to lease, buy, and build apartments throughout New York City for rental to Negroes. Through such acquisitions, the Afro-American Company sought to make it possible for a Negro to live anywhere in the city. The only requirement put upon tenants was ability to pay the rent; hence it was presumed that Negroes and whites could live not only in the same neighborhoods, but in the same buildings. By the end of 1904 the Afro-American Company owned four five-story flats and had five-year leases on eleven other buildings. This number grew to six owned and fourteen leased in 1905. The Company, though, limited its rentals to the so-called better class of Negroes. In 1907 the *Age* praised Afro-American Realty for securing "desirable homes in localities which are not infested with crime, sin, and death-breeding tenement houses." [72]

The *New York Times,* though, opposed the Company's plan. It will "depress real estate values," argued the newspaper, "in order to bring desirable apartment houses into the market as homes for negroes." The Negro Company's proposal would "intensify" rather than reduce prejudice, by causing "neighborhood deterioration," contended the paper as it concluded with a diatribe against the Negro tenant:

> The negro has not yet established his status as a desirable tenant, and while he has been the recourse of owners who have unprofitable apartments on their hands, negro settlements are rarely invited if other use can be made of what are designed to be permanent improvements. [73]

Because of attitudes such as that of the *Times,* Afro-American Realty was forced to abandon its plans for integrated houses and seek separate but fairly equal homes for the Negro. In the future, when Afro-American Realty and other companies acquired a house occupied by whites, they evicted the white tenants and replaced them with Negroes. [74]

The Company's real estate agent, the leading Negro realty man in the city, was Philip A. Payton, Jr. Payton was born in Massachusetts in 1876. Upon coming to New York City, he worked as a porter and barber. Before long, however, he opened a real estate office. Young Payton was given credit for opening Harlem to Negro settlement. While Negroes had arrived in Harlem before Payton's activities, it was through his diligent work that the race was furnished with extensive housing accommodations in the area. In 1917, for example, his firm bought six modern elevator buildings in Harlem for "better class" Negroes. In peopling those houses he managed or owned, Payton demanded references from prospective tenants. He believed that it was through the Negro real estate agent, not the disinterested white landlord, that housing conditions for Negroes would be improved.[75] Another active Negro real estate firm was that of John E. Nail and Henry C. Parker. Within seven years, these men were managing more than 75 pieces of real estate that brought in $35,000 in monthly rentals. Other Negroes entered the real estate field; by 1920 some 21 such persons had offices in Harlem.[76]

Better housing for Negroes also received some assistance from Negro churches. Many of the more financially secure houses of worship invested portions of their funds in real estate. St. Mark's Methodist Episcopal Church purchased an apartment house on Lenox Avenue, between 140th and 141st streets. St. Philip's Protestant Episcopal Church, which catered to the more affluent members of the city's Negro community, made the largest real estate investments of any New York Negro church. By 1911 it was reported that this church owned or controlled 20 six-story buildings on West 135th Street. Not all Negro investment in real estate was limited to New Yorkers; southern Negro groups, like the Wage Earners' Savings Bank of Savannah, Georgia, put portions of their savings into New York property. In 1918 it was estimated that Negroes owned some $20 million in Harlem real estate.[77]

The National Urban League, too, worked for better Negro housing accommodations. Formed in 1910 as the League on Urban Conditions Among Negroes, it created a housing bureau not only to find decent homes for Negroes but to improve living conditions in Negro neighborhoods. The League established a "certified list" of decent houses for Negroes and a "suspicion list" for those buildings that failed to maintain adequate living standards. As part of its work, it instructed Negroes in the proper method of "sanitation and upkeep of properties." Through the development of a "moral consciousness," the League believed Negroes would not tolerate bad management of the houses they occupied and would prevent the deterioration of their living quarters and neighborhoods. In regard to the latter, the League encouraged Negroes to develop community pride. The Utopia Neighborhood Club was organized to fulfill this purpose in one section of Harlem. The League enrolled youths in its Juvenile Park Protective League to report on obstructed fire escapes, unlighted hallways, and street littering.[78]

Outside of the Urban League, which was composed of Negroes and whites, white reform groups did little to furnish or locate decent housing facilities for Negroes. The Charity Organization, for example, limited its activities to instructing Negroes in better health habits and establishing a kindergarten for Negro children.[79] In general, Negroes were forced to rely on the resources of their own community for any improvement in housing accommodations. The city's Department of Health, as indicated earlier, informed Negroes of the latest health practices; however, Negroes complained that municipal authorities were indifferent to the plight of their community. The city failed to provide regular garbage collection and to prosecute housing violations in Negro neighborhoods. Mayor John F. Hylan did appoint a Negro to a committee investigating the housing shortage problem after World War I.[80] Yet Negroes only benefited indirectly from the service performed by the city. As one Negro commentator remarked in 1920, those in power would do little for the Negro unless "the Negro himself takes the initiative and attempts to work out his own salvation by bringing his case to the direct attention of those who are in position to help him." In this way, Negroes, only after a period of continual protestation to the city fathers, obtained a play street and bathhouse in Harlem.[81]

Mainly through self-help, therefore, housing conditions for some Negroes improved. But even with these improvements the average Negro still had to endure inferior living quarters and face the discriminatory practices of most landlords and tenants. The disinterest exhibited by municipal officials and the ever increasing Negro population of the city further impeded attempts by the Negro community to secure decent housing accommodations. This was attested to by an Urban League study of 1927 that found housing and neighborhood deterioration on the rise in Harlem.[82]

Notes

[1] W. E. B. Du Bois, *Some Notes on the Negroes in New York City* (Atlanta, 1903), p. 1; Ernst, "The Economic Status of New York City Negroes," p. 132; Johnson, *Black Manhattan*, pp. 58–59; Harry A. Williamson, "Folks in Old New York and Brooklyn," unpublished paper, Arthur A. Schomburg Collection, New York, 1953, p. 10; *New York Times*, April 14, 1889.

[2] New York City Board of Education, *Annual Report from the Committee on Colored Schools for 1866* (New York, 1867), p. 4, and *Annual Report for 1868* (New York, 1869), unpaged appendix.

[3] A few of the more wealthy

Negroes found it possible to live in white neighborhoods of Brooklyn. They owned their houses and in some cases had white servants. *New York Times,* July 14, 1895. Du Bois, *Notes on Negroes,* p. 1, contended that residential segregation began in 1850. Increased immigration in the 1840s, he went on to argue, had "formed a cordon" around the Negro; *New York Tribune,* July 22, 1906. Mary White Ovington, *Half A Man: the Status of the Negro in New York* (New York, 1911), p. 34, selected 1860 as the year segregation began; however, George E. Haynes, *The Negro at Work in New York: a Study in Economic Progress* (New York, 1912), p. 48, went as far back as 1800 to find the start of New York City segregation.

⁴ *New York Times,* April 14, 1889; *New York Tribune,* January 27, 1889; George E. Haynes, "Conditions Among Negroes in the Cities," *Annals of the American Academy of Political and Social Science,* XLIX (September, 1913), 109; Ovington, *Half A Man,* pp. 49–50.
⁵ *Ninth Census, Statistics of Population,* pp. 212–14.
⁶ New York City Board of Education, *Directory for 1865* (New York, 1866), pp. 165–69; *Directory for 1867* (New York, 1868), pp. 139–43; *Directory for 1868* (New York, 1869), p. 138; *Journal for 1872* (New York, 1873), pp. 396, 656–57; *Annual Report for 1877* (New York, 1878), p. 32; *Tribune Monthly* (March, 1896), 51.
⁷ *Ninth Census, Statistics of Population,* p. 212; *Eleventh Census, Population,* I, 471.
⁸ Jacob A. Riis, *The Children of the Poor* (New York, 1892), p. 10; *New York Times,* April 14, 1889; *New York Tribune,* October 13, 1895.
⁹ *New York Times,* April 14, 1889; *New York Tribune,* October 13, 1895; Jacob A. Riis, *A Ten*

Years' War: an Account of the Battle with the Slum in New York (New York, 1900), p. 65.
¹⁰ *New York Tribune,* January 27, 1889.
¹¹ *Ibid.* See also October 13, 1895, and July 18, 1901; New York *Sun,* August 6, 1905; Ovington, *Half A Man,* pp. 34, 50; Federation of Churches and Christian Workers in New York City, *Sociological Canvass No. 2* (New York, 1897), p. 21; David Graham Phillips, "A Walk on Seventh Avenue," *Harper's Weekly,* XXXV (June 20, 1891), 466.
¹² *New York Tribune,* March 6, April 10, October 13, 1895.
¹³ *Ibid.,* April 1, 1900; *Ninth Census, Statistics of Population,* pp. 212–14; *Eleventh Census, Population,* I, 471; *Twelfth Census, Population,* I, 631–32; *Thirteenth Census, Population,* III, 253–55.
¹⁴ *New York Age,* March 23, 1889; June 5, 14, 1890; February 28, 1891.
¹⁵ *New York Times,* December 26, 1901.
¹⁶ *Ibid.,* March 8, 22, 1914, and October 8, 1916; *New York Age,* April 25, October 3, 1912; August 7, 14, 1913; February 12, June 11, 1914; *Crisis,* VII (February, 1914), 174–75.
¹⁷ *New York Age,* May 11, 1913; March 19, 1914; December 6, 1919; New York *Post,* July 14, 1917; *Crisis,* II (June, 1911), 51; Frances Blascoer, *Colored School Children in New York* (New York, 1915), p. 70; The Charity Organization Society of the City of New York, *Twenty-Eighth Annual Report, 1910* (New York, 1910), p. 38; Victor R. Daly, "The Housing Crisis in New York City," *Crisis,* XXI (December, 1920), 61; *Thirteenth Census, Population,* III, 253–58; *Fourteenth Census, New York State,* pp. 66–67.
¹⁸ Blascoer, *Colored School Children,* pp. 75–76; Rollin Lynde Hartt, "I'd Like to Show You Harlem,"

Independent, CV (April 2, 1921), 334.

[19] *New York Times,* November 17, 1901.

[20] *Ibid.,* April 28, 1889; July 14, October 13, 1895; November 17, 1901; *New York Tribune,* April 1, 1900, and August 14, 1910; *New York Age,* August 18, 1910; Ovington, *Half A Man,* p. 43; Williamson, "Folks in New York," p. 11.

[21] *New York Globe,* March 8, 1884; *New York Age,* November 1, 1890 and May 16, 1891.

[22] Riis, *The Children of the Poor,* p. 10.

[23] *Ninth Census, Statistics of Population,* pp. 211–14; *Eleventh Census, Population,* I, 470–71; *Twelfth Census, Population,* III, 253–58; *Fourteenth Census, New York State,* pp. 66–67; Federation of Churches, *Canvass No. 2,* p. 21.

[24] Ovington, *Half A Man,* pp. 34, 50. For further comment on conflict between Negro and other groups, see chapter five.

[25] *New York Times,* April 14, 1889; *New York Tribune,* August 14, 1904; *New York Age,* August 24, 1905; Mary White Ovington, "The Negro Home in New York," *Charities,* XV (October 7, 1905), 29–30.

[26] *New York Age,* December 5, 1912; August 14, 1913; June 11, 1914; E. F. Dyckoff, "A Negro City in New York," *Outlook,* CVIII (December 23, 1914), 948–51; National League on Urban Conditions Among Negroes, "Housing Conditions Among Negroes in Harlem, New York City," *Bulletin,* IV (January, 1915), 7–8.

[27] *New York Age,* January 19, 1911; Harry J. Carman, *The Street Surface Railway Franchises of New York City* (New York, 1919), pp. 53, 73, 75–76, 113–14, 177; Greater New York Federation of Churches, *The Negro Churches of Manhattan* (New York, 1930), p. 5; Haynes, *Negro at Work,* pp. 48–49; Johnson,

Black Manhattan, p. 148; Ovington, *Half A Man,* pp. 35–38.

[28] *New York Times,* November 17, 1901; The Charity Organization Society of the City of New York, *Twenty-Ninth Annual Report, 1911* (New York, 1911), p. 32; Glenn Frank, "The Clash of Color: the Negro in American Democracy," *Century,* XCIX (November, 1919), 88.

[29] *Ninth Census, Statistics of Population,* p. 211; *Eleventh Census, 1890, Vital Statistics of New York City and Brooklyn* (New York, 1894), pp. 238–41.

[30] *Eleventh Census, Vital Statistics of New York City and Brooklyn,* pp. 238–41; *New York Age,* June 22, 1889; *New York Times,* October 1, 3, 1894; *New York Tribune,* August 14, 1910; Ovington, *Half A Man,* p. 29.

[31] *Twelfth Census, Population,* I, 631; *Thirteenth Census, Population,* III, 256–58; *Fourteenth Census, New York State,* pp. 64–65; *New York Age,* August 6, 1908.

[32] *New York Times,* July 14, 1895; *New York Age,* September 3, 1908; *New York Tribune,* August 14, 1910; *Thirteenth Census, Population,* III, 256–58; *Fourteenth Census, New York State,* pp. 64–65.

[33] *New York Globe,* January 20, 1883; Jacob A. Riis, *How the Other Half Lives: Studies Among the Tenements of New York* (New York, 1890), p. 150; *New York Times,* April 14, 1889; *Survey,* XXXIV (April 17, 1915), 66.

[34] *New York Times,* March 2, 1869, April 14, 1889; New York Colored Mission, *Annual Report for 1871* (New York, 1872), p. 8; *New York Globe,* January 20, 1883; Congress of Colored Catholics of the United States, *Proceedings of Three Catholic Afro-American Congresses . . . 1889* (Cincinnati, 1893), p. 70.

[35] Riis, *The Children of the Poor,* p. 10; Riis, *How the Other*

Half Lives, p. 150; Riis, *Ten Years'
War,* pp. 75–76; *New York Age,* December 20, 1890.

³⁶ *New York Tribune,* January
27, 1889.

³⁷ *New York Age,* March 23,
1889, and February 28, August 22,
1891.

³⁸ *Ibid.,* July 27, 1916; New
York *Post,* August 18, 1900; *New
York Times,* August 16, 17, 1900,
and November 17, 1901; *New York
Tribune,* August 16, 17, 1900; New
York *Sun,* August 6, 1905; Haynes,
Negro at Work, p. 52.

³⁹ New York *Sun,* August 6,
1905.

⁴⁰ Helena Titus Emerson, "Children of the Circle: the Work of the
New York Free Kindergarten Association for Colored Children,"
Charities, XV (October 7, 1905),
82; G. L. Collins, "The City Within
the City," *Outlook,* LXXXIV (September 29, 1906), 274; Ovington,
"The Negro Home in New York,"
p. 25.

⁴¹ New York *Sun,* August 6,
1905. The article in which these
statements appeared was entitled
"The Naughty Negroes of San Juan
Hill." It was accompanied by stereotype cartoons of the Negro. In one
line, though, the writer of the article
admitted that only a small part of
the colony was "bad."

⁴² Ovington, *Half A Man,* p. 41;
Free Kindergarten Association for
Colored Children, *Annual Report for
1904* (New York, 1904), p. 3; Federation of Churches, *Canvass No. 2,*
p. 85; New York *World,* August 19,
1900; Emerson, "Children of the
Circle," p. 82.

⁴³ Ovington, *Half A Man,* p. 47;
J. Gilmer Speed, "The Negro in New
York," *Harper's Weekly,* XLIV (December 22, 1900), 1249–50; *New
York Age,* July 30, 1908.

⁴⁴ *New York Times,* July 14,
1903; Ovington, "The Negro Home
in New York," p. 25. Also see *New
York Age,* August 10, 1911, and
August 1, 1912; The Charity Organization of the City of New York,
Thirtieth Annual Report, 1912 (New
York, 1912), p. 45; Mary White
Ovington, "The Gunpowder of Race
Antagonism," *American City,* XXI
(September, 1919), 248–51.

⁴⁵ Percentage of families in each
nationality having boarders: Austrian–54.3; Negro–40; Italian–32.6;
Irish–18.3; American–16.6; German–10.7. Percentage of families in
each nationality having nonrelative
boarders: German–47.9; Negro–
44.5; Italian–36.4; Irish–28.3; American–24.7. Federation of Churches,
Canvass No. 2, p. 26.

⁴⁶ *New York Age,* December 23,
1915; National League on Urban
Conditions, "Housing Conditions
Among Negroes in Harlem," pp.
19–20.

⁴⁷ *New York Times,* November
24, 1901; Tucker, "Negro Craftsmen
in New York," p. 546.

⁴⁸ Ovington, *Half A Man,* pp.
53–55; *Charities,* XIV (June 10,
1905), 825; Mary White Ovington,
"Fresh Air Work Among Colored
Children in New York," *ibid.,* XVII
(February, 1906), 115–17.

⁴⁹ Mary White Ovington, "Vacation Days on San Juan Hill — a New
York Negro Colony," *Southern Workman,* XXXVIII (November, 1909),
633–34; New York City Department
of Health, *Weekly Bulletin,* VI
(April 7, 1917), 105, and *Columbus
Hill Chronicle,* I (April, 1915), 3;
Survey, XXVII (December 30,
1916), 37–38.

⁵⁰ *New York Times,* March 2,
1869.

⁵¹ *Ibid.,* April 14, 28, 1889.

⁵² Riis, *How the Other Half
Lives,* p. 150; New York *Post,* August
17, 1900; *New York Tribune,* March
15, 1903; Mary Rankin Cranston,
"The Housing of the Negro in New
York City," *Southern Workman,*
XXXI (June, 1902), 327–32; Col-

ored American Magazine, VIII (May, 1905), 242; Dyckoff, "A Negro City in New York," p. 949.

[53] New York *Sun,* August 6, 1905; Emerson, "The Children of the Circle," p. 82; Ovington, "The Negro Home in New York," pp. 29–30; *Half A Man,* p. 85; *New York Tribune,* July 28, 1901, and August 10, 1906; *New York Age,* November 26, 1908, and September 2, 1909; *New York Times,* August 22, 1903.

[54] *Crisis,* II (October, 1911), 232, and VII (February, 1914), 174–75; *New York Age,* August 7, 14, October 3, 1913, and February 12, March 19, June 11, 1914; *New York Times,* January 7, 1913; March 22, 1914; October 8, 1916; January 18, 1919.

[55] *New York Age,* April 25, June 27, August 25, October 3, November 7, December 5, 1912; March 6, August 14, 1913; June 11, 1914; July 12, 1917; *New York Times,* July 11, 1917; New York *World,* February 23, 1913; National League on Urban Conditions, "Housing Conditions Among Negroes in Harlem," p. 8.

[56] *New York Globe,* January 20, 1883; *New York Times,* April 14, 1889; *New York Tribune,* January 27, 1889.

[57] New York Colored Mission, *Annual Report for 1871* (New York, 1872), p. 8. For Negro rents, see *New York Freeman,* September 17, October 1, 1887; *New York Age,* October 29, 1887; March 3, August 25, September 22, 1888; April 13, June 1, November 2, 23, 1889. For rents paid by whites, see *New York Tribune,* November 6, 1887, and February 24, 1889.

[58] Riis, *Ten Years' War,* p. 64. Also see Charles Martin, "The Harlem Negro," *A.M.E. Zion Quarterly Review,* XXVI (Fourth Quarter, 1916), 3; National League on Urban Conditions, "Housing Conditions Among Negroes in Harlem," pp. 7,

15–17; *Crisis,* XIII (January, 1917), 147; New York *World,* February 23, 1913; *New York Age,* December 5, 1911; June 11, 1914; October 12, 1916.

[59] See Federation of Churches, *Canvass No. 2,* p. 85; *New York Times,* November 24, 1901; *New York Tribune,* October 13, 1895; Tucker, "Negro Craftsmen in New York," p. 546; Speed, "The Negro in New York," p. 1249; Claude McKay, *Harlem: Negro Metropolis* (New York, 1940), p. 17.

[60] *New York Age,* February 23, March 9, August 3, December 28, 1905; January 11, May 24, October 4, December 20, 1906; January 7, February 7, August 1, 1907; February 20, November 19, 1908; September 16, 1909; October 6, 13, 1910.

[61] *New York Tribune,* January 27, 1889, and October 13, 1895; *New York Times,* April 14, 1889; Riis, *How Other Half Lives,* p. 151.

[62] *New York Times,* September 12, 1900; Tucker, "Negro Craftsmen in New York," p. 546; Ovington, *Half A Man,* p. 33; Sir Harry H. Johnston, *The Negro in the World* (London, 1910), p. 475; *New York Age,* August 7, 1913, and April 19, 1919.

[63] *New York Age,* March 23, June 15, November 2, December 7, 1889, and February 28, August 22, 1891.

[64] *Ibid.,* February 21, 1890.

[65] *New York Times,* April 28, 1889.

[66] *New York Age,* November 26, 1887.

[67] *Eleventh Census, Population,* II, 581. In 1920 Negro home ownership by boroughs was .7 per cent for Manhattan; 6.1 for Brooklyn; 7.8 for the Bronx; 17.9 for Richmond; and 31.5 for Queens. Thomas J. Woofter, *Negro Problems in Cities* (Garden City, N.Y., 1928), p. 141.

[68] Brooklyn Urban League for

Social Service Among Negroes, *Annual Report, 1919* (New York, 1919), p. 2; *New York Age,* March 31, 1910. Also see *ibid.,* September 3, 1908; *New York Times,* November 11, 1903; *New York Tribune,* August 14, 1910.

[69] *New York Age,* January 26, 1905; New York *Sun,* August 6, 1905; *New York Times,* February 28, 1905; Ovington, *Half A Man,* p. 41.

[70] *New York Age,* October 13, 1910; August 1, 1912; July 27, 1916; *New York Tribune,* August 14, 1910; Ovington, *Half A Man,* p. 47; National League on Urban Conditions, "Housing Conditions Among Negroes in Harlem," p. 949; Hartt, "I'd Like to Show You Harlem," p. 334.

[71] Ovington, *Half A Man,* p. 45; *New York Tribune,* August 14, 1910, and July 11, 1917; *New York Age,* February 9, December 28, 1905; January 11, May 24, 1906; August 1, 1907; February 20, November 19, 1908; September 16, 1909; June 27, 1912; *New York Times,* November 21, 1920; New York *Post,* July 14, 1917.

[72] Cranston, "The Housing of the Negro in New York City," p. 331; *New York Times,* July 26, 1904; *New York Tribune,* July 26, August 14, 1904, and August 13, 1905; Roscoe Conkling Simmons, "The Afro-American Realty Company," *Colored American Magazine,* VIII (July, 1905), 269–70; Booker T. Washington, *The Negro in Business* (Boston, 1907), pp. 197–98; *New York Age,* February 28, 1907; *Crisis,* I (December, 1910), 9; City and Suburban Homes Company, *Negro Housing: a Sound Economic Plan to Solve a Social Problem of the Greatest Importance to Every Citizen* (New York, 1916), unpaged.

[73] *New York Times,* July 27, 1904.

[74] *Ibid.,* October 9, 1913, and

July 11, 1917; *New York Age,* February 28, 1907; October 3, June 27, 1912; October 9, 1913; *Crisis,* II (May, 1911), 5; Daly, "The Housing Crisis in New York," p. 62.

[75] Dyckoff, "A Negro City in New York," p. 948; *New York Age,* July 12, 1917; *Crisis,* I (January, 1911), back cover.

[76] *New York Age,* August 14, 1913, and July 31, 1920; *Colored American Review,* I (May, 1916), 202; Dyckoff, "A Negro City in New York," p. 951.

[77] *New York Age,* February 9, 1918; November 7, 1912; March 6, 1913; *New York Times,* March 10, 1920; National League on Urban Conditions, "Housing Conditions Among Negroes in Harlem," pp. 12–13; *Crisis,* II (May, 1911), 5.

[78] *New York Age,* November 6, June 26, 1913; National League on Urban Conditions Among Negroes, *Report for 1912* (New York, 1912), and *Report for 1913–1914 and 1914–1915* (New York, 1915), pp. 18–19.

[79] Ovington, "Fresh Air Work Among Colored Children," pp. 115–17; Ovington, "The Negro Home in New York," pp. 25–30; Emerson, "The Children of the Circle," pp. 81–83; *New York Age,* December 29, 1917. The City and Suburban Homes Company made available two model tenement houses on West Sixty-third Street, see City and Suburban Homes, *Negro Housing,* unpaged.

[80] Blascoer, *Colored School Children,* pp. 23, 71; *New York Age,* June 26, 1890; February 22, 1917; June 12, 1920; National League on Urban Conditions Among Negroes, "Housing Conditions Among Negroes in Harlem," pp. 28–29.

[81] Daly, "The Housing Crisis in New York City," p. 61; New York City Department of Health, *Everybody's Chronicle,* I (August, 1915),

1; *New York Age*, August 10, 1911, and July 24, 1920.

[52] New York Urban League, "Twenty-Four Hundred Negro Families in Harlem," unpublished paper, Schomburg Collection, 1927, p. 3.

.2.

The Negro at Work

LACKING FREEDOM of choice during their period of enslavement, New York's Negroes were severely limited in their selection of an occupation. A few Negroes had been trained as artisans during their years of slavery. But given the nature of slavery, the average Negro was prepared for little more than domestic service outside of farming. Nor was there any appreciable improvement in the Negro's status once the shackles of slavery had been broken. Freedom of person did not mean freedom of choice. His former master once again determined the Negro's occupational status. The Negro was left those jobs that whites considered distasteful and menial.[1]

Most New York Negroes worked as domestics and common laborers in the pre-Civil War period. They could be found in the homes of affluent whites working as butlers and coachmen, cooks and waiters, gardeners and general domestics. In the public sphere, they were employed as bootblacks, porters, waiters, cooks, longshoremen, hod carriers, seamen, washerwomen, dressmakers, and seamstresses.[2] At first Negroes and whites worked side by side, but before long prejudice developed and whites refused to work with the man of the darker skin. Economic competition drove a wedge between the two groups. Fearing the occupational challenge of the Negro laborer, white workers pressured the state into refusing licenses to Negro carmen and porters. With the great migration of Irish immigrants to New York City in the 1840s and 1850s, prejudice between white and Negro workers increased. The German immigrant, on the other hand, who was not the Negro's economic competitor, never developed the antipathy for Negroes that the Irish newcomer manifested.[3]

Initially, white employers professed a preference for Negro to Irish workers. The Irish were considered too truculent and independent. No doubt Protestant employers looked contemptuously upon Irish-Catholic employees. Advertisements in the New York press reflected this sentiment: "A Cook, Washer, and Ironer; who perfectly understands her business; any color or country except Irish." [4] Thus, two of New York society's outcasts struggled for the more menial jobs reserved for them. They developed a mutual antipathy that manifested itself in a number of pitched battles. When the Irishman forced the Negro out of certain jobs, the darker race was impelled to resort to strikebreaking when Irish employees went on strike. This precipitated a number of riots that culminated in the great draft riots of 1863.[5]

Despite the early preference of white employers for Negro labor, the Negro was displaced gradually by the Irish newcomer. In addition, economic innovations created new jobs that were filled by the Irish rather than the Negro. By 1850 there were more Irish servants than the entire Negro population of the city, whereas twenty years earlier Negro labor constituted a majority of the servant class. Hence, the Negro's already precarious position was made even more insecure. Still, a few Negroes were able to enter the skilled trades. Of the 3,688 employed Negroes in 1855, some 200 were in the trades. Most of these trained workers engaged in occupations that catered to the Negro community. Ministers, teachers, druggists, doctors, and musicians comprised the bulk of the skilled Negro class.[6] Discussions of Negro workers, however, were limited to those who serviced the white community, for the white commentator rarely entered the Negro's world. The Negro caterer was the man most whites turned to when they planned a banquet. On the streets of the city, the Negro coachman, in private employment, was a common sight. A white man wishing a haircut or shave would most likely have gone to a Negro barber. Serving the white man, according to the Negro barber, caterer, and coachman, was more respectable than catering to the Negro community. Believing themselves superior to other Negro workers, these men formed their own organizations. Negro caterers, for instance, established the United Waiters' Mutual Beneficial Association in 1869. Despite its title, waiters were not admitted until the 1880s. The organization had a three-fold purpose: first, it was to provide sick and death benefits for its members; second, it sought to maintain a high degree of proficiency among Negro caterers; and third, it served as an outlet through which its members manifested their higher status.[7]

After the Civil War, catering, barbering, and coaching among Negroes declined. The majority of the city's Negro domestics worked as waiters and servants. In 1874, an Irish traveler, Fergus Ferguson, commented on the frequent employment of Negro waiters in New York City. This observation was confirmed four years later by another visitor to Gotham, Sir George Campbell. Other foreign visitors commented on the high quality of service given by Negro waiters. According to George Rose, visiting the city in 1868, the Negro was "far better mannered and attentive" than the white servant. In 1870 another traveler touring the United States was pleasantly surprised to find Negro waiters "more active and obliging" than Irish waiters.[8]

The minority of New York City Negroes who worked outside of the domestic field in the late 1860s were generally unskilled laborers. According to a report of the National Labor Convention of 1869, the few skilled Negro workers were employed in such occupations as tobacco twisting, carpentry, masonry, and printing. However, this was a small number when compared to the 500 Negro longshoremen working on New York City's waterfront in that year. Before the Civil War, Negroes had been used as strikebreakers on the city's piers and a few of these men were retained after a strike was settled. By 1865 Negroes had secured a small place on the docks of New York City.[9]

A change, though, occurred in the Negro's economic status in the post-Civil War period. In 1884 the Negro *Globe* reported that many hotels had replaced Negro workers with white help. French, German, and Irish immigrants had been substituted for many Negro coachmen, footmen, valets, chambermaids, and waiters. Edward Money, an Englishman visiting New York in 1885, noted that Negroes were employed in second-class hotels. Jacob Riis wrote in 1890 that the Negro barber was becoming a "thing of the past." [10]

Though foreign-born workers had replaced some Negro domestics in the 1880s, most Negroes continued to work in the domestic and personal service field. According to the Census of 1890 — the first such report to list the occupations of New York City Negroes — about 70 per cent of the city's Negro men were in domestic and personal service. On the other hand, only 20 per cent of the city's male population and 25 per cent of the foreign-born males were so employed. Negro women also were employed as domestic servants to a greater degree than the other elements of Gotham's population.[11] In 1890 most Negro domestics were employed as servants, waiters, laundresses, and janitors. Negroes constituted 19.9 per cent of the city's male servants and 5.3 per cent of the female servants. Some 20.3 per cent of the laundresses in New York City were Negro as were 15.1 per cent of the janitors. Only 30 per cent of the city's Negro men, however, made their living outside of the domestic and personal service fields. This was far less than the 75 per cent for foreign-born males and the 80 per cent of the total male population. Most Negro men were unskilled workers. Some 68 per cent of those working in the trade and transportation field were draymen, hackmen, teamsters, hostlers, porters, packers, and messengers. As the Colored Mission had remarked in 1885, Negroes were "shut out from nearly all of the trades." [12]

The European immigrant was the main competitor of the Negro. In 1890 the foreign-born element of New York City accounted for at least 50 per cent of the persons employed in occupations that contained a high percentage of Negroes. Not only did Negroes still vie with the Irish and German immigrant for jobs, but they now had to compete, to a lesser degree, with the Italians. Between 1890 and 1900 Italians became New York's bootblacks and barbers, positions that had been the province of the Negro. In addition, French cooks and German waiters replaced Negro help in the better New York restaurants. But foreign displacement of the Negro occurred in only a few areas. Negro workers continued to enter most of the positions they had held in previous years, and in those did so at a faster rate than did the European immigrant.[13]

Between 1890 and 1900 male Negro domestics increased by 109 per cent as opposed to 45 per cent for the foreign-born male. In 1900 Negroes constituted a larger percentage of the city's draymen, hostlers, housekeepers, and servants than in 1890, while the foreign-born proportion of workers in these occupations declined. Only among the city's barbers and seamstresses was there a decrease in the Negro's share and an increase in the foreign-born portion. Thus, in the 1890s the migration of southern and eastern Europeans to New York City failed to result in any sizable displacement of Negroes from occupations that they had acquired in earlier years. When they were supplanted, it was by west European immigrants — the Irish, German, and French. As in the 1880s, they continued to replace Negro servants and cooks in the better hotels and restaurants of the city. It was only as barbers, bootblacks, and whitewashers that the Italian gave the Negro serious competition, for most Italians entered the unskilled occupations of trade and industry where only a few Negroes worked.[14]

Though few Negroes were employed outside of the domestic trades, the number of Negroes in the professions, trades, and industry increased between 1890 and 1900. Negro professionals expanded by over 500 per cent as opposed to about a 200 per cent rise for both the entire population of the city and the foreign-born element. In the trade, transportation, and manufacturing fields the Negro also increased at a more rapid rate than the other major elements of New York City's population. These percentages, nevertheless, can be misleading. For example, Negro professionals increased by 600 persons, whereas foreign-born professionals rose by 12,000. For Negroes this was a greater percentage growth; however, as indicated, they were proceeding from a smaller base. Of the 8,000 Negroes employed outside the domestic field in 1900, a majority worked as unskilled laborers. For example, draymen, hucksters, teamsters, messengers, and porters accounted for 79 per cent of the Negroes in the trade and transportation field as opposed to 68 per cent in 1890. Thus, while the number of Negroes in the skilled trades had increased in actual numbers between 1890 and 1900, their share of the city's Negro working force had either decreased, or, at best, remained stationary.[15]

Oscar Handlin has taken the position that Negroes "had made considerable progress" between 1870 and 1900. He has asserted that "they had earned a minor but secure economic position in the service trades of the city. There were few unskilled workers among them to compete for factory jobs against the hordes of poor immigrants." While the findings of this study cast doubt concerning the "secure position" of the Negro domestic and his "considerable progress" between 1870 and 1900, they do agree with Professor Handlin's argument that the small number of unskilled Negro factory workers limited the effect of the foreign-born laborer's competition. H. D. Bloch, on the other hand, has argued that there was wholesale displacement of the Negro worker between 1870 and 1900. He also has made no mention of any economic progress on the part of the Negro. As will be seen, the author takes a position between Handlin and Bloch.[16]

Between 1900 and 1910 there was a decline in domestic employment throughout the United States.[17] By 1910 male Negro domestics were reduced to 50.3 per cent of New York City's Negro work force.[18] While Negro men engaged in the trades or manufacturing had increased by almost 100 per cent, those in domestic service decreased by about 4 per cent. Although some 1,700 had become waiters or servants between 1890 and 1900, less than 250 entered those occupations between 1900 and 1910. This reflected the movement of Negro men from the home and restaurant to the factory and the store. The years spent by the Negro in domestic service, it appears, may have prepared him for industrial labor. As Harold U. Faulkner has written, "much personal service had become industrialized" between 1900 and 1910. It must be remembered, though, that the majority of Negro men continued to work as domestics. In fact, the city's domestic work force contained a higher percentage of Negro workers in 1910 than in 1900. The vast majority of Negro women, too, still were working in domestic service. Most New York City Negroes, therefore, were still domestic workers; however, by 1910 there was a distinct tendency on the part of Negro men to enter into the trades and industry. The number of male Negroes listed as engaged in manufacturing and mechanical pursuits increased from 1,774 in 1900 to 4,504 in 1910, and the percentage of Negroes so employed from about 7 per cent to 14 per cent of the total Negro working force.[19] Hence, to a greater degree than is often supposed, Negroes had begun to enter the industrial life of New York City during the early 1900s rather than the World War I years.[20]

In the first decade of the twentieth century, more Negroes became skilled artisans than in any previous decade since the Civil War. This large increase in actual numbers, however, only resulted in a small growth in the percentage of Negroes engaged in skilled jobs. Negro entrance into the trades as well as industry was restricted to some degree by foreign competition. Between 1900 and 1910 Negroes had become far more conscious of their foreign competitors than in the last thirty-five years of the nineteenth century. European immigrants continued to be at least 50 per cent of those employed in occupations that contained a large portion of New York City's Negro population. Comparison with earlier census reports, however, is not possible. The 1910 Census gave a more detailed listing of occupations than any previous report, and because of this change comparison with earlier documents has been impossible. For example, longshoremen were listed in the 1910 Census; however, in the reports for 1890 and 1900 they were included in the broad category of common laborers. Consequently, one must turn to the opinions of Negroes and whites of the 1900s to determine the degree of competition between Negroes and European immigrants.[21]

In 1904 the *Tribune* commented on the "persistence" of European immigrants in "seeking and keeping employment." Hungarians, Bohemians, and Italians, according to the newspaper, were the main competitors of the Negro. In the same year, Samuel Scottron, a Negro businessman, noted that Italians and Greeks had replaced Negro waiters. D. Macon Webster, a Negro lawyer, told the National Negro Business League Convention of 1905 that the New York Negro experienced his severest economic rivalry from immigrants. One year later Mary Ovington reported that "no first class hotels" and few "good restaurants" employed Negro help. William Archer, traveling through the United States in the same year in which Mary Ovington wrote her article, observed that Negroes were "no longer at the best hotels and clubs."[22] In the first decade of the twentieth century, therefore, southern and eastern Europeans had replaced the immigrant from western Europe as the chief economic rival of the Negro. In the 1900s the "new" immigrants gave the Negro more serious competition as waiters, servants, and stewards than the west Europeans, for, while the Negro portion in these trades was declining, the foreign-born share was increasing. In addition, it appears that they vied with the Negro for industrial occupations as well as domestic jobs.[23]

Following the outbreak of World War I, the massive flow of foreign immigrants to the United States came to a virtual halt. Negroes entered industry to fill both the gap left by the decrease in foreign immigration and the needs of the expanding American industrial machine. James Weldon Johnson, Negro author, poet, musical composer, social critic, and race leader, reported that the demand for Negro labor was so great that the members of his race found little trouble in obtaining employment.[24] Negro women for the first time entered industry in large numbers. Employers who had never before used Negro labor were compelled to employ the black worker. As a result, the number of New York Negroes in the manufacturing, mechanical, trade, and transportation fields more than doubled in the decade 1910–1920. The proportion of employed male Negroes in these fields rose from 43.9 per cent in 1910 to 56.4 per cent in 1920. At the same time, the proportion of Negro men employed as domestics fell from 50.3 in 1910 to 37.4 in 1920. The war years also had their effect on Negro women. There was a decided decline in the proportion of New York's Negro women working in domestic service — from 86.9 per cent in 1910 to 74.2 per cent in 1920. Consequently, there was a rise in the number of women in industry. New York Negro women in manufacturing and mechanical pursuits increased almost fourfold in the decade. Nevertheless, the smaller proportion of the Negro population engaged in domestic service had increased in its share of the city's domestic work force. Where Negro men constituted 8 per cent of the city's domestics in 1890, in 1910 they accounted for 11 per cent, and 14 per cent in 1920. A similar trend was evidenced among Negro women. But it was not as waiters and servants that Negroes showed the greatest increase — in fact, in these occupations the Negro proportion declined — it was in the more menial fields such as janitoring and portering that they made their greatest gains.[25]

Although more Negroes than ever were entering skilled trades, a still larger number were finding positions that required less training. Skilled workers accounted for 53 per cent of the Negroes in manufacturing and mechanical pursuits in 1910, but fell to 48 per cent in 1920. The difference was filled by the semi-skilled and unskilled.[26] Negroes had entered new fields, but, in general, they were restricted to the lower paying and least skilled positions. Even many of the new-won positions in the skilled trades were limited to servicing the Negro community. Economic progress for the Negro race in the fifty-five years since the Civil War came to only a few. Many of the positions that Negroes had held in previous years, especially in domestic service, became the province of other groups. New York Negroes still found themselves restricted to the more menial occupations.

Foreign competition not only displaced the Negro from certain jobs, but was one factor in limiting the Negro's entrance into the skilled trades. Discrimination, however, appears to have had a greater effect than competition on excluding Negroes from the skilled trades. Throughout the fifty-five year period between 1865 and 1920, attempts by Negroes to enter the skilled occupations were met with constant obstructions. In 1868 a Brooklynite, Frederick Belson, remarked that Negroes were excluded from the mechanical trades. According to the Colored Mission in 1879, Negroes were "entirely excluded from the more lucrative branches of employment" and were "debarred from the trades." One year later, the Mission reported that "many of the various industries open to the foreigner" were closed "to the native colored man." [27] Restrictions upon the Negro's entrance into the skilled trades continued during the 1880s. In 1885 the Colored Mission took this view of the Negro's economic predicament:

> The condition of the colored people of New York City is one that should claim the serious consideration of our citizens . . . shut out from nearly all of the trades (on account of color) there seems to be no career open to them except that of a less lucrative character which affords them a bare subsistence.[28]

Though some Negroes in the 1880s were employed as carpenters and masons, Negro leaders considered the number too small and contended that further entrance was next to impossible. In 1890 Jacob Riis stated that the average Negro was forced to take the "lower level of menial service"; but he blamed the Negro's "past tradition and natural love of ease" for his condition.[29]

During the 1890s some commentators reported Negro advancement in the trades and professions. In 1891 the *Age* noted that Negroes were entering the professions in greater numbers; however, it complained that there "was a scarcity of skilled laborers . . . in comparison to the vast number" of Negroes engaged in the professions. "Those who imagine that the negro population of this city is composed of peddlers, whitewashers, and boot-blacks," wrote the *Times* in 1895, "would be considerably enlightened if they could observe the real progress which the race has made." At about the same time, the Colored Mission observed that "prejudice against" the Negro was "steadily waning" into the past.[30] But not all comments indicated that the Negro had improved his position in the 1890s. The *Age* in 1891 still complained that the Negro was limited to "menial employment." According to the New York *Post* in 1900, Negroes were excluded from most employments. In the same year, J. Gilmer Speed contended that the prospects for the New York Negro were not "very encouraging"; in fact, they were "less" bright than they ever had been.[31]

In the first two decades of the twentieth century, observers continued to mention both the Negro's exclusion from and entrance into the skilled trades. W. E. B. Du Bois, writing for the *Times* in 1901, complained of the obstacles "placed in the way" of attempts by Negroes to improve their position. A Joshua Barton, in a letter published in the *Tribune* of March 25, 1901, asserted that Negro "opportunities for advancement" were practically at a standstill. Three years later, the *Tribune* agreed with Barton's comments, declaring that "better class" Negroes were limited to working as elevator operators or porters. Also in 1904, Charles Morris, minister of the Abyssinian Baptist Church, spoke of the "barred doors" that New York Negroes faced in labor and business. "Outside of domestic employment," declared another Negro clergyman in 1913, "there is very little opportunity . . . except within the limited circle of their own people." Negroes complained that they were excluded from public transportation employment above the rank of porter. "The Negro gets a chance to work only when there is no one else," wrote the *New Republic* in 1916 of the New York Negro's occupational plight. "He is the last served; his are the industrial leavings and scraps." [32]

Negro leaders such as the educator William L. Bulkley, writing in 1906, contended that employment restrictions had a deleterious effect on Negro youths. The Negro boy had run "up against a stone wall in his attempts to learn a trade," argued Bulkley. Negro women, too, found the factory door closed to them, declared Mary Ovington.[33] Even when Negro women entered industry, they were limited to the "most poorly paid and the least desirable kinds of work." Many employers admitted that they employed the Negro female only when they could find no one else.[34] Though the prejudice of employers and even unions may have restricted the employment of Negro women in skilled jobs, their lack of training for industry as well as the trades was a serious impediment to their economic progress. Limited in the past to domestic service and the most menial positions in other fields, they lacked the background that was needed in the trades. But again, it was prejudice rather than the female's own predilection that was responsible for her inadequate training. For where there was no employment opportunity, there was little motivation to seek training.[35]

Those Negroes who had received training in the skilled trades fared little better than the untutored members of their race. Negro artisans who migrated to New York City in the 1900s experienced difficulty in obtaining jobs in their chosen occupations.[36] In 1907 the *Age* warned southern Negroes to "think carefully" before coming to New York. It asserted that native New York Negroes were severely limited in their choice of "responsible positions of any sort." The steady stream of newcomers only complicated a difficult situation, the paper concluded. This opinion was supported one year later by Samuel Scottron. The Negro businessman said that Negro newcomers were arriving in the city "faster than they can be assimilated and adjusted." These people have discovered that "expressions of sympathy" are more "plentiful than employment," Scottron declared. According to a report of the *Times* in 1917, only one of about 2,800 skilled Negroes obtained employment in his chosen occupation.[37]

Though most Negroes in the first twenty years of the twentieth century experienced difficulty in their search for better employment opportunities, a few were able to enter the skilled trades. In 1907 the *Colored American Magazine* asserted that "despite the general belief to the contrary, now and then" a Negro mechanic was employed in the construction industry. According to Mary Ovington, by 1909 some Negroes had obtained skilled jobs. In support of Mary Ovington's observation, the *Age* in 1910 reported that Negroes were "not only holding their own," but they were "making progress." George Haynes, who was making a study of Manhattan's Negroes at this time, concluded that the "slight" entrance of Negroes into the trades was "prophetic of a probable widening scope of the field of employment open to them." [38]

Because of the opportunities afforded by industry during World War I, Negroes entered skilled jobs in greater numbers than ever before. But these gains were few. When compared to the status of most Negroes, they were more illusory than real. By 1920 the vast majority of the city's Negro population remained outside or on the periphery of the skilled trades.[39] The few Negroes who entered the skilled occupations were a small portion of the expanding Negro population of Gotham. This fact was illustrated by the Negro artisans who migrated to New York City but were unable to find employment in the fields for which they had been trained. Thus, although the Negro skilled worker increased in actual numbers, the proportion of skilled workers in the city's work force had expanded only slightly.

Even those gains made in the unskilled and semiskilled industrial positions during World War I were not guaranteed. Negro leaders feared that a renewed wave of European migration to the United States would deprive their race of those jobs they had obtained during the war. For this reason some Negroes supported immigration restriction proposals.[40] Still another threat to the Negro's industrial position was the returning white soldier. The first to feel the effects of a change from a war to a peace economy were Negro women. Negro war veterans, too, discovered that jobs were hard to come by. In cooperation with the Urban League, governmental agencies established employment offices in Harlem to help returning soldiers as well as civilian Negroes in their postwar adjustment. Athough some Negroes retained those industrial positions secured during the war, others found themselves the "first fired and the last hired" when the nation was struck by a recession.[41]

Unemployment was not a new phenomenon for the Negro worker; it was something that he had faced for years. In the nineteenth century the seasonal nature of his work made for unemployment. In 1869 the *Times* reported that job opportunities were better for Negro servants and waiters during the summer than the winter. This compelled Negroes to live for an entire year on one season's pay, the paper asserted. The Colored Mission in 1871 took a position directly opposite to that of the *Times*. It claimed that Negro unemployment was greatest in the summer when the well-to-do families who used Negro help left the city.[47] Hence, it may have been possible for a Negro to find a job in the city for the winter and at the resorts in the summer. But the concern of the *Times* and the Mission for the unemployed Negro indicated that not all Negroes found both summer and winter work; in fact, it appears that Negro unemployment was high throughout the year. When the economic situation of the city deteriorated, the Negro faced more difficult times. During the panic of 1893, according to the Colored Mission, the Negro was subjected to trying days — "some were found actually dying of want." Negroes were so hard hit by the recession of 1915 that the Mayor's Unemployment Committee worked with the Urban League to assist Negro workers. Relief was provided, work projects were established, and some training of the unemployed was conducted by the League. When the industrial slump of 1921 occurred, Howard D. Gregg, industrial secretary of the Urban League, reported that Negro workers were the first to feel its effects. Their late entrance into industrial occupations and the prevalence of unskilled workers among the race contributed to the high rate of Negro unemployment.[43]

The high incidence of unemployment and the low wages among Negro workingmen shifted a large part of the burden of supporting the family upon the mother. She may have worked as a servant in the home of a white family, or converted her home into a workshop, where she was either a laundress, seamstress, or dressmaker. In 1897 a church survey of a West Side district of Manhattan reported that the largest number of working mothers were Negro. Among working fathers, on the other hand, the Negro father was third largest. A similar study in 1910 found that 31.4 per cent of married Negro women in the city worked, whereas for their white counterparts it was 4.2 per cent.[44] The Negro's precarious economic position compelled the children of the family as well as the mother and father to work. The Board of Education wrote in 1871 that Negro children were "called from school at a very early age" and were "placed temporarily wherever their services" brought a few dollars "to aid in the support of themselves and their parents." The Federation of Churches reported in 1897 that two Negro boys and girls were employed for every one of any other group.[45]

The high rate of widowhood was another factor that forced

Negro women to seek employment. Between 1890 and 1920 there was a higher percentage of widowhood among Negro women than among the native-born and foreign-born residents of the city.[46] Accordingly, many Negro children lived in homes without the influence of a father. The Colored Mission in 1871 and Mary Ovington in 1905 contended that this had a deleterious effect on the moral upbringing of the children.[47]

Many commentators blamed the "lazy" Negro husband for the high proportion of working wives. Most Negro men "do nothing but lounge about street corners," wrote the *Tribune* in 1895, while their women slave over washtubs "making their apartments perpetual 'steam rooms.'" The "lounging" male, however, may not have been lazy or unemployed but part of a large group of Negroes who worked nights. Indolence is not always attributable to shiftlessness and indifference, but more often is the result of factors beyond the control of the so-called indolent male.[48]

In time, both Negro and white groups formed various organizations for the purpose of improving the Negro's economic position. It was not until the 1900s, though, that these groups became numerous. Before 1900 the Negro's efforts to obtain employment were assisted mainly by employment agencies — both commercial and philanthropic. Shortly after the Civil War, the American Freedmen's Friend Society established an agency in Brooklyn to help Negroes find employment. In 1871 the New York Colored Mission opened an employment service. By 1890 the Mission was placing over 1,000 persons a year.[49] Other groups went beyond finding employment for Negroes. The Colored Orphan Asylum in 1885 created a sewing school for Negro girls. Five years later, a few of New York City's leading Negro citizens formed the Professional and Business Men's Social Club. Their aim was to improve "the proficiency of colored men engaged in the professions, trades and business" and to make public opinion more receptive to Negro labor and business. At the same time, two other leading Negroes — T. Thomas Fortune, journalist, and Jacob Simms, lawyer — set up the Young Men's Industrial League. The League assisted Negro youths to find positions where they could learn a trade. It encouraged these young men to invest their savings in a business. Fortune and Simms agreed with Booker T. Washington that industrial training was the most useful education for Negroes. Whether these two organizations helped to improve the

Negro's economic position cannot be determined. In the years following their formation, their meetings were mentioned in the press, but nothing was said of their work. They were, however, the precursors of the organizations that emerged in the 1900s.[50]

Between 1900 and 1910 whites as well as Negroes doubled their efforts to aid the Negro worker. White citizens — possibly as an extension of their philanthropic activities in behalf of southern Negroes and as part of the social reform activity of urban progressives — played an increasing role in the battle to improve the plight of the New York Negro.[51] In 1905 the New York City Board of Education opened an evening school on Fifty-third Street, under the direction of William L. Bulkley, "to train [Negro] men and women for larger industrial wealth to themselves and the community." It offered classes in dressmaking and stenography, typing and bookkeeping, carpentry and electricity. Two years later, a similar school was opened in Brooklyn.[52] In 1906 a group of leading New York Negroes and whites formed the Committee for Improving the Industrial Conditions of Negroes in New York. One of the foremost white reformers in the city, William J. Schieffelin, was chairman and two Negroes, Samuel Scottron and Seth T. Stewart, were vice-chairmen. Other members were T. Thomas Fortune, Mary Ovington, and two white philanthropists, Felix Warburg and Isaac N. Seligman. The Committee attempted to find places for skilled Negroes in trade and industry. It concerned itself with the industrial training of Negroes, and maintained an unofficial connection with the two Negro evening schools in the city.[53] According to Samuel Scottron in 1908, the Committee realized that industrial education was the "gateway by which the colored people" were "to enter into the full activities of our city life." [54]

The Committee for Improving the Industrial Conditions of Negroes reported in 1909 that new areas of employment had been opened to the Negro. By virtue of its cooperation with the evening schools of the city, over 1,000 Negroes had acquired a trade. Other groups, though not as large as the Committee, helped the Negro to learn a trade. In 1908 St. Cyprian's Church opened a class to teach Negro boys shoemaking. The Henrietta Evening Trade School was established in 1909 to train West Indian Negroes who had migrated to the city.[55]

In 1910 the Committee for Improving the Industrial Conditions of Negroes, the League for the Protection of Colored Women, and the recently organized Committee on Urban Conditions agreed to merge into one organization — the National League on Urban Conditions Among Negroes which in a few years became known as the National Urban League — to "promote and to do constructive and preventive social work for improving the social and economic conditions among Negroes in urban centers." [56] The League for the Protection of Colored Women had been established in 1905 to combat the unethical practices of certain northern employment agencies. [57] The League, with a chapter in New York City, attempted to prevent "irresponsible agencies" from using false claims to lure Negro girls to the North. For those who came to New York, the League provided lodging and attempted to find jobs. By 1909 it reported that it had given aid to over 2,000 women. [58]

In the next decade the Urban League continued to work for the improvement of the Negro's occupational status. It maintained connections with agencies of the local, state, and national governments to obtain employment for Negroes. This alliance was most active during periods of high unemployment and in the period of postwar adjustment. The League also continued to work with other organizations. In 1918 it cooperated with the Russell Sage Foundation, the Young Women's Christian Association, the Consumers' League, and the Manhattan Trade School to study the industrial position of Negro women. [59] But the League's most far-reaching work was performed on its own. It formed organizations of Negro laborers. Those groups that had been formed in the past had become nothing more than social clubs and beneficial societies. [60] In 1912 the League assisted in the organization of the Colored Public Porters Association. This group sought to protect the public from unscrupulous porters and to raise the "reliability and efficiency" of those engaged in this work. Negro elevatormen, hallmen, musicians, and chauffeurs formed their own societies under the direction of the League. The Urban League also attempted to find jobs for Negro men and women. In 1912 it established a Vocational Exchange to serve as clearing house through which Negro job applicants were referred to reliable employment agencies. When unemployment among Negroes assumed frightening proportions, the League created a workshop in which the unemployed Negro worker made goods for which he was paid. [61]

By 1920, therefore, more organizations than ever before were working in behalf of Negro laborers. Philanthropic agencies composed of whites as well as blacks showed a greater interest in the Negro. The Negro community, outside of some cooperation with whites, restricted its self-help activities to private schools, private employment agencies, and the church. Of the three, the church contributed the least.[62] Employment agencies became a thriving business for their owners and to a lesser degree helped the Negro worker.[63] A necessary service was performed by Negro trade schools. Mme Beck's School of Dressmaking held day and evening classes. Negroes interested in chauffeuring and repairing automobiles could attend such trade schools as the Harlem River Auto School and Repair Shop, the Broadway Auto School, and the Cosmopolitan Automobile School.[64] But these educational institutions, despite all their efforts, could not fill the needs of a population that was deprived of training and employment because of the color of its skin. Little could be done for the Negro's economic plight before the most influential elements of the American economic system and the American public changed their attitudes toward the Negro. It is doubtful whether these agencies would broaden their outlook by themselves. Negro organizations and governmental agencies would have to conduct a massive campaign in behalf of Negro equality before there would be any appreciable improvement in the Negro's occupational situation.

Notes

[1] Haynes, *Negro at Work*, p. 47; Olson, "Negro Slavery in New York," pp. 57–58; *Weekly Anglo African*, August 12, 1865.

[2] Sterling D. Spero and Abram I. Harris, *The Black Worker: the Negro and the Labor Movement* (New York, 1931), pp. 12–18; Haynes, *Negro at Work*, pp. 67–68.

[3] Ernst, "The Economic Status of the New York City Negro," pp. 131–32; Arnett G. Lindsay, "The Economic Condition of the Negroes of New York Prior to 1861," *Journal of Negro History*, VI (April, 1921), 193–94; Litwack, *North of Slavery*, pp. 159, 167.

[4] Ernst, "The Economic Status of the New York City Negro," p. 140.

[5] Litwack, *North of Slavery*, pp. 163–64; Albon P. Man, Jr., "Labor Competition and the New York Draft Riots," *Journal of Negro History*, XXXVI (October, 1951), 384–402.

[6] Ernst, "The Economic Status of the New York City Negro," p. 142; Litwack, *North of Slavery*, pp. 165–66; Samuel R. Scottron, "The Industrial and Professional Pursuits of the Colored People of Old New York," *Colored American Magazine*, XIII (October, 1907), 265–67.

[7] *Weekly Anglo African*, August 12, 1865; Speed, "The Negro in New York," p. 1249; *New York*

Times, March 2, 1869; Haynes, *Negro at Work,* p. 68.

⁸ *Weekly Anglo African,* August 12, 1865; *National Anti-Slavery Standard,* January 15, 1870; Fergus Ferguson, *From Glasgow to Missouri and Back* (Glasgow, 1879), p. 24; Sir George Campbell, *White and Black: the Outcome of a Visit to the United States* (London, 1879), p. 206; George Rose, *The Great Country; or, Impressions of America* (London, 1868), p. 70; James Macauley, "First Impressions of America and Its People," *The Leisure Hour,* XX (1871), 206.

⁹ *National Anti-Slavery Standard,* January 15, 1870; *New York Times,* March 2, 1869; Spero and Harris, *The Black Worker,* p. 197. Negroes usually were relegated to the least skilled jobs on the waterfront. Charles B. Barnes, *The Longshoremen* (New York, 1915), p. 3.

¹⁰ *New York Globe,* March 8, 29, 1884; Edward Money, *The Truth About America* (London, 1886), p. 41; Riis, *How the Other Half Lives,* p. 149.

¹¹ See tables 6 and 7.

¹² See table 6; *Eleventh Census, Population,* I, 640, 704; New York Colored Mission, *Annual Report for 1885* (New York, 1886), p. 10.

¹³ *Eleventh Census, Population,* I, 640, 704; Speed, "The Negro in New York," pp. 1249–50; *New York Age,* May 16, 1891; *New York Times,* November 17, 1901. H. D. Bloch, "The New York City Negro and Occupational Eviction, 1860–1910," *International Review of Social History,* V (Part 1, 1960), 28–32, has taken a position opposite the one presented here. Mr. Bloch has made the conclusion that because there was competition between Negroes and European immigrants for jobs the Negro was displaced. The mere existence of competition did not mean displacement.

¹⁴ *Eleventh Census, Population,*
I, 640, 704; *Twelfth Census, Occupations,* pp. 634–41.

¹⁵ See table 6.

¹⁶ Handlin, *Newcomers,* p. 46; Bloch, "The New York City Negro and Occupational Eviction," pp. 30–33.

¹⁷ Harold U. Faulkner, *The Decline of Laissez Faire, 1897–1917* (New York, 1951), p. 241.

¹⁸ See tables 6 and 7. H. D. Bloch, "The New York City Negro and Occupational Eviction," p. 36, has concluded that 70.1 per cent of the city's Negro population were domestics. This is correct when the figures for men and women are combined; however, a clearer picture of the Negro worker is obtained when the sexes are studied separately.

¹⁹ See tables 6 and 7; *Twelfth Census, Occupations,* pp. 634–41; *Thirteenth Census, Population,* IV, 571–74; Faulkner, *Decline of Laissez Faire,* p. 241.

²⁰ Faulkner, *Decline of Laissez Faire,* p. 100; John Hope Franklin, *From Slavery to Freedom: a History of American Negroes* (rev. ed.; New York, 1960), p. 464.

²¹ *Twelfth Census, Occupations,* pp. 636, 638; *Thirteenth Census, Population,* IV, 571–74.

²² *New York Tribune,* August 14, 1904; *New York Age,* August 24, 1905; Mary White Ovington, "The Negro in the Trade Unions in New York," *Annals of the American Academy of Political and Social Science,* XXVII (June, 1906), 557; William Archer, *Through Afro-America: an English Reading of the Race Problem* (London, 1910), p. 7.

²³ *Thirteenth Census, Population,* IV, 571–74.

²⁴ *New York Age,* June 7, 1917.

²⁵ See tables 6 and 7 and sources cited there. *New York Age,* January 4, 1912; New York *Herald,* December 10, 1911; Consumers' League of the City of New York, *Report for 1918* (New York, 1919), pp. 6–8;

George E. Haynes, "The Negro at Work: a Development of the War and a Problem of Reconstruction," *Review of Reviews,* LIX (August, 1919), 390.

[26] *Thirteenth Census, Population,* IV, 571–74; *Fourteenth Census, Population,* IV, 1157–62.

[27] Frederick Belson, *Considerations in the Interests of the Colored People* (Brooklyn, 1868), p. 4; New York Colored Mission, *Annual Report for 1879* (New York, 1880), p. 5, and *Annual Report for 1880* (New York, 1881), p. 5.

[28] New York Colored Mission, *Annual Report for 1885,* p. 10.

[29] *New York Age,* March 16, 1889; Riis, *How Other Half Lives,* p. 149.

[30] *New York Age,* February 28, 1891; *New York Times,* July 14, 1895; *Milestones* (April, 1896), unpaged.

[31] *New York Age,* September 5, 1891; New York *Post,* August 17, 1900; Speed, "The Negro in New York," p. 1249.

[32] *New York Times,* November 17, 1901, and June 15, 1904; *New York Tribune,* August 14, 1904; New York *World,* August 17, 1918; "The Superfluous Negro," *New Republic,* VII (June 24, 1916), 187.

[33] William L. Bulkley, "The Industrial Condition of the Negro in New York City," *Annals of the American Academy of Political and Social Science,* XXVII (June, 1906), 592; Ovington, *Half A Man,* pp. 43, 162.

[34] Kennedy, *Negro Peasant Turns Cityward,* pp. 90–91.

[35] Consumers' League, *Report of 1918,* pp. 6–8.

[36] Bulkley, "Industrial Conditions of the Negro in New York City," p. 591; Helen A. Tucker, "Negro Craftsmen in New York," *Southern Workman,* XXXVI (October, 1907), 545–51 and XXXVII (March, 1908), 139–44.

[37] *New York Age,* February 14,

April 4, 1907, and May 24, 1908; *New York Times,* October 7, 1917.

[38] *Colored American Magazine,* XIII (August, 1907), 87; Ovington, *Half A Man,* pp. 107–108; *New York Age,* August 18, 1910; Haynes, *Negro at Work,* p. 57.

[39] *Fourteenth Census, Population,* IV, 1157–62.

[40] *New York Age,* November 23, 1918, and February 8, 1919.

[41] *Ibid.,* January 24, 1917; December 21, 1918; January 1, 1921; *Survey,* XLII (September 27, 1919), 900; *Crisis,* XVII (May, 1919), 13–14; Haynes, "The Negro at Work: a Development of the War and a Problem of Reconstruction," p. 390; United States Department of Labor, Women's Bureau, *Negro Women in Industry* (Washington, D.C., 1920), p. 15; U.S. Department of Labor, Division of Negro Economics, *The Negro at Work During the World War and During Reconstruction* (Washington, 1921), pp. 95–96; Kennedy, *Negro Peasant Turns Cityward,* pp. 130–31.

[42] *New York Times,* March 2, 1869; New York Colored Mission, *Annual Report for 1871,* p. 8.

[43] New York Colored Mission, *Annual Report for 1893* (New York, 1894), pp. 14, 17; *New York Age,* April 22, 1915, and October 25, 1917; National League on Urban Conditions, *Report for 1913–1914 and 1914–1915,* p. 14.

[44] New York Colored Mission, *Annual Report for 1875* (New York, 1876), p. 6; Ovington, "The Negro Home in New York," pp. 26–27; Tucker, "Negro Craftsmen in New York," XXVI, 546–47; Ovington, *Half A Man,* pp. 56–57. More Negro fathers, mothers, and children worked a seven-day week than did any other group. See Federation of Churches, *Canvass No. 2,* pp. 90–92.

[45] *Ibid.,* p. 90; New York City Board of Education, *Annual Report*

for 1871 (New York, 1872), p. 43.

⁴⁶ *Eleventh Census, Population,* I, 883; *Twelfth Census, Population,* II, 332; *Thirteenth Census, Population,* I, 629; *Fourteenth Census, Population,* II, 501. The Federation of Churches, *Canvass No. 2,* p. 25, found a similar situation in its survey of 1897.

⁴⁷ New York Colored Mission, *Annual Report for 1871,* p. 8; Ovington, "The Negro Home in New York," p. 27.

⁴⁸ *New York Age,* July 14, 1888, and March 21, 1907; *New York Tribune,* October 13, 1895; Ovington, "Vacation Days on San Juan Hill," p. 630; Blascoer, *Colored School Children,* p. 81.

⁴⁹ *Weekly Anglo African,* August 12, October 14, 1865; *New York Globe,* September 29, 1882; *New York Age,* October 12, 1889; New York Colored Mission, *Annual Report for 1871,* p. 7, and *Annual Report for 1890* (New York, 1891), p. 7.

⁵⁰ Colored Orphan Asylum and Association for the Benefit of Colored Children, *Annual Report for 1885* (New York, 1886), p. 6; *New York Age,* December 14, 1889; January 4, 11, February 15, June 21, 1890; June 20, 1891.

⁵¹ For philanthropic assistance to the southern Negro, see Franklin, *From Slavery to Freedom,* pp. 377–84.

⁵² *Milestones,* II (May, 1910), 9; *Colored American Magazine,* XIII (August, 1907), 95.

⁵³ *New York Age,* July 12, 1906; *New York Tribune,* June 20, 1906; *Colored American Magazine,* XIII (September, 1907), 210; *Milestones,* II (May, 1910), 10.

⁵⁴ *New York Age,* May 14, 1908.

⁵⁵ *New York Age,* March 12, May 14, 1908, and May 25, 1909; *Milestones,* II (May, 1910), 8.

⁵⁶ National League on Urban Conditions Among Negroes, *Report for 1910–1911* (New York, 1911), pp. 4–8.

⁵⁷ The League had its origins in the White Rose Industrial Association which was formed in 1897 to assist southern Negro girls who had migrated to New York. *Colored American Magazine,* XIII (September, 1907), 210; *Milestones,* II (May, 1910), 8.

⁵⁸ *Charities,* XIV (June 10, 1905), 826; *Milestones* (May, 1905), 10–11, and II (May, 1910), 10; National League for the Protection of Colored Women, *Annual Report for 1910* (New York, 1910), p. 6.

⁵⁹ *New York Age,* October 25, 1917, and April 20, 1918; U. S. Department of Labor, Division of Negro Economics, *Negro at Work During the War,* pp. 95–96; *Survey,* XLII (September 27, 1919), 900; National League on Urban Conditions, *Report for 1913–1914 and 1914–1915,* p. 14, and *Report for 1917–1918* (New York, 1918), p. 14.

⁶⁰ *New York Age,* August 7, 1913.

⁶¹ *Ibid.,* April 22, 1915; National League on Urban Conditions, *Report for 1912–1913,* pp. 12–13, and *Report for 1913–1914 and 1914–1915,* p. 13.

⁶² *New York Age,* February 19, April 30, 1914; *Crisis,* IV (May, 1912), 24–25.

⁶³ *Colored American Review,* I (October 1, 1915), 8–9, 15.

⁶⁴ *Ibid.,* I (December, 1915), 13; *New York Age,* March 2, 1911, and February 13, 1913; *Crusader,* V (November, 1921), 3.

. 3 .

Labor and Capital

ENTRANCE into labor unions presented still another problem for the New York Negro. Since unionization in its earlier years usually was limited to the skilled trades, the majority of Negroes remained outside the mainstream of the labor movement. But the lack of Negro skilled workers in itself fails to provide a complete explanation for the sparsity of Negro union members. The prejudice of many white union members must assume a large share of the responsibility for the Negro's exclusion from the labor movement. Before the Civil War most white unions denied Negroes membership in their organizations. A group of white barbers, for instance, refused to combine with Negro barbers in a labor union. Many Negro workers because of their exclusion from unions resorted to strikebreaking when white workers went on strike.[1]

Following the Civil War, labor began to organize with greater vigor. At first glance the policies of these unions seemed to indicate a better day for Negro workers: the National Labor Union and the Knights of Labor declared that their membership roles were open to white and black. These national pronouncements, however, either were not enforced or were incapable of enforcement on the local level. Accordingly, Negroes experienced difficulty in obtaining membership in local chapters of both national organizations.[2] Like its predecessors, the American Federation of Labor failed to provide equal membership opportunities for Negro workers. The federated structure of the AF of L impeded attempts to adhere to a national policy of welcoming as members all skilled workers regardless of race or color. To make matters worse for Negroes, the AF of L shifted from its early statements on equality. Samuel Gompers, the union's president, gave voice to this change when he told the United States Industrial Commission in 1899 that his union did not look favorably upon Negro membership because Negroes "so conducted themselves as to be a continuous convenient whip placed in the hands of the employers to cow the white men and compel them to accept abject conditions of labor." Even Gompers' earlier pro-Negro statements, according to Bernard Mandel in his study of labor and the Negro, were not made from conviction but with a desire "to keep Negroes from competing with white labor." [3]

Within New York City, the prospective Negro union member faced constant bars to his enrollment in many a labor group. Before 1900 very few Negroes obtained a union card. Negroes as well as whites commented upon labor's hostility toward the Negro.[4] When Negroes were admitted to the union movement, it was usually in all-Negro or predominantly Negro chapters. In 1884 a group of Negro waiters affiliated with the Knights of Labor. A New York Negro became an officer in a machinists local composed mostly of Negroes. Before the turn of the century small groups of Negro engineers, masons, and clerks were granted union membership.[5]

It was not until Negroes entered industry and the trades in greater numbers after 1900 that they gained wider admission to labor's ranks. The asphalt workers union asserted that one-third of its membership was Negro and that one of its organizers was a Negro. In 1906 Mary Ovington reported that at least 1,400 New York City Negroes were union workers. Among this group were asphalt workers, teamsters, rock drillers, tool sharpeners, cigarmakers, and waiters. Negroes also became members of the International Ladies Garment Workers' Union in 1909. On one occasion a union made up of both whites and Negroes struck to force an employer to rehire Negro union workers whom he had fired.[6] But these gains, though an improvement over earlier years, were few and too often were obtained on a segregated basis. Only a limited number of Negro carpenters, printers, machinists, mechanics, and plumbers were admitted to white locals. They often were forced to organize all-Negro chapters if they wished to become part of the labor movement. In 1910 the *Age* declared that labor discrimination was responsible for the small number of Negro unionists.[7]

The influx of Negroes into industry during World War I, however, caused labor to reevaluate its attitude toward Negro membership. Facing the competition of nonunion Negro labor, various northern locals persuaded the national body to campaign for the organization of southern Negro workers. Although certain northern locals were more responsive to Negro membership in the postwar period, a number not only refused to admit the Negro but retained white only provisions in their charters.[8] For all its public statements on wanting equality, the national body was unable to enforce its national pronouncements upon recalcitrant locals because of its federated structure. Convention after convention affirmed the national organization's belief in the equality of man; still, Negro leaders demanded deeds not words. Permitting Negroes to organize their own local chapters where the local union refused to admit Negroes failed to appease the race's leaders. Segregation in union membership, like segregation in education, meant second-class results. The best that Negro protestations could obtain from the AF of L was a resolution by the 1920 convention that the parent body would recommend that its affiliates eradicate discriminatory practices and eliminate the word white from their constitutions. Despite this position of the national organization, the autonomy allowed local chapters prevented many Negroes from achieving union membership.[9] Certainly, the claim of the *New York Times* in 1919 that the AF of L opened its doors to Negroes only when it was "absolutely necessary" appears justified.[10]

Against this background of labor reluctance to admit Negro members, New York City's Negro community advanced a myriad of proposals to counteract labor's discriminatory ways. Some Negroes condemned the intolerance that permeated the union movement and urged labor's adherence to a policy of equality for all workers. The National Association for the Advancement of Colored People, for example, asserted in 1912 that the anti-Negro practices of many unions forced Negroes to resort to the "pitiable" and "cutthroat" practice of strikebreaking. It exhorted unions to remove obstacles barring Negro entrance into the ranks of the labor movement.[11] A number of Negro workers resigned themselves to participating in the unionization process through segregated local chapters.[12] Others attempted to form Negro labor organizations. In 1850 the American League of Colored Laborers was formed in New York and a similar group was organized shortly after the Civil War. In the 1900s a series of such groups burst forth upon the New York City scene. Negro labor groups of stenographers, musicians, porters, elevatormen, hallmen, and longshoremen were formed. In 1917 a Negro graduate of New York University formed the Associated Colored Employees of America. These organizations, however, usually failed because they were developed apart from the mainstream of the union movement, their leaders sought to convert them into political vehicles, and too often were concerned more with the development of Negro business enterprises than with establishing organizations to improve the plight of the Negro workingman.[13]

In many cases, Negroes accepted positions as strikebreakers to obtain employment. Even before the Civil War, Negroes had been used as strikebreakers on the waterfront of New York.[14] Employers who developed a degree of tolerance during labor troubles continued this practice after the war. In 1887 the National Steamship Line hired Negroes to replace strikers. The Ward Lines followed the same procedure in 1892 and 1895. On at least three other occasions between 1893 and 1907 Negroes were employed as strikebreakers on the piers of New York City. In 1903 subway contractors imported some 2,000 Negroes from Maryland and Virginia to break a strike. Negro waiters who had lost their jobs in the city's hotels because of employer and employee prejudice became strikebreakers when the International Hotel Waiters' Union struck in 1912. In 1920 Negro strikebreakers battled with striking white longshoremen along the city's waterfront.[15]

Another influential segment of the city's Negro community advanced an anti-labor philosophy. At times, this position was motivated by reaction to labor's anti-Negro actions, and, at others, by a belief that labor threatened both Negro and white business interests. In 1886, for instance, a Negro newspaper, the New York *Enterprise,* encouraged Negroes to answer the Third Avenue Railroad Company's appeal for workers to replace its striking employees. The newspaper contended that too many Negro workmen had been "idle too long"; now was their chance to gain decent employment. But this position failed to receive uniform support from the Negro press. The *New York Freeman*, another Negro newspaper, asserted that if Negroes "scabbed" it would injure their opportunity of becoming union members – a status, the Negro paper insisted, that had been improving in recent years.[16] But this pro-labor sentiment of the *Freeman* disappeared from its pages when it changed its name to the *Age*. According to the *Age*, in 1888, arbitration should be the "first and last resort" of labor disputes. If an "amicable settlement" could not be reached by arbitration, a worker should resign rather than strike. In 1905 the paper condemned a New York subway strike as wasteful, a "folly," and an "abuse of public generosity and patience." [17] A speaker at the National Negro Business League Convention, meeting in New York City in the same year, seconded these sentiments when he praised those Negro laborers who accepted employment as strikebreakers.[18] Two years later, after a group of Italian strikers had assaulted their Negro replacements, the *Age* censured the practice of honoring picket lines. In 1910 the paper delivered a scathing editorial against both the anti-Negro practices of unions and the labor movement in general. Unions, it charged, were a "damaging influence" upon property and liberty as well as posing a "dangerous menace to the well-being of the people"; they were "agents of terror" who were "inconsiderate of the rights of both capital and the people." Strikes fomented "upon large as well as small pretense" were "one of the worst of the growing evils of the day." In the second decade of the twentieth century, the *Age* continued its attacks on the union movement. It complained that business interests were "gagged by labor unions and legislation favoring them." The paper included in such legislation state and federal antitrust laws. It asserted that government was at the "dictation of labor unions" – when labor unions did not control business, federal or state commissions did.[19]

No doubt labor's discriminatory ways fostered this Negro hostility to unions; however, a large portion of New York City's Negro community developed an economic philosophy that had the businessman as its hero and the labor leader as its villain. Although limited to the Negro quarter of the city, the Negro businessman believed that financial success could mitigate the inconveniences of ghetto life. Within the Negro community, the entrepreneur was advanced as the ideal for Negro youths to follow. As early as 1883, the *New York Globe* advised Negroes to invest their savings in a business instead of squandering them on frivolities. The *Age* counseled the race: "Don't work for wages; make a business of your own and pay wages to others." [20] T. McCants Stewart, a Negro lawyer, told Negroes that if they wished to be in "elbow touch with other races," they must imitate the enterprise of the "despised Jew, the representative of business and money." Fred R. Moore, who was to become editor of the *New York Age,* told the National Negro Business League Convention of 1904 that Negroes must "learn to value money and study thoroughly the plan of investment." [21] In the next fifteen years such statements increased in fervor. Henry S. Creamer, a Negro, maintained that only through education and ownership could the Negro secure his constitutional rights. A Negro journal considered real estate "the foundation of national power." A. Clayton Powell, pastor of the Abyssinian Baptist Church and the father of Adam Clayton Powell, asserted that although Negroes had been denied political equality, they retained "the right to save money, buy property and engage in business." [22]

To implement these suggestions, organizations were formed to foster the creation of Negro business enterprises. Both the Professional and Business Men's Social Club of New York in the early 1890s and the local chapter of the National Negro Business League in the 1900s urged Negroes to become entrepreneurs. In 1916 the New York Colored Business Men's Association was created to encourage Negroes to invest in business enterprises. [23]

The advocate of Negro capital investment, however, came to the realization that the mere establishment of a business was inadequate — a separate Negro economic community was needed to insure the success of the Negro businessman. Even though the creation of Negro Harlem increased Negro business opportunities, the race was still a small element of the city's business community. A survey of Harlem in 1916 showed that there was a sparsity of Negro stores. [24] Negro proponents of business investment attributed this situation, in part, to the failure of Negro consumers to patronize stores owned by members of their race. [25] Accordingly, Negro shoppers were beseeched to shop at Negro-owned business establishments. In 1886 a Lewis C. Jenkins advised his fellow Negroes to "do as the Irish and German — patronize your own race." Almost two decades later, Fred Moore declared that "Jews support Jews; Germans support Germans . . . and Negroes should begin to support Negroes." Shortly before Moore's statement, the New York Family Supply Company, a Negro concern, informed "every race loving" Negro that it was his duty to buy from his "own people." It concluded with a battle cry: "Let us spend our pennies with ourselves."[26] Booker T. Washington entreated a gathering of New York City Negroes in 1914 to patronize Negroes rather than whites.[27] "As long as Negroes talk race loyalty and race rights," declared A. Clayton Powell in the same year as Washington's address, "and then spend their money with white business and professional men" the race problem would never be solved. Powell was alluding to the "double duty" dollar — buying from Negro merchants provided more jobs for Negro workers. A Negro periodical referred to this plan in 1915 when it asserted that it was a "sad commentary" that Negroes patronize white business establishments "that give the race nothing in return." To spend money with the white man, continued the journal, was "assinine and senseless." It rebuked Negroes for filling "the coffers of the Jew and the Italian" who failed to hire even a Negro porter.[28]

Such statements appear to have been a combination of the frustration Negroes developed because of the discriminatory practices of the white community and a rationalization to assure Negro merchants the patronage of the city's Negro community. Gunnar Myrdal in his notable study of the American Negro has taken cognizance of the paradox Negro businessmen faced: "On the one hand, they find that the caste wall blocks their economic and social opportunities. On the other hand, they have, at the same time, a vested interest in racial segregation since it gives them what opportunity they have."[29] This outlook hardened the pro-business and anti-labor orientation of a vocal element of the city's Negro population. Here was what E. Franklin Frazier referred to as an attempt by the Negro businessman "to identify with the white propertied classes," to accept not only the mores of the white entrepreneur but to embrace his basic philosophical orientation. Booker T. Washington, for example, as Samuel R. Spencer has observed, was a self-made man who subscribed to the white businessman's "gospel of wealth." One of Washington's leading supporters, A. Clayton Powell, seconded the Tuskegee Wizard's beliefs when he asserted that wealth was "an adjunct to Christianity . . . it makes a man more manly." [30] Negro hostility to unions, therefore, combined reaction to the anti-Negro practices of labor, philosophical adherence to the laissez-faire ideas of a business community that viewed increased unionization as a threat, and insecurity created and nourished by discriminatory practices on the part of labor, business, and the general public.

But this rejection of unions ran into a dilemma. The same men who condemned unions urged the race to acquire training in the skilled occupations.[31] If Negroes entered the trades they would be involved in that area of American life where unions had their greatest success in the four decades between 1880 and 1920. Those Negroes who rejected the labor movement failed to recognize the role that unions were playing in the American economy. They overemphasized the defeats suffered by labor along the path to victory. Southern Negroes who were reared in the southern setting of anti-unionism and who witnessed many of labor's failures in the South looked skeptically at any possible future for the labor movement in the American economy. Washington maintained in 1907 that Negroes were "not given to 'strikes' " and the South "was largely free from the restrictive influences of the Northern trade unions." In the main, those southern Negroes who migrated northward brought with them the southern antipathy for unions.[32]

These anti-labor statements did not go unchallenged. In 1906 James L. Wallace, Negro union agent, rebuked those Negroes who opposed unionization. He said that the Negro "weeps and wails about the bad [working] conditions, but supports the men and methods that create them." [33] In an attempt to improve the Negro's status within unions, the Committee for Improving the Industrial Conditions of Negroes in New York — later known as the National Urban League — worked to eradicate the discriminatory practices of employee groups. In light of the increased unionization in skilled occupations, the Committee realized that Negroes must achieve wider membership in unions if they were to improve their economic position. During World War I, it held conferences with the American Federation of Labor so that the union "might become fairer and more generous in its attitude toward Negro workingmen." At the same time, it cooperated with various educational institutions in preparing Negroes for skilled employment. Through an increased supply of skilled Negro labor and a labor market devoid of anti-Negro policies on the part of business and labor, the Committee hoped to improve the Negro's position in society.[34]

This recognition of the important role of unions in the American economy also was reflected in the thinking of the National Association for the Advancement of Colored People.[35] Shortly after its formation in 1910, the NAACP asserted that anti-unionism was an "old attitude" which was out of place in a modern economic system. In contraposition to Booker T. Washington's disdain for unions, the NAACP considered the labor movement a positive good. "The standard of living among workers," according to the organization's publication, the *Crisis*, "has been raised in the last half century through the efforts and sacrifice of laborers banded together in unions." While this position failed to obtain unanimous support from the Negro community — in the 1920s anti-labor thought once again flourished among a substantial element of the Negro community — it marked a decided shift in Negro thinking.[36]

Not only did the NAACP and the Washington school disagree as to the utility of unions, they differed as to the nature of the country's economic system. The NAACP repudiated the simple capitalism which permeated the thinking of the Tuskegee educator. Where Washington counseled Negroes to begin a business "in the humblest way, the simplest way" rather than start with a "complicated enterprise," the NAACP subscribed to the modern capitalistic system.[37] It realized that the Negro could not rely on the small business establishment for salvation. Where Washington believed that the financial success of the Negro businessman would benefit the entire Negro community, the NAACP concluded that the race only could move forward together under the leadership of the "Talented Tenth." Equal opportunity for all, not economic accomplishments for a few, was the answer to the Negro's situation.[38] As it rejected the "trickle-down" concept that was an implicit part of the "gospel of wealth," so did it repudiate the laissez-faire attitude contained in Washington's economic theory. For the NAACP, Washington's National Negro Business League symbolized the materialism of the so-called robber baron. It rejected what it considered the League's advocacy of "a career of individual selfishness." Like the progressive of the early 1900s, the NAACP stressed moral values rather than materialism, social service rather than self-aggrandizement, equal opportunity rather than special interest. Negroes, asserted the *Crisis,* must not reproduce "in the twentieth century the lying, stealing and grafting which characterized the white race in the nineteenth century." What a business paid, it declared, was no "test of its social value"; it was only through "social service" that businessmen contributed to the Negro community and society.[39]

Negro thought, therefore, had traveled a long way from the simple past of Booker T. Washington. The transformation from Washington's principles to the philosophy of the NAACP was the movement from the nineteenth to the twentieth century. As part of this change, the NAACP recognized the important role that labor unions were to play in the American economic system; and, as with other institutions, demanded equal treatment of Negroes. Nor was this changed attitude without its effect on the Washington school. Views enunciated by the progressive movement — which was more akin to the thinking of the NAACP than of Washington — found their way into the laws of the nation. In 1915 the conservative wing of the Negro community suffered another blow when Washington died. But even before his death, Washington had altered somewhat his earlier thinking on the value of labor unions. In 1913 he wrote that it was "not to the advantage of organized labor to produce among the Negroes a prejudice and a fear of labor unions such as to create in this country a race of strike-breakers." [40] This more moderate position was followed by his successor, Robert R. Moton. The *Age,* while still directing an occasional disparaging remark toward unions, accepted labor organizations as a necessary part of the American economy.[41] But in the postwar period the pro-business point of view was revived in the Negro community. The nation's political pendulum had swung in the direction of conservatism. Business, which before the war had been the villain in the piece, now emerged as the protector of the nation against the alleged rise of bolshevism in the world and the United States. The stigma of radicalism, deserved or undeserved, injured the position of labor unions in the America of the 1920s. This national mood had its effect on Negro thinking. The pro-business and anti-labor viewpoint once again became an important part of Negro thought. According to those who advanced this belief, the well-being of the Negro was intertwined with the interests of business not labor, laissez-faire not government intervention, free enterprise not collectivism, the capitalist not the workingman.[42] The leading Negro spokesman for this position was the educator, Kelly Miller. "At present the capitalist class possess the culture and conscience," wrote Miller in 1925, "which hold even the malignity of race passion in restraint." He found nothing "in the white working class to which the Negro can appeal." It is this group, the Negro educator continued, that "lynch and burn and torture" the Negro. The race "must look to the upper element for law and order." [43]

Ironically, the pro-business group was joined in its anti-labor thinking by the extreme Negro nationalist Marcus Garvey. Garvey, who founded the Universal Negro Improvement Association in 1914, regarded the capitalist and unionist, the Democrat and Republican, the Socialist and Communist as the enemy of the Negro. He accepted the ideal of a separate Negro economy and carried it to its logical extreme — a separate Negro nation.[44] Although Garveyism gained a large following after World War I, it was condemned by various segments of the Negro world. One such group was the small aggregation of Negro Marxists. On the surface, these radicals appeared to be the antithesis of black nationalism as well as the "buy black" movement. But in reality there were striking similarities between these groups. The ideal of a separate economic community seemed to permeate the thinking of the Negro Socialist as well as the Negro nationalist, the Negro Communist as well as the Negro businessman.

In 1917 the Marxists founded the *Messenger,* a periodical edited by the young and alert A. Philip Randolph — later the organizer of the Brotherhood of Sleeping Car Porters — and Chandler Owen. While the journal advocated "more wages, shorter hours and better working conditions," it charged that the American Federation of Labor was a capitalistic tool. Randolph and Owen also discovered that working with the more Marxist orientated labor unions failed to answer the Negro's predicament. Consequently, they proceeded to encourage the formation of a series of all Negro labor unions. If these organizations were to be one of the means by which a socialist society would come to the United States or were to facilitate the Negro's attainment of equality within capitalist America, is not clear.[45] Whatever their purpose, these labor groups were short-lived. Socialism, national and state investigating committees to the contrary, never was able to establish firm roots in the Negro community. Similarly, the mass of Negroes refused to accept completely the idea of a separate Negro community — whether in Africa or New York City. When separatism did occur, it was in reaction to the discriminatory practices of a hostile section of the white community. This caused a dichotomy in Negro thinking. The same Negro who demanded equality, very often advocated separatism. This apparent dilemma could be attributed to the position that white society had placed the Negro community. The second-class status imposed upon the Negro forced many a Negro into a quandary that continued beyond the 1920s. And, as in earlier years, Negro leaders debated the advisability of a separate Negro economy as well as the place of labor unions in American society.

Despite the debate over the place of business in the economic life of the New York Negro, the race continued to establish business enterprises. Even before the Civil War, Negroes had won a small place in the business community of the city. As indicated earlier, before 1865 Negroes were the leading caterers in New York. Many of the leading social functions of the white community were catered by Negroes. Fraunces Tavern, which the leading citizens of the Revolutionary period patronized, was operated by a Negro. George Washington held a farewell dinner for his officers at this restaurant.[46] Negroes also owned such diverse businesses as barber shops and coal yards, drugstores and secondhand clothing shops. By 1819 it was estimated that 100 of the leading Negro families in the city had total capital investments of at least $10,000. This sum rose to $836,000 by the end of the Civil War. In that year, it was also estimated that the race had more than $1,000,000 in the savings banks of the city and $1,500,000 in taxable real estate.[47]

Increased competition from whites prompted many Negro businessmen to form organizations to preserve as well as enhance their economic position. For instance, in 1869 the 12 leading Negro caterers in the city met to organize the United Public Waiters' Mutual Beneficial Association. They pledged themselves to control and maintain their high quality of service and to expand their businesses. They resolved to prevent "irresponsible men from catering affairs." So successful were the leading Negro caterers that three members of the Association — Daniel Brooks, Jacob Day, and Jeremiah Bowers — claimed total capital investments of over $200,000 in 1871. Another group of Negroes organized the Excelsior Land Association of Brooklyn in the 1870s to facilitate real estate investments.[48] Real estate ownership was common among affluent Negroes, for those men who made a profit in business found that investment in land was not only profitable, but carried with it a sense of economic security. In the decade after the Civil War the white press, when discussing well-to-do Negroes, referred to the real estate investments of these men.[49]

The limited amount of available evidence for the two decades between 1865 and 1885 indicates that the position of the Negro businessman was similar to that before 1865.[50] Some growth in capital investments must have occurred in this period, for the New York *Sun* estimated the wealth of the Negro community at approximately $3,000,000 in 1887. The paper listed Negro real estate owners, druggists, and physicians among the affluent Negroes. Catering as a Negro enterprise, however, had declined in importance. Whites now serviced most of the social events held by the well-to-do members of the non-Negro community.[51] On the one hand, Negro business enterprises were going forward, whereas, on the other hand, they were losing ground. Negro leaders were dissatisfied with the race's position in the city's business community. They condemned most of their fellow Negroes for squandering their money rather than using it to advance the economic status of the race. Investment in business, as indicated earlier, was advanced by many Negroes as the solution to the plight of the race. Practical application of these beliefs were attempted through the formation of a number of companies and societies. The Professional and Business Men's Social Club and the Young Men's Industrial League, both formed in 1890, attempted to improve the business status of New York Negroes. The Keystone Loan and Investment Association was organized in 1891 to facilitate the acquisition of capital for Negro business ventures.[52] But outside of their propaganda effect, these groups did little to enhance the status of business in Negro New York. Those Negro enterprises that were created in the years that followed were individual undertakings and bore little relation to the groups mentioned.

As the Negro population of the city grew, so did its business enterprises. Such gains were recorded in a study of Negro business made by W. E. B. Du Bois in 1899.[53] The Negro sociologist listed some 63 Negro-owned businesses. Among this number were six caterers and five moving van companies, three newsdealers and four real estate agencies, four undertakers and two printers. Only two Negroes were listed as hotel owners in 1899, while in 1888 five hotels advertised in the Negro press.[54] More Negroes appear to have operated business establishments than owned them. During the 1900s Negroes made further advances into the business world.[55] In 1901 Du Bois reported that Negroes had invested at least $1,500,000 in business endeavors. Most of this sum was in real estate, catering, restaurants, undertaking, drugstores, and hotels. In 1907 the *Age* announced that more Negroes were entering business than at any time since the Civil War.[56] By 1910 there were nine Negro printing companies, whereas only two existed in 1899. More than 16 real estate companies were operating in 1910, while only four were functioning 11 years earlier. Similar increases occurred in grocery, moving van, coal, wood, and ice enterprises. In 1910, too, such Negro business ventures in the fields of photography, upholstery, and electric supplies were in operation. At least 16 Negro-owned funeral parlors were in operation at the end of the first decade of the twentieth century. Although Negro barbers had lost their white trade, more than 56 such shops serviced the Negro community. These gains caused Mary Ovington to remark in 1910 that Negro participation in business was on the increase. This advance continued in the next five years. The growing Negro community of Harlem provided further opportunity for the Negro storekeeper. In 1915 a selected list of Negro business establishments in Harlem recorded more than 100 enterprises. Taking this limited survey, it is apparent that Negro business operations were on the rise.[57]

Most Negro business ventures were one- or two-man enterprises.[58] Those that enjoyed the greatest success provided facilities denied the Negro in the wider community. Although there were state laws prohibiting discrimination in public places, Negroes found themselves excluded by subtle practices that skirted the law. Many white-owned restaurants discouraged Negro patronage by poor service and high prices.[59] For this reason, restaurants owned by Negroes thrived in the Negro community.

Constant reference was made to restaurants of all descriptions that catered to the race. As the *Age* observed in 1913, "Eating places are springing up like mushrooms in Harlem." Negro neighborhoods were filled with taverns and cabarets, lunchrooms and elegant restaurants. One of the largest eating places in Harlem was the Empire Restaurant on West 135th Street. The Bradford, a hotel and restaurant on West 134th Street, catered to the more affluent Negro. Southern cooking, too, was a feature of many Negro eating establishments.[60] Certain of the cabarets, hotels, and restaurants were centers for Negro entertainers. James Weldon Johnson portrayed the Negro Bohemia that centered in the Maceo and Marshall hotels of West Fifty-third Street.[61]

Another successful Negro enterprise was the funeral parlor. Like the white restaurateur who disliked the Negro's patronage while alive, so the white undertaker manifested no preference for the Negro after death. Consequently, there developed a prosperous group of Negro undertakers.[62] One of the most successful Negro undertakers was John C. Thomas. Thomas worked his way to New York City in 1881 on a southern steamer. His early years in the city were spent working as a hotel steward. In 1897 he opened an undertaking parlor. This small firm expanded to one of the largest in the Negro community. As Thomas' profits increased, he invested a portion in real estate.[63] Other Negroes enjoyed prosperous business careers in real estate. Philip A. Payton, Jr., whose activities were discussed in chapter one, was the leading Negro real estate man in the city for many years.[64] Another very profitable enterprise in the Negro community was the sale of cosmetic preparations. The most popular was hair straightening tonic. The Negro press was filled with advertisements of beauty parlors and retail establishments that offered this preparation.[65] Still other Negroes opened dress and millinery shops that offered the latest styles. Odessa Warren Grey's hat shop in Harlem provided the latest Parisian fashions.[66] To a lesser degree, Negroes invested in dance halls, theaters, and casinos that met the recreational predilections of the Negro community.[67] A large owner of property in Negro areas was the Negro church. Not only did the church use money to build lavish and ornate houses of worship, but they bought many apartment houses in Negro communities.[68]

The successful Negro businessman, however, was more the exception than the rule. Most Negro store owners had to compete with white shopkeepers. In Harlem the most flourishing stores were owned by whites. This situation prompted the *Age* to conduct an investigation of Negro business enterprises in Harlem. In general, it not only found that there were too few Negro shops in Harlem, but that the race was denied the better locations. On Fifth Avenue, between 131st and 138th streets, Negroes constituted 98 per cent of the consumers, according to the newspaper, but they owned only 12 per cent of the stores. In addition, most Negroes of this section patronized stores owned by whites. Where Negroes accounted for almost all of the shoppers, Negro storekeepers received only between 15 and 20 per cent of the race's trade. Similar conditions were found in other parts of Harlem.[69] The failure of Negro shoppers to "buy black" was partially attributable to an absence of race loyalty. Business consideration, however, offered a better explanation for this situation. Negroes were restricted to the least desirable location, which, in part, was explained by their late entrance into Harlem's business world. A limited supply of capital also restricted the size and the stock of the Negro store. The wholesale merchant because of the Negro shopkeeper's limited capital and trade was reluctant to extend credit. This combination of factors prevented the Negro entrepreneur from offering both a varied stock and credit to prospective customers. On the other hand, Negro shoppers found that they could get credit and a greater variety of goods at white-owned stores. Appeals to race loyalty fell on deaf ears when the offerings of the Negro merchant were inferior to those of his white competitor.[70] Negroes, therefore, were urged to do more than open "a little shop." They were implored to make it a "bigger shop," to increase their capital, to vary their stock, and to improve their business practices.[71]

To this end, organizations were created. Early in the twentieth century a local chapter of the National Negro Business League was formed. It advised Negroes to expand their business activities. Too often, however, its proposals were hampered by an antiquated conception of a nation of small shopkeepers. Yet, it did, on occasion, urge the combination of capital into larger enterprises.[72] Other groups, including the Urban League, also stressed the necessity of Negroes combining their financial resources. The New York Colored Business Men's Association worked with the Urban League to foster cooperative business investment.[73] The work of these groups and the opportunities afforded by Negro Harlem impelled many Negroes to go beyond the traditional small shop. The *Age* in 1920 noted that the race was "acquiring the capital and courage to try newer fields" in the business world. It reported that "five- and ten-cent" stores, furniture companies, markets, and even clothing factories were owned and operated by Negroes.[74] These advances, according to the Negro newspaper, could be attributed to the higher prevalence of sound business principles. Negro customers now had greater confidence in Negro store owners. One of the greatest beneficiaries of this change was the Negro groceryman. These stores grew in number and size; they offered a more varied stock and employed modern selling practices. This change led James Weldon Johnson to remark in 1925 that Harlem was "gradually becoming more and more of a self-supporting community." In 1921 the New York *Dispatch,* a Negro newspaper, contended that Negro Harlem's "professional and business men are among the best in the country." [75] Yet whites continued to control a sizable portion of the shops in Negro neighborhoods. The Negro businessman, therefore, faced strong competition from whites within the Negro ghetto, while finding it next to impossible to run a successful business in white neighborhoods. Against this background, many Negro leaders continued to urge the race to invest in business operations as well as to "buy black." [76]

Notes

[1] Ernst, "The Economic Status of the New York City Negro," pp. 140–41; Robert Ernst, *Immigrant Life in New York City, 1825–1863* (New York, 1949), pp. 104–105.

[2] Herman D. Bloch, "Craft Unions and the Negro in Historical Perspective," *Journal of Negro History,* XLIII (January, 1958), 11–13; Sidney H. Kessler, "The Organization of Negroes in the Knights of Labor," *ibid.,* XXXVII (July, 1952), 248–76; Charles L. Franklin, *The Negro Labor Unionist of New York: Problems and Conditions among Negroes in the Labor Unions in Manhattan with Special Reference to the* N.R.A. *and Post-N.R.A. Situations* (New York, 1936), pp. 68–69.

[3] Bernard Mandel, "Samuel Gompers and the Negro Workers, 1886–1914," *Journal of Negro History,* XL (January, 1955), 40, 48–49. Also see Rayford W. Logan, *The Negro in American Life and Thought: the Nadir, 1877–1901* (New York, 1954), pp. 148–53; Charles H. Wesley, *Negro Labor in the United States, 1850–1925* (New York, 1927), pp. 256–64. Gompers, on occasion, claimed that he was not anti-Negro and that his statements had been quoted out of context. See, for example, his letter to

the National Association for the Advancement of Colored People in the *Crisis*, I (January, 1911), 13.

⁴ *New York Freeman,* May 7, 1886; *New York Age,* November 24, 1910; *New York Times,* July 14, 1895; March 14, 1898; August 4, 1913; Speed, "The Negro in New York," p. 1250.

⁵ *New York Times,* November 20, 1898; Kessler, "The Organization of Negroes in the Knights of Labor," p. 257; John Stephens Durham, "The Labor Unions and the Negro," *Atlantic Monthly,* LXXXI (February, 1898), 230.

⁶ Ovington, "The Negro in the Trade Unions in New York," pp. 551–57; Spero and Harris, *The Black Worker,* p. 337; *New York Age,* July 12, 1906; Ray Stannard Baker, "The Negro's Struggle for Survival in the North," *American Magazine,* LXV (March, 1908), 479.

⁷ Ovington, "The Negro in the Trade Unions in New York," pp. 551–57; *New York Age,* March 28, 1907, and November 24, 1910; Herbert R. Northrup, *Organized Labor and the Negro* (New York, 1944), p. 46; Haynes, *Negro at Work,* p. 82.

⁸ *Southern Workman,* XLIX (September, 1920), 433–34; Spero and Harris, *The Black Worker,* pp. 102–106; Haynes, "The Negro at Work: a Development of the War and a Problem of Reconstruction," pp. 390–91.

⁹ Spero and Harris, *The Black Worker,* pp. 89–112; Wesley, *Negro Labor in the United States,* pp. 272–73; *New York Tribune,* July 5, 1917; *New York Age,* December 8, 1917; Kennedy, *Negro Peasant Turns Cityward,* pp. 111–12.

¹⁰ *New York Times,* December 1, 1919.

¹¹ *Ibid.,* July 14, 1895; March 14, 1898; June 15, 1904; *New York Age,* November 24, 1910; *Crisis,* I (January, 1911), 13; IV (July, 1912), 13.

¹² *New York Age,* March 28, 1907; *New York Freeman,* March 20, 1884; Kessler, "The Organization of Negroes in the Knights of Labor," pp. 257, 272; Northrup, *Organized Labor and the Negro,* p. 46.

¹³ Wesley, *Negro Labor in the United States,* pp. 55–56, 168–89; *New York Age,* June 5, 1913, and January 11, 1919; *New York Times,* October 7, 1917; National League on Urban Conditions, *Report for 1912–1913,* pp. 12–13, and *Report for 1913–1914 and 1914–1915,* p. 13.

¹⁴ Ernst, "The Economic Status of the New York City Negro," pp. 140–41; Man, "Labor Competition and the New York Draft Riots," pp. 384–402; Barnes, *Longshoremen,* p. 8; Spero and Harris, *The Black Worker,* pp. 198–99.

¹⁵ *New York Age,* May 30, 1907, and June 6, 1912; *New York Times,* August 17, 1920; *New York Tribune,* May 20, 1903; Barnes, *Longshoremen,* p. 8; Spero and Harris, *The Black Worker,* pp. 198–99; David Bryant Fulton [pseud., Jack Thorne], *Eagle Clippings* (Brooklyn, 1907), p. 8; Ovington, "The Negro in the Trade Unions in New York," p. 556.

¹⁶ *New York Freeman,* May 7, 1886.

¹⁷ *New York Age,* February 25, 1888, and March 23, 1905.

¹⁸ Ovington, "The Negro in the Trade Unions in New York," p. 555.

¹⁹ *New York Age,* May 30, 1907; November 24, 1910; November 30, 1911; June 18, July 2, 1914.

²⁰ *Ibid.,* August 24, 1905; *New York Globe,* November 3, 1883.

²¹ *New York Age,* March 1, 1890; National Negro Business League, *Report of the Fifth Annual*

Convention, 1904 (Pensacola, 1904), p. 48.

[22] *New York Age,* July 11, October 3, 1912; *Colored American Review,* I (October 1, 1915), 4, 12.

[23] *New York Age,* January 4, June 21, 1890; March 7, December 26, 1907; April 13, October 5, 1916.

[24] *Ibid.,* April 21, 1910; October 19, 1911; September 11, 1913; March 23, 30, April 6, 1916.

[25] *Colored American Review,* I (October 1, 1915), opposite p. 1.

[26] *New York Freeman,* April 3, 1886; National Negro Business League, *Report of the Fifth Annual Convention, 1904,* p. 46; *New York Tribune,* May 4, 1903.

[27] *New York Times,* April 20, 1914.

[28] *New York Age,* January 8, 1914; *Colored American Review,* I (October 1, 1915), 1–2, 15.

[29] Gunnar Myrdal, *An American Dilemma: the Negro Problem and Modern Democracy* (20th Anniversary ed.; New York, 1962), p. 305.

[30] E. Franklin Frazier, *Black Bourgeoisie* (Glencoe, Ill., 1957), p. 168; Samuel R. Spencer, Jr., *Booker T. Washington and the Negro's Place in America* (Boston, 1955), pp. 116–17; *Colored American Review,* I (October 1, 1915), 4.

[31] See *New York Age,* February 28, September 5, 1891; August 24, 1905; February 14, April 4, 1907; May 14, 1908; *New York Times,* June 15, 1904.

[32] Booker T. Washington, *Negro in Business* (Boston, 1907), pp. 333, 355; Ovington, "The Negro in the Trade Unions in New York," p. 554.

[33] *New York Age,* August 30, 1906.

[34] *Ibid.,* December 19, 1907; May 14, 1908; May 25, 1909; *Colored American Magazine,* XIII (September, 1907), 210; National League on Urban Conditions, *Re-*

port for 1910–1911, pp. 4–6, and *Report for 1913–1914 and 1914–1915,* p. 13.

[35] Residents of New York City constituted a majority of both the general committee and the executive committee. *Crisis,* I (November, 1910), 12.

[36] *Ibid.,* IV (July, 1912), 131, and V (November, 1912), 20 and (January, 1913), 124–25. For the 1920s, see Spero and Harris, *The Black Worker,* pp. 128–46.

[37] National Negro Business League, *Report of the Eleventh Annual Convention, 1910* (Nashville, 1910), p. 83; *Crisis,* II (June, 1911), 64–65, and VI (October, 1913), 290. Washington, Spero and Harris have stated, "was a small capitalist, an eighteenth-century individualist, in an era of corporate wealth and industrial integration." *The Black Worker,* pp. 51–52.

[38] *Crisis,* II (June, 1911), 64–65.

[39] *Ibid.,* II (June, 1911), 64–65, and VI (October, 1913), 290.

[40] "The Negro and the Labor Unions," *Atlantic Monthly,* CXI (June, 1913), 763.

[41] *New York Age,* May 4, 1918, and June 19, 1920.

[42] Spero and Harris, *The Black Worker,* pp. 134–46.

[43] *Ibid.,* p. 134.

[44] *Ibid.,* pp. 135–36, 388.

[45] *Ibid.,* pp. 388–97.

[46] Johnson, *Black Manhattan,* p. 44.

[47] Hirsch, "The Negro and New York," pp. 433–38; Payne, "The Negro in New York Prior to 1860," pp. 62–64; Haynes, *Negro At Work,* pp. 94–98; Scottron, "The Industrial and Professional Pursuits of the Colored People of Old New York," pp. 265–67; Charles H. Wesley, "The Negroes of New York in the Emancipation Movement," *Journal of Negro*

History, XXIV (January, 1939), 66, 102.

[48] *New York Times*, March 13, 1871; *New York Globe*, November 10, 1883; *New York Freeman*, January 22, 1887; Haynes, *Negro at Work*, p. 68.

[49] *New York Times*, March 2, 1869, and March 13, 1871.

[50] See article by Samuel Scottron in *New York Age*, October 19, 1905.

[51] New York *Sun*, June 5, 1887; Scottron, "The Industrial and Professional Pursuits of the Colored People of Old New York," pp. 265–67; Speed, "The Negro in New York," p. 1250.

[52] *New York Age*, February 15, June 21, 1890, and February 14, 1891.

[53] W. E. B. Du Bois, ed., *The Negro in Business* (Atlanta, 1899), p. 27.

[54] *Ibid.*, *New York Age*, November 24, 1888.

[55] Samuel Scottron was one Negro who believed that Negro business opportunities had declined: "Years ago it was a common thing for our people to engage in business. There existed no feeling in the community averse to trading with us." *New York Age*, October 19, 1905.

[56] *Ibid.*, February 28, July 15, 1907; *New York Times*, November 17, 1901.

[57] Du Bois, *Negro in Business*, p. 27; Ovington, *Half A Man*, pp. 111–14; *Colored American Review*, I (October 1, 1915), 8–9, 15.

[58] Haynes, *Negro at Work*, p. 100; Kennedy, *Negro Peasant Turns Cityward*, pp. 85–87.

[59] *New York Age*, April 19, July 19, 1906; *New York Tribune*, February 23, 1903; New York *World*, February 23, 1913; *Crisis*, III (February, 1912), 158.

[60] *New York Age*, March 2, 1911; January 30, 1913; March 23, 1916; *New York Times*, September 2, 1917; *Colored American Review*, I (October 1, 1915), 16; Blascoer, *Colored School Children*, p. 72.

[61] James Weldon Johnson, *Along This Way* (New York, 1933), pp. 175–76.

[62] Ovington, *Half A Man*, p. 110. See advertisements in *New York Age*, March 2, 1911.

[63] *Colored American Review*, I (January, 1916), 12; Washington, *Negro in Business*, pp. 104–109.

[64] See, for example, *New York Times*, September 2, 1917; Dyckoff, "A Negro City in New York," p. 951; *New York Age*, March 23, 1916.

[65] *New York Times*, September 2, 1917; *New York Age*, February 9, 1911, and November 26, 1914. See almost any issue of the *Age* for hair tonic advertisements.

[66] *New York Age*, December 19, 1912.

[67] *Ibid.*, July 11, 1912; *New York Times*, June 8, 1914.

[68] National League on Urban Conditions, "Housing Conditions Among Negroes in Harlem," pp. 12–13.

[69] *New York Age*, March 9, 16, 23, 30, April 6, 1916.

[70] *Ibid.*, October 19, 1911, and March 30, April 13, 1916; *Colored American Review*, I (October 1, 1915), opposite p. 1; Haynes, *Negro at Work*, p. 122.

[71] *New York Age*, August 26, 1915; March 30, April 13, 1916; March 22, 1917.

[72] *Ibid.*, August 31, 1918; *New York Tribune*, October 2, 1903, and January 11, 1906; National Negro Business League, *Report of the Fifth Annual Convention*, 1904, p. 18, and *Report of the Eleventh Annual Convention*, 1910, p. 83.

[73] National League on Urban Conditions, *Report for 1913–1914 and 1914–1915*, p. 13; *New York Age*, April 13, October 5, 1916, and January 4, 1917.

[74] *New York Age*, August 7, 1920.

[75] *Ibid.*, February 9, 1918, and July 17, August 14, 1920; James Weldon Johnson, "The Making of Harlem," *Survey Graphic*, LIII (March 1, 1925), 635–39; New York *Dispatch*, January 7, 1921.

[76] Kelly Miller, "The Harvest of Race Prejudice," *Survey Graphic*, LIII (March 1, 1925), 711–12.

.4.

Negro Society

BARRED in general from the white community's neighborhoods, social life, and economic affairs, New York Negroes developed their own society. They created a separate world; a world with its own churches, its own societies, its own recreational facilities, its own cultural life. The activities of this Negro society conformed to the basic social pattern of New York City, for the Negro patterned his social and cultural institutions upon his American background rather than his African inheritance.[1] As Richard Bardolph has noted: the Negro built a "black replica of white American culture on his own side of the line." Still, by the very fact of his exclusion from the wider community, the Negro gave his own interpretation to the dominant culture of the white man. These differences, though, were only minor variations of prevailing social habits.[2]

Behind the walls of the Negro ghetto, the church was the major institution about which the life of the Negro community revolved. By virtue of the Negro's exclusion from white society — both during and after bondage — the church had to meet the needs of its adherents. Consequently, the church provided many of the facilities which Negroes could not receive outside the confines of their segregated world. In the course of the period 1865 to 1920, the Negro church in New York City and the nation played a multifold role. It ministered to religious needs, served as a social center, supplied relief to the orphaned and aged, promoted educational and cultural activities, stood in the vanguard of many race enterprises, and fostered the expression of a Negro point of view through the leadership of the clergy. Given the nature of Negro religion, it is not surprising that the Negro preacher was concerned with almost every aspect of his constituency's life. He was the politician and the social worker, the moral counselor and the employment agent of the Negro community.[3] In the course of this period, however, the church declined somewhat as a central force in the Negro world because of the growth of secular agencies as well as its own inability to adjust to the ramifications of the urbanization process. While it was still the single most influential institution in Negro society in 1920, it had declined from its earlier preeminence.

In 1865 there were 13 Negro churches in Manhattan and Brooklyn; by the 1920s this number had increased to more than 200. This growth can be attributed to the constant migration of Negroes to the city, the changing residential pattern, the frequent schisms within churches, and the rise of the storefront church. These factors also contributed to changes in the relative size of the various denominations. Where the Methodist church claimed the largest number of Negro adherents in the city during the nineteenth century, it was surpassed in the twentieth century by the Baptist church. The large majority of the city's Negroes belonged to one of these two sects; a smaller number adhered to the Episcopalian, Presbyterian, and Catholic faiths.[4]

The first Negro church organized in the city was the African Methodist Episcopal Zion Church. Established by a group of Negroes who separated from the predominantly white John Street Methodist Episcopal Church in 1796, it held its early meetings in the shop of a Negro cabinet maker. Before long, the congregation moved to a more permanent structure on West Tenth and Bleecker streets.[5] In 1808 another group of Negroes left the First Baptist Church on Gold Street because of the white leadership's discriminatory ways. They opened the Abyssinian Baptist Church on Anthony Street. In the years that followed, this house of God gained in membership as well as financial resources and became one of the most influential and wealthiest Negro churches in the city. It erected an impressive edifice on Waverly Place where it remained until the 1900s when it relocated on West Fortieth Street and, finally, in Harlem.[6] One decade after the formation of the Abyssinian Baptist Church, a small band of Negro Episcopalians organized St. Philip's Protestant Episcopal Church. During the Civil War the church house was used as a soldiers' barracks. In the years following the war, St. Philip's came to cater to the more affluent element of the Negro population. Like other Negro churches it moved slowly northward until it finally located in Harlem. There it built an impressive house of worship and invested a large portion of its income in real estate. In 1919 the *Age* reported that St. Philip's was the richest Negro church in the world with holdings in the area of $1,000,000.[7]

Following the establishment of these and other early Negro churches, Negroes as well as whites accepted segregated worship. Negroes rarely joined a white congregation; instead they organized their own religious institutions. Segregation of the city's churches became the rule. This was attested to by an Englishman visiting the city in 1886, John Kirkwood, who noted that he rarely saw Negroes worshipping alongside whites. Negroes, Kirkwood asserted, preferred "to draw together and worship with their own people." [8]

As New York's Negro population increased more churches were created to minister to the race's religious needs. Between 1865 and 1900 the number of Negro churches increased more than threefold; in the next two decades the number increased fivefold.[9] In 1871 St. Mark's Methodist Episcopal Church opened its doors for Negroes residing in the West Thirty-fifth Street area. A few years later Mount Olivet Baptist Church, which was to appeal to southern newcomers, was holding religious services in the Tenderloin district. And, in 1883, the first Negro Roman Catholic Church in the city, St. Benedict the Moor, was established in the Greenwich Village neighborhood.[10]

Contributing to this proliferation of Negro religious houses was not only the growth in the size of the Negro population of New York, but the race's constant movement within the city. Although many Negro churches followed the movement of the city's Negro population, they did so only after the new community had existed for a number of years. Older Negro residents of

the city as well as newcomers were compelled to travel downtown for religious services until churches were established in the
new communities. For a brief period of time, then, many Negro
citizens were left without the benefits of a church in their immediate neighborhood. This temporary absence of religious min-
istration resulted in a decline in church membership. In 1896 a
church survey of a Negro district in the west Forties discovered
that Negro church attendance exceeded church membership.
After comparing the Negro to other nationality groups, the
church report concluded that the Negro had the lowest rate of
church membership. This movement of population also affected
the appeal of certain churches among the Negro citizenry. Between 1882 and 1887, for example, Mount Olivet Baptist Church
recorded a threefold increase in membership, whereas the Abyssinian Baptist Church in lower Manhattan suffered a 50 per cent
decline.[11]

Seeing their congregations dwindle in size, many clergymen
realized that they must follow the uptown movement of their
fellow Negroes. During the late 1880s and 1890s, St. Mark's
Methodist Episcopal, Mount Olivet Baptist, and St. Benedict the
Moor transferred to new quarters on West Fifty-third Street. The
influx of Italians into the Greenwich Village area caused St.
Philip's Protestant Episcopal Church to sell its property on Mulberry Street to an Italian group. It then proceeded to purchase
new quarters on West Twenty-fifth Street.[12] In the 1900s many
of the churches that had relocated at least once began to move
into Harlem. The Bethel African Methodist Episcopal Church,
which had been organized in 1819, moved to West 132nd Street
from West Twenty-fifth Street in 1914. The church fathers admitted that the decline in attendance was responsible for their
decision to find new quarters in Harlem.[13]

The effects that population movement had on church membership was at least partially responsible for the revival services
that were conducted in the late 1880s and 1890s. Clergymen used
the meetings to attract those who had strayed from the flock as
well as to gain new adherents from the mass of southern Negroes
who had migrated to New York. In addition, certain churches
conducted missionary activities. In 1891 the Bronx Mission of the
Union African Methodist Episcopal Church of Manhattan was
ministering to the needs of that borough's Negro citizens. St.

Mark's Methodist Episcopal Church, by 1905, had missions in Harlem, Brooklyn, and the Bronx. The Highways and Hedges Society of the Abyssinian Baptist Church and the Mite Missionary Society of the Bethel African Methodist Episcopal Church went into the street to bring the wayward back to God.[14]

Also working toward the proliferation of Negro churches in New York City was the rise of the storefront church. The spread of this type of religious institution reached a high point in the 1900s. More substantial edifices took time to erect but the storefront church could be set up virtually overnight.[15] Some of these religious houses grew out of disagreements within older churches. These disputes, which had been taking place since the early nineteenth century, have been attributed more to a desire on the part of many Negroes for positions of leadership than to theological differences.[16] These schisms did not merely add to the number of Negro churches in the city, but limited the membership potential of many and spread thin their financial resources. It reduced the influence of the clergy, for even with few churches the Negro's economic deprivation reduced the financial support that could be given the church.[17]

Inasmuch as most Negro churches had limited financial resources, they were severely restricted in their charitable activities. "These superfluous churches," wrote James Weldon Johnson in 1920, "create such a financial drain that the race does not build and maintain hospitals, old folks' homes, orphan asylums." Lack of money was not the only reason given for the inadequate philanthropic activities of the Negro church; it was alleged that the church was preoccupied with frivolous undertakings or in erecting ostentatious structures. In 1913 Mary Martel charged that Negro churches devoted too insignificant a portion of their Sunday contributions to assisting the needy. Writing in the 1900s, the *Age* maintained that many churches had become "a drain upon the time and small money of their membership." The paper asserted that church fathers considered "church building and money raising as the principal business of a preacher, the primary question of saving the wayward from bad associations and making a good reputation for himself and his people in his community being subordinated." James Weldon Johnson charged in 1915 that a "gross mercenary spirit" permeated the thinking of church elders. "And for what purposes is the money gathered? Does it go to feed the hungry? to clothe the naked? to care for the widow and the orphan? To some extent yes; but the great bulk of it goes to maintain costly temples." What the church needs, concluded Johnson, is a "new baptism of Christ-like simplicity." [18] The *Age* echoed the thoughts of the Negro leader when it wrote that preachers should teach "more the way to live and less the way to die." It urged church leaders to "make the precepts of religion an active force in the right living of the community," to "be a directing force in the neighborhood activities of the people." The *Crisis* in 1912 complained that the clergy devoted more time to "inveighing against dancing and theatre going" than in "positive programs of education and social uplift." [19]

The Negro church despite these criticisms did perform some much needed charitable services. As will be seen in chapter six, though, the major philanthropic activities in behalf of the city's Negro residents came from agencies operated either by whites or whites in conjunction with Negroes. It must also be pointed out in defense of Negro clergymen that many worked with non-Negro organizations. They realized that they faced "the alternative of either responding to these social needs of the membership or seeing . . . [their] constituency gradually drawn away by agencies which would." [20] But the Negro church that did extensive social work among the Negro masses was the exception. In general, the charitable programs of most Negro churches were erratic. Two exceptions to the general rule were St. Philip's Protestant Episcopal and Salem Methodist Episcopal. They manifested an interest in all aspects of life. In addition to the usual adult organizations, these institutional churches initiated organized activities for youths in Negro neighborhoods. W. E. Cullen, Salem's pastor, worked for the eradication of crime among Negro juveniles. He exhibited deep concern in the problem of prostitution. Working with white reformers, the Reverend Cullen attempted to wipe out this vice in the vicinity of his church. St. Philip's social work activities were far more extensive than those of the Salem Church. Hutchens C. Bishop, the pastor, was an active member of both the NAACP and the Urban League. Under his leadership, St. Philip's became a center through which certain programs of these organizations were administered. A number of St. Philip's male members participated in the Big Brother program established by the Urban League. The women of the church, through the Dorcas Society, gave clothing to the Negro poor. In 1875 the church was operating a home for the aged and infirm in the Bronx.[21]

Although few Negro churches engaged in activities as extensive as those of St. Philip's or Salem, almost every Negro church offered some sort of charitable and educational program to its adherents. The Abyssinian Baptist Church conducted a Vacation Training School to teach students a trade. The Union Baptist Church also operated an industrial school; however, in 1892 the Children's Aid Society assumed direction of the school. Nurseries and kindergartens, both affiliated and unaffiliated with churches, were a common feature in Negro neighborhoods. A few houses of worship opened summer camps outside of the city to take Negro youths from New York's streets. Other than this, the Negro community had to depend for education on facilities provided by white philanthropic organizations and upon the public school system (see chapter six).

While assistance was given to the aged and needy, most Negro churches attacked the problems of the deprived elements in a haphazard manner. Too often assistance was restricted to sickness and death benefits or such inconsequential ventures as sending flowers to the sick. On the whole, then, the charitable work of the average Negro church failed to fulfill the social needs of the Negro masses.[22]

The influence of the church on the life of the New York Negro was affected in time by the rise of fraternal societies and social clubs. Churches had their own fraternal societies and benevolent organizations, but between 1865 and 1920 those groups that were not affiliated with religious institutions became the more influential. During their early history these secular societies met in churches, but as they augmented their treasuries they rented or purchased meeting halls and relied less on the church as a place to congregate.[23] Like the church, fraternal societies and social clubs compensated for the Negro's exclusion from the activities of white society. Because they could not take part in the political, religious, and social life of the wider community, Negroes magnified the secret rituals, the formal regalia, the pomp and splendor, the high-sounding titles of fraternal and social associations. Through these organizations Negroes gained an expression of race consciousness, a feeling of self-fulfillment, a sense of achievement denied them beyond the walls of the ghetto. Negro societies and clubs bore a striking resemblance to those of the outside world; but, as Gunnar Myrdal observed in 1940, they were a pathological replica of white society, for these organizations displayed exaggerated manifestations of the American norm. Furthermore, Negroes fought the struggle for class status within the institutions of the ghetto — different societies had different appeals to different classes. As E. Franklin Frazier remarked: For the Negro elite " 'social' life has not only provided a form of participation; it has represented an effort to achieve identification with upper-class whites by imitating as far as possible the behavior of white society." [24]

The early fraternal societies were established to provide sickness and death benefits for their members. The Saloonmen's Protective Union, for instance, was organized in 1863 to provide benefits for sick members and payment for burial costs. The large number of Negro coachmen in New York City about the time of the Civil War formed a mutual relief society to provide similar features. Before long, however, these and other associations — the Southern Beneficial League, the Hotel Bellmen's Beneficial League, and the West Indian Benevolent Association — opened their membership roles to the Negro community at large. Moreover, the sickness and death benefits gradually took a back seat to the social aspects of these groups. [25]

Shortly after the Civil War the *New York Times* reported that societies drawing their membership exclusively from Negroes included six lodges of the Society of Good Samaritans, four branches of the Grand United Order of Odd Fellows, and 14 chapters of Colored Freemasons. All told, these organizations had a membership of almost 2,000. They were not connected with similar white organizations; in fact, the Odd Fellows had received its charter directly from England. Negro women also formed organizations. In most cases, the female groups were auxiliaries of the male societies. Chapters of the Grand Army of the Republic — the Thaddeus Stevens and William Lloyd Garrison posts — also were organized. The profusion of Negro organizations, as early as 1871, caused the *New York Times* to report that Negroes possessed "a readiness to enter into every new society." Scarcely was there a Negro who did not belong to a society, the newspaper asserted. [26]

The fifty-five year period between 1865 and 1920 saw the continued establishment of Negro fraternal and benevolent societies. During the 1880s the Negro Elks came into existence, and by 1908 had at least ten lodges. Similar gains were recorded by other societies. The Negro Odd Fellows had 22 lodges and more than 4,000 members by the close of the first decade of the twentieth century. At the same time the United Order of True Reformers claimed 44 meeting places. In 1916 Negro Masons, sporting a large treasury as well as a growing membership, opened a lavish Masonic Temple in Harlem.[27] Natives of different states banded together in their own organizations. In 1884 a group of New York-born Negroes established the Society of the Sons of New York; two years later a sister society was created. In the next decade the Society bought a $20,000 clubhouse on West Fifty-third Street. Since a considerable portion of the Negro leadership class of the city was drawn from Negroes born and raised in sections of the nation other than New York (T. Thomas Fortune in Florida, A. Clayton Powell in Virginia and Connecticut, T. McCants Stewart in South Carolina, and Alexander Walters in Kentucky), the Sons of New York failed to exert a far-reaching influence on Negro life. Other groups, though, followed the lead of the Sons of New York in forming organizations. There were the Sons of Virginia, the Sons of North Carolina, and the Sons and Daughters of South Carolina. So great was the growth and popularity of fraternal organizations that the *Age* in the 1900s carried a regular calendar of society meetings. Charles Martin wrote in 1916 with some misgivings that Negroes "are lodge mad." [28]

As indicated earlier, not all the fraternal organizations and social clubs appealed or wished to appeal to the same elements of Negro society. Certain clubs catered to certain classes. The Ugly Club listed among its members some of the wealthiest Negroes in the city. A leading group in the Sons of Virginia and the Sons of North Carolina were professional men. The New York Social Club appealed to the young adult offspring of well-to-do New York Negroes. The Manhattan Club claimed many of the city's leading professionals and educators. In 1892 the Brooklyn *Eagle* reported the existence of a Negro "400." [29]

The fraternal society went beyond sickness and death benefits; along with the social club, they provided a very active social life. One of the most popular social diversions was the ball or promenade. At these events, the participants socialized and displayed the latest clothing fashions. Social affairs helped to defray the heavy expenses of these organizations. Where fraternal organizations usually held social events to commemorate an annual occasion, social clubs engaged in these activities at more frequent intervals. The Negro press contained numerous announcements of masquerade balls, dances, and promenades of such groups as the Tempo Club, the Monte Carlo Social Club, and the Still Alarm Social Club.[30] Along with balls and promenades, picnics were popular diversions in the Negro community. Churches, fraternal organizations, social clubs, and various ad hoc associations held these events in neighboring parks or distant resort areas. Negroes celebrated the customary holidays and added the commemoration of such events as the signing of the Emancipation Proclamation and Lincoln's Birthday.[31]

In time the social offerings of the fraternal society and the social club had to compete with public recreational facilities. This was particularly so in the case of the lower-class Negro, who had failed to gain significant entrance into organized Negro society. As the period 1865–1920 progressed, many Negroes turned to the theater, amusement parks, sporting events, and other forms of public entertainment. Negroes displayed special interest in theatrical performances. Early in its history, the New York Negro community, especially the upper- and middle-class sections, attended presentations of serious plays and classical music. As far back as 1820, Negro actors performed Shakespearean plays before both white and Negro audiences.[32] Concerts, which were first offered before the Civil War, were given at churches and rented public places such as Steinway Hall. In 1883 a Negro contralto performed at the African Methodist Episcopal Zion Church. The Shiloh Presbyterian Church presented frequent concerts such as one in 1886 offering works by Mozart, Rossini, and Wagner. Flora Batson, the "Jenny Lind of the Race," held recitals in Steinway Hall during the 1880s. Also appearing in New York City during this decade was the "Sweet Singing Robin," soprano Edna E. Brown. One of the most popular Negro vocalists was Sissieretta Jones, better known as the "Black Patti." During the eighties and nineties she performed at Madison Square Garden and in the Academy of Music. Despite suggestions that "Black

Patti" play the "dark roles" in *Aida* and *L'Africaine*, she had to settle for her own company — "Black Patti's" Troubadours — which followed the format of the minstrel show rather than that of the opera hall. In the 1900s, however, there rose to preeminence the all-Negro Drury Opera Company. In 1905 the *Age* praised the Company's performance of Carmen.[33] Among both the white and Negro masses, though, the classics never achieved the high level of popularity enjoyed by lighter forms of entertainment.

In the 1860s Negro entertainers made their first significant appearance on the New York stage in minstrel shows. Before that decade whites in black face had dominated minstrel presentations. Unfortunately, according to James Weldon Johnson, minstrelsy created a picture of the Negro as "an irresponsible, happy-go-lucky, wide-grinning, loud-laughing, shuffling . . . sort of being." Yet, argued Johnson, it had its good side, for it provided Negro entertainers with theatrical experience. In general, the shows were performed before white audiences. In the 1880s the Callendar Minstrels performed at the Madison Square Theatre and whites flocked to see Hicks and Sawyer's Refined Colored Minstrels. The rage for minstrel shows even extended to the city's Negro community. In 1887 a reporter for the *Freeman* wrote that he had "frequently encountered a band of genuine colored minstrels in my evening walks." [34]

In 1891 Negro entertainment made its first significant departure from the minstrel pattern when the *Creole Show* opened in Chicago. While it retained many of the basic minstrel features of the stage, it discarded the plantation ones that had come to dominate Negro shows and adopted instead the more modern techniques of burlesque. Within three years the *Creole Show* opened at the Standard Theatre on Greeley Square in New York City. Then, in 1898, the complete break from the minstrel past came with the presentation of *A Trip to Coontown*. Written by Bob Cole, a Negro composer as well as entertainer, it was the first musical comedy written, produced, directed, and performed by Negroes. After this show, Negro songwriters and composers "began to appear as if by magic." [35]

This break from the minstrel format was facilitated by the emergence of a Negro Bohemia in New York City. Beginning in the 1880s Negroes frequented clubs in the Tenderloin district. Whether centered in Joe Stewart's Criterion, Johnny Johnson's, or Ike Hines's, "early Negro theatrical talent created for itself a congenial atmosphere, an atmosphere of emulation and guildship . . . an atmosphere in which new artistic ideas were born and developed." Of these clubs, the best known and most popular was that of Ike Hines. Its walls were lined with pictures of Negro historical figures, sports personalities, and theatrical performers. Entertainers used part of the club for rehearsing their acts. About 1900 this black Bohemia shifted uptown to Fifty-third Street. On this street such leading Negro artists as the writer Paul Laurence Dunbar, the jazz musician Ford Dabney, and the vaudeville team of Williams and Walker congregated in the Marshall and Maceo hotels. George Walker and Bert Williams came to New York in 1896. Beginning as minstrels on the white stage, they were responsible for originating and making popular the cakewalk. Before Walker's untimely physical breakdown while performing *Bandana Land* in 1907 at the Majestic Theatre on Columbus Circle, this team was the most popular Negro one performing before white audiences. Following the loss of his partner, Bert Williams went out on his own to become in time a leading comedian on the white stage. In 1910 he began a ten-year tour with the Ziegfeld Follies.[36]

Williams' career illustrated the frustrations experienced by many Negro performers who achieved success on the white stage. His triumphant appearances before non-Negro audiences never gave him the opportunity to "interpret the real Negro." Since the Negro theater was virtually nonexistent before 1910, Negro entertainers, if they hoped to obtain employment, had to satisfy the tastes of white audiences — play the buffoon. Some solace, though, was afforded by the Marshall and Maceo hotels as well as the cabarets and nightclubs of black Bohemia. Here Williams and other Negro artists could perform unhampered by restrictions placed upon them by the white stage. Here they could express their dream of interpreting the real Negro.[37]

About 1910 a change was in the offing: Negroes discovered that the white stage had dropped a curtain barring Negro entertainers. At the same time, a Negro community was developing in Harlem that thirsted for entertainment. It provided a place devoid of the prejudices facing Negro entertainers as well as theatergoers in other sections of the city. Frequently, white actors had refused to work on the same stage as Negroes. Negroes had

even encountered similar insults when attempting to buy tickets
for all-Negro shows at white patronized theaters.[38] Accordingly,
the emergence of a sizable Negro community in Harlem as well
as the exclusion of Negro artists from the white stage was a
blessing in disguise. Theaters operated by Negroes, featuring
Negro entertainers, and playing before Negro audiences dotted
Harlem during the second decade of the twentieth century. Burst-
ing forth, then, was a Negro theater free of the buffoonery of the
past, free of white taboos against certain types of Negro show-
manship, free of the restrictions placed on potential Negro patrons
at downtown show places. Negro music, for example, at this time
was emerging from "a broken, musically illiterate dialect" into a
"national and international music." [39]

Before long theaters lined the streets of Harlem. As early as
1908 stage shows had been given at the Family Theatre on 125th
Street. In 1911 advertisements appeared in the Negro press an-
nouncing vaudeville shows at the Crescent Theatre. The leading
Negro playhouse in Harlem was the Lafayette Theatre. Here was
performed the *Darktown Follies,* written by a former member of
the Williams and Walker company — Leubrie Hill. Also presented
at the Lafayette were serious plays — in many cases, they were
Negro versions of shows appearing at downtown theaters. As
theater attendance became a favorite pastime of New York's Negroes, more and more theaters were opened. Most of these places
of entertainment lined Lenox Avenue between 125th and 145th
streets. The popularity of the Negro stage soon spread across the
East River to the Negro community of Brooklyn. Here also could
be found a multiplicity of Negro theaters.[40] Negro entertainers
also performed in the numerous nightclubs and cabarets that
catered to Negroes. Along with their other offerings, these clubs
as well as the theaters featured jazz bands. In 1905 one of the
most popular jazz organizations — the Memphis Students — performed at Proctor's Theatre. This form of music reached its pin-
nacle with the appearance of the Clef Club Orchestra at Carnegie Hall in 1912.[41]

As the popularity of public entertainment spread through
the Negro community, the Negro press devoted more space to
amusements than to the activities of churches and social organizations. The "Music and the Stage" column of Lester A. Walton,
who produced Negro shows, became a regular feature of the

Age.[42] This newspaper also reported that Negro artists were forming their own organizations. In the 1900s the Frogs, a Negro
vaudeville company, opened a clubhouse for Negro entertainers.
The United Colored Vaudeville Exchange and the New Amsterdam Musical Association furnished Negro acts. Employment services as well as relief benefits were provided for members of the
Colored Vaudeville Benevolent Association.[43]

The dominance of live entertainment did not go unchallenged. Many Negro theaters shifted to motion pictures. Generally, the films featured white actors (one notable exception was
the all-Negro Frederick Douglass Film Company), thereby working to the detriment of Negro entertainers. But because of the
great popularity of vaudeville, Harlem show places featured live
acts along with movies.[44] In addition, after World War I, Negro
performers discovered that because of a change in attitude of the
white stage they could once again perform at downtown theaters.
But the readmission of Negroes to the white stage was not without change — some of the old buffoonery was gone. During their
exile from the white world of entertainment, Negroes had the
opportunity to express their racial identity free of previous stereotypes.[45] Through the stage Negroes were able to develop a cultural ingredient that gave cohesion to Negro society. Once again,
being barred from the wider community worked toward the
creation of a separate society.

Sporting events, too, enjoyed great popularity in the Negro
community. Negroes accounted for many of the leading jockeys
and boxers of the nineteenth century, but they usually performed
before white audiences. Still the Negro press took great pride in
their exploits. Isaac Murphy, the leading jockey of the 1880s,
won 49 of his 51 races at Saratoga in 1882 and on three occasions
rode Kentucky Derby winners. But with the coming of the twentieth century, the Negro jockey was replaced by his white counterpart.[46] The most popular Negro spectator sports, naturally, were
those that could be performed before Negro audiences. Since
Negro ballplayers could not enter the major leagues of the white
world, they formed their own teams. The first Negro baseball
team in the city, Gorhams of New York, was formed in the 1880s.
This group was replaced by the very popular Cuban Giants. The
Giants brought to the sport a combination of serious baseball and
comical antics. On occasion, it played some of the leading white

clubs. Soon Negro teams from other parts of the nation came to play the New York clubs. In 1920 two leading Negro baseball nines — the Lincoln Giants and the Bacharachs — played at Ebbets Field before 16,000 spectators. Also rising in popularity was basketball. Spectator sports enjoyed such a high degree of approbation in the Negro community that the *Age* devoted a full page to the exploits of Negro athletes.[47]

The spread of secular entertainment disturbed elements of the Negro community, especially the clergy. As early as 1883, the Rev. James Peyton, of the Fleet Street African Methodist Episcopal Church, declared that dancing was "of heathen origin" and had "demoralizing effects" on the Negro. A. Clayton Powell contended in 1914 that "The Negro race is dancing itself to death." Such dances as the Tango, the Turkey Trot, and the Chicago are destroying "grace and modesty." The young people, he concluded, are "too frivolous because they feed on too much trash." Many clergymen condemned "the quantity of profanity and lager beer indulged in" at social gatherings. They complained that the sole purpose of social clubs and societies was pleasure rather than to promote good in the Negro community.[48] But most Negroes disregarded the advice of their preachers. Not only did dancing increase in popularity, but new dances were created. The message contained in the sermons of the clergy was lost in the rafters of the church. At least partially responsible for the failure of these appeals was the antiquated nature of the clergy's reactions. Preoccupation with puritanical values and failure to display interest in many of the race's social problems impaired the influence of the church. The New York Negro had become urbanized, but his church had not. R. R. Wright wrote in 1907 that where the small town offered little more social life than what the local church could supply, in the city the house of God had to compete with diverse forms of amusement for the Sabbath. The fraternal society and the social club, which were in their youth in the 1880s, contained the seeds of the urban alternative to the church. This independence permitted the societies to develop activities outside of the religious institution. When the preacher condemned their diversions, he drove the social life of the Negro farther from the church. It was said that rural Protestantism had no place in a Negro urban society, which was copying the habits of the white community that surrounded it.[49]

From the Negro press it is apparent that there was a very considerable cultural activity available to the Negro community between 1865 and 1920. Like other aspects of Negro society, the early cultural life of the New York Negro was centered in the church. He could attend concerts, lectures, discussions, reading rooms, and literary societies held under its auspices. As the years progressed, cultural activities extended beyond the confines of the church.

The early center of Negro cultural life was in Brooklyn rather than Manhattan. Almost every Negro church in Brooklyn had a literary society. According to the Brooklyn *Eagle* in 1892, there was no class of its city's citizens "fonder of literary pursuits than the Afro-American." The Brooklyn Literary Union of the Siloam Presbyterian Church offered concerts, lectures, and discussions. In 1887 Seth Low delivered a paper before the group on the subject of libraries. Like most Negro literary societies, the Literary Union had a lending library and a reading room. Cultural activities similar to those provided at the Siloam church were available at other Negro churches. Whether it was a lecture at the Concord Literary Circle, a concert at the Turner Lyceum, or a discussion of books at the Progressive Literary Union, Negroes welcomed the opportunity to attend the functions.[50]

Though most Negro literary societies of the nineteenth century were located in Brooklyn, a number were organized in Manhattan. One such association was connected with the Abyssinian Baptist Church where T. McCants Stewart delivered a lecture entitled "Heredity and Character." The Zion Literary Society of the African Methodist Episcopal Zion Church took great pride in its musical and literary jubilees. St. Mark's Methodist Episcopal Church opened a lyceum for Negro students. Cultural organizations also were established outside of the church. The meetings of the Lincoln Literary and Musical Association were conducted in the homes of its members. Similar sessions were held by the Ladies' Progressive Literary Circle; there stories and plays were read and musical selections were performed. In 1907 the Progressive Club was formed to discuss "economic and current questions." As an adjunct to the Negro Business League of New York, the Gregory W. Hayes's Literary Circle was organized.[51] These organizations became so widespread that the *Age* remarked in 1890 that "it would make your head swim to count them." In 1907 the paper noted with pride the beneficial effect that these cultural activities had on the family life of the Negro:

> Education and culture have found it's [sic] way into our home life, and have left their imprint. Subjects of a higher order, pertaining to education and literature, have become part of the family circle. Libraries, pianos, are a part of the household, and the general home life is becoming improved.[52]

Cultural activities also were expanding beyond the confines of organized societies. In the twentieth century a distinct Negro literature came into being. Before the present century most Negro literary efforts were either unknown to the general public or bore little relation to the realities of Negro life. The best known Negro novelist and poet of the late nineteenth century — mainly because of a review of his works by William Dean Howells — was Paul Laurence Dunbar. Born in Dayton, Ohio, in 1872, Dunbar came to New York City around 1900. Dunbar's "folk and dialect poetry is picturesque, often amusing," but it is part of the "apologist" tradition. Dunbar through his use of the plantation character fostered the stereotype of the fumbling, easygoing, and shiftless Negro. As Benjamin Brawley, a leading student of Negro literature has noted, "black was not fashionable" in Dunbar's writings.[53] But during the second decade of the 1900s, a change occurred in Negro writing. Here were the beginnings of the Negro literary Renaissance that was to burst into full bloom in the 1920s. Negro poetry and writing became more realistic; it sought themes in the realities of Negro life; it evinced a "race consciousness divested of the older apology or self-pity." Succinctly put by James Weldon Johnson, the new literature

> discarded traditional dialect and the stereotyped material. . . . Its members did not concern themselves with the sound of the old banjo and the singing round the cabin door; nor with the succession of the watermelon, possum, and sweet potato seasons. They broke away entirely from the limitations of pathos and humour. Also they broke away from use of the subject material that had already been over-used by white American poets of a former generation. What they did was to attempt to express what the masses of their race were then feeling and thinking and wanting to hear. . . . And so the distinguishing notes of their poetry were disillusionment, protest, and challenge — and sometimes despair.[54]

Coming to the forefront of this movement were poets such as Claude McKay who, while writing of the despair of his race, urged his fellow Negroes to strike back.

> O kinsmen! We must meet the common foe!
> Though far outnumbered, let us show us brave,
> And for their thousand blows deal one death-blow!
> What though before us lies the open grave?
> Like men we'll face the murderous, cowardly pack,
> Pressed to the wall, dying, but fighting back! [55]

Intellectual curiosity spread like wildfire through New York's Negro community. There emerged a burning interest to read the works of this new generation of writers so that one could transform himself into the "New Negro." Book clubs and stores selling books appeared throughout Negro New York. The Negro press featured lists of books by Negroes. Harlem became the literary and art center of the Negro world. The leading Negro bookstore in Harlem was Young's Book Exchange on West 135th Street. There could be found volumes of the *Journal of Negro History*, Du Bois' *Darkwater* and *Souls of Black Folk*, works on Africa, and *A Negro Explorer at the North Pole*. The desire to learn about Negro contributions to the history of mankind — especially the American past — reached monumental proportions. Societies to study the Negro heritage were created. In 1911, for example, the Negro Society for Historical Research was organized by leading New York Negroes in Yonkers, New York.[56]

Interest in their historical background gave Negroes a sense of identity. Their common heritage provided a medium through which they could express their race consciousness. As Alain Locke, a leading literary figure of the Negro Renaissance, stated in an address before the Negro Society for Historical Research in 1911, Negroes must destroy the stereotypes created by the antebellum period and the Reconstruction years; instead they should reconstruct their history along the lines of a racial loyalty that transcends national boundaries.[57] Elements of race loyalty could be seen in the "buy black" movement; in the plays, musicals, poems, and writings of the "New Negro"; in the satisfaction taken in the exploits of Negro athletes, stage performers, and leading figures of the past. Still further, race loyalty was present in the fetish for Negro dolls in the 1900s. Beginning about 1908 the Negro press carried advertisements for Negro dolls. One typical advertisement ran: "Why should a negro child play with a white doll?" Or as one Negro wrote in calling for the purchase of these toys: "Other races teach their children to admire and adore their own. Why should we not do likewise?" The Negro doll, the writer concluded, would "instill and cultivate race pride." [58]

The Negro's interest in his African inheritance was another example of this race consciousness. In the 1900s books relating to the history and culture of Africa were among the best sellers in Negro New York.[59] Looking to the African past, whether it took the form of reading works pertaining to African history or of advocating a return to Africa, was based on the Negro's second-class position in American society and his consequent desire and need to identify with a particular group. The Back-to-Africa movement reached its high point under the direction of Marcus Garvey.

Garvey was born in Jamaica in 1887. After traveling in Latin America and England, he came to New York in 1916. There he established a branch of his Universal Negro Improvement Association formed two years earlier in Jamaica. At first, he was greeted coldly as another street corner orator. Before long, however, he began to catch the public eye. He brought his opinions before the public both from the rostrum and through the pages of his weekly newspaper, the *Negro World*. Soon he organized the Black Star Steamship Company and purchased a few ships to send skilled technicians, goods, and a few American Negroes to Africa. In 1920, at the International Convention of the Negro People of the World held in New York, Garvey was elected provisional president of Africa. At its peak, the Garvey movement had somewhere between one and six million adherents with some 30,000 in New York City. Even though Garvey's economic enterprises were unsuccessful, he came into conflict with the United States government. After a prolonged trial, he was convicted of mail fraud. Garvey served two years of his sentence before he was released and deported to his native Jamaica as an undesirable alien. From Jamaica he went to London where he stayed until his death in 1940.

Garvey urged Negroes to seek their place in the sun. He told his followers "to assist in civilizing the backward tribes of Africa." In Africa would be located the parent black nation to which the Negro people of the world would look for direction.

Through the efforts of the Negro world community, Africa would be redeemed from colonialism. In time, all Negroes would relocate on the African continent. In the meantime, Garvey believed that Negroes should do their utmost to preserve racial purity.[60]

Well before the emergence of the Garvey movement, American Negroes had exhibited an interest in Africa. Negro societies and the Negro press held frequent discussions on the subject of colonization in Africa.[61] Yet most Negroes opposed colonization. Africa appealed to Negroes not as a future home but as a link with their lost past. In 1892 T. Thomas Fortune wrote that American Negroes were not Africans — they knew practically nothing about Africa except for "a sentimental interest in it and its people." As editor of the *Freeman,* he referred to Africa as "our Fatherland" but opposed Negro emigration to that continent. The Literary Union held a Liberian Coffee Party in 1887, pronouncing the coffee "delicious," but said nothing of moving to Liberia. Frequently, articles were carried in the Negro press describing life in African countries and reporting on the visits of leading Negroes to those nations. Interest in the countries of Africa became especially strong following World War I. The NAACP supported what it believed were attempts by President Woodrow Wilson to secure independence for African colonies from European domination. It contended that the League of Nations was "absolutely necessary to the salvation of the Negro race." W. E. B. Du Bois' plan for a Pan-African movement earned the support of many outstanding Negroes.[62]

But this interest in Africa was concerned more with the plight of fellow blacks and less with a desire to form a world union of Negroes. Where this sentiment reached nationalistic proportions, it exhibited the "cultural alienation and social estrangement" of American Negroes from white society and "the confusion, apathy, frustration, and disillusionment which" arose "in their attempt to adjust to these conditions." It was a defense against the discrimination that Negroes faced at the hands of white society.[63] This position was present in the thinking of Marcus Garvey:

> If you cannot live alongside the white man in peace, if you cannot get the same chance and opportunity alongside the white man even tho you are his fellow citizen . . . then find a country

of your own and rise to the highest position within that country.[64]

When Negro writers expressed nationalistic pride in the accomplishments of their race, they reflected a racial consciousness as well as a desire to show the white world that the Negro could be the white man's equal. Arthur A. Schomburg, the founder of the Negro library that bears his name today, declared in 1898 that the study of the Negro past would "form an effective breakwater against the ever-increasing and cumulative tide of prejudice and discrimination." [65] New York Negroes, as will be seen in the next chapter, were more desirous of becoming part of the American dream than part of the African past.

Still another medium through which New York Negroes expressed their racial identity was the Negro press. Since the white press generally ignored the activities of the Negro community, the pages of the Negro newspaper served as a format for the display of Negro accomplishments and for the expression of a Negro point of view. In 1827 the first Negro newspaper in the city — *Freedom's Journal* — was published; before the Civil War approximately ten more Negro papers were started. The period from 1865 to 1920 saw the publication of at least 35 newspapers edited by Negroes. Many of these were short-lived, and, moreover, few of these weekly papers have been preserved.[66] It was not until the arrival in New York City of a young Florida-born Negro, T. Thomas Fortune, that a paper of any appreciable influence and notable duration served the New York Negro community.

Fortune was born in 1856 in Marianna, Florida. After the Civil War, young Fortune's father served as a member of the Florida legislature where he secured a position for his son as a page. At the age of eighteen, Fortune was employed as the mail route agent between Jacksonville and Chattahoochee. In 1876 he entered Howard University. After two years at Howard, Fortune returned to Florida to work as a journalist and teacher. In 1879 he decided that his future was in the North. Thus, at the age of twenty-three, young Fortune left Florida for the larger vistas that awaited him in New York City. Once in New York, Fortune entered the newspaper business. His first paper, the *Rumor,* was a failure; however, his second newspaper venture, the *New York Globe,* was more successful. The *Globe,* which began publication in 1882, became the *Freeman* in 1884, and it in turn was converted to the *Age* in 1887.

During Fortune's editorship of the *Age*, the paper came under the influence of Booker T. Washington. Despite Washington's economic contributions to the *Age*, Fortune retained a degree of independence and remained the paper's editor until 1907 when he resigned because of poor health. After Fortune's resignation, Booker T. Washington gained complete control of the newspaper.[67]

The *Age* and other New York Negro newspapers followed similar formats. In general, they were four pages in length. Page one was devoted to national news and important local matters. Editorials, letters to the editor, local news, and articles from other newspapers were placed on pages two and four. The third page contained descriptions of social activities and excerpts from religious sermons. In the 1900s religious news received less coverage, and more space was devoted to local news and entertainment. Interspersed through the pages were columns of advice, such as one for women.

The Negro newspaper, therefore, served as a forum for the expression of a Negro point of view, as a cohesive force for Negro society, as a medium through which Negro protests could be expressed. Although the actual number of newspapers sold was small, their influence extended beyond the immediate buyer.[68] They were passed from person to person; and were consulted at reading rooms of literary societies and fraternal organizations, as well as such meeting places as churches, barber shops, and social clubs. During the 1900s the militancy of the Negro press increased. As the Negro community expanded and as it manifested greater interest in its problems, the number of papers in circulation increased — by 1920, Harlem alone had five.[69]

By 1920, then, there had emerged in New York City a Negro society centered in Harlem. Shut off from white society, it had developed its own churches, fraternal and social organizations, a common culture, and a sense of racial self-consciousness. W. E. B. Du Bois' description of Negro society in 1901 held true for 1920: "Here . . . is a world of itself, closed in from the outer world and almost unknown to it . . . with its own social distinctions, amusements, and ambitions." And, in 1920 another Negro remarked that "no community in New York has become so complete a city as Harlem." What Harlem was to be to the Negro world in the future — its pulse — had already been established by 1920.[70]

Notes

[1] Here I have followed the position advanced by E. Franklin Frazier, *The Negro in the United States* (rev. ed., New York, 1957), chapter I. For an opposing point of view, see Melville J. Herskovits, *The Myth of the Negro Past* (New York, 1941).

[2] Richard Bardolph, *The Negro Vanguard* (Vintage ed., New York, 1961), p. 12; Myrdal, *American Dilemma*, pp. 645–47, 982; article by W. E. B. Du Bois in the *New York Times*, November 24, 1901.

[3] For a discussion of the role of the Negro church, see Carter G. Woodson, *The History of the Negro Church* (2d. ed., Washington, 1921), especially pp. 220–21; W. E. B. Du Bois, *The Souls of Black Folk* (12th ed., Chicago, 1935), p. 190; Benjamin C. Mays and Joseph Nicholson, *The Negro Church* (New York, 1933), *passim*.

[4] *Weekly Anglo African*, August 12, 1865; *New York Times*, March 2, 1869; Ovington, *Half A Man*, p. 118; Greater New York Federation of Churches, *Negro Churches in Manhattan* (New York, 1930), pp. 17–21.

[5] *New York Age*, May 29, 1913; Woodson, *Negro Church*, pp. 78–80; Payne, "The Negro in New York Prior to 1860," p. 60; *New York Tribune*, March 6, 1895.

[6] *New York Age*, February 21, 1891, and April 17, 1913; Abyssinian Baptist Church, *The Ninety-Fourth Anniversary* (New York, 1902), p. 2.

[7] *New York Age*, December 9, 1909, and December 20, 1919; *New York Times*, November 24, 1901; National League on Urban Condi-

tions, "Housing Conditions Among Negroes in Harlem," pp. 12–13; Dyckoff, "A Negro City in New York," pp. 951–52; George F. Bragg, *History of the Afro-American Group of the Episcopal Church* (Baltimore, 1922), pp. 81, 86–87.

[8] John Kirkwood, *An Autumn Holiday in the United States and Canada* (Edinburgh, 1887), p. 30. A few Negroes still remained in white churches; however, they were usually segregated. *New York Age*, February 5, 1912, and April 24, 1913.

[9] *Weekly Anglo African*, August 12, 1865; *New York Times*, November 24, 1901; *Milestones*, II (May, 1910), 8; Federation of Churches, *Negro Churches in Manhattan*, pp. 19–21.

[10] *Colored American Magazine*, X (June, 1906), 381; *New York Globe*, December 1, 1883; *New York Age*, March 6, 1913; Mount Olivet Baptist Church, *Mortgage Liquidation Journal* (New York, 1946), p. 7.

[11] New York City Mission and Tract Society, *Annual Report for 1888* (New York, 1889), pp. 115–20; *Annual Report for 1890* (New York, 1891), pp. 128–42; *Annual Report for 1896* (New York, 1897), pp. 93–105; Federation of Churches and Christian Organizations in New York City, *The Redemption of Our City* (New York, 1902), unpaged; Federation of Churches and Christian Workers in New York City, *Sociological Canvass No. 1* (New York, 1896), p. 43, and *Canvass No. 2*, pp. 59, 66–67.

[12] *New York Age*, February 23,

1889; *New York Tribune,* January 25, May 20, 1894, and March 6, April 10, June 3, 1895.

[13] *New York Age,* May 8, 1913, and May 21, 1914; *New York Tribune,* January 25, May 20, 1894, and March 6, April 10, June 3, 1895.

[14] *New York Age,* February 2, 1889; March 15, 22, 1890; February 14, 1891; January 5, March 25, 1909; April 17, May 8, 1913; *New York Tribune,* March 19, 1894, and June 12, 1899; Maude K. Griffin, "The Negro Church and Its Social Work — St. Mark's," *Charities,* XV (October 7, 1905), 75–76.

[15] Compare church statistics in Du Bois' article in *New York Times,* November 24, 1901 with those in Federation of Churches, *Negro Churches in Manhattan,* pp. 17–21.

[16] Woodson, *Negro Church,* pp. 80–81; *New York Age,* September 6, 1890, and February 21, 1891; *New York Tribune,* January 25, 1894.

[17] Mays, *Negro Church,* p. 224; Kennedy, *Negro Peasant Turns Cityward,* p. 208.

[18] *New York Age,* June 24, 1909; July 4, 1912; February 13, 1913; February 19, April 30, 1914; October 14, 1915; February 14, 1920.

[19] *Ibid.,* September 3, 1908; June 24, 1909; November 21, 1912; April 24, 1920; *Crisis,* IV (May, 1912), 25.

[20] Woodson, *Negro Church,* p. 274. Also see the *New York Age,* May 24, 1919.

[21] Blascoer, *Colored School Children,* pp. 56–59; *Milestones,* II (May, 1910), 7; St. Philip's Parish House, *Annual Report for 1887–1888* (New York, 1888).

[22] *New York Age,* February 22, 1890; July 14, 1910; December 26, 1912; April 17, May 8, 29, 1913; Dyckoff, "A Negro City in New York," pp. 951–52; National League on Urban Conditions, "Housing Conditions Among Negroes," pp. 12–13;

Siloam Presbyterian Church, Semi-Centennial, May 2 to July 25, 1899 (Brooklyn, 1899), pp. 47–48.

[23] Compare Reverdy C. Ransom, *The Pilgrimage of Harriet Ransom's Son* (Nashville, 1949), p. 206 with the *New York Times,* November 24, 1901.

[24] Myrdal, *American Dilemma,* pp. 952–53; E. Nelson Palmer, "A Note on the Development of Negro Lodges in the United States," unpublished manuscript, prepared for Carnegie-Myrdal study of the Negro in America, Schomburg Collection, New York, 1940, pp. 11–12; Frazier, *Black Bourgeoisie,* p. 204.

[25] *New York Times,* March 13, 1873; *New York Age,* July 21, November 24, 1888; January 12, 1905; February 23, 1908.

[26] *New York Times,* March 2, 1869; March 13, 1871; April 2, 1872; *New York Age,* April 12, 1890.

[27] *New York Age,* August 6, 1908, and August 14, 1913; *Crisis,* XI (February, 1916), 166; Ovington, *Half A Man,* p. 175.

[28] George E. Wibecau, "New York Negro Clubs," *Souvenir Program of the National Negro Exposition* (New York, 1915), unpaged; Society of the Sons of New York, *Second Annual Report, 1886* (New York, 1887), *passim; New York Tribune,* January 27, 1889, and March 20, 1892; *New York Age,* March 23, 1889; January 12, July 27, 1905; November 21, 1907; Martin, "The Harlem Negro," p. 6.

[29] Wibecau, "Negro Clubs," unpaged; *New York Times,* March 13, 1871; *New York Freeman,* June 5, 1886; Brooklyn *Eagle,* September 16, 1892.

[30] *New York Globe,* May 5, 19, 1883, and February 9, 1884; *New York Freeman,* February 12, March 2, April 2, May 14, 21, 1887; *New York Age,* February 22, March 22, 1890; February 9, 1905; April 20,

27, 1911; March 15, 1917; *Colored American Review*, I (October 1, 1915), 8.

[31] *New York Age*, August 3, 1889; January 19, 1905; January 7, 1915; *New York Times*, September 23, 1898, and October 23, 1913.

[32] Johnson, *Black Manhattan*, pp. 78–86.

[33] *Ibid.*, pp. 98–101; *New York Globe*, April 14, 1883, and March 8, 1884; *New York Freeman*, July 10, September 25, December 18, 1886; *New York Age*, March 31, 1888; March 25, 1889; April 18, 1891; May 18, 1905; March 2, 1911; *Colored American Magazine*, I (August, 1900), 190.

[34] Johnson, *Black Manhattan*, pp. 87–94; *New York Globe*, May 12, 1883; *New York Freeman*, May 21, July 23, 1887.

[35] Johnson, *Black Manhattan*, pp. 96–98, 102; Margaret Just Butcher, *The Negro in American Culture* (New York, 1956), pp. 64–65.

[36] Johnson, *Black Manhattan*, pp. 74–78, 104–108, 118–120; Ovington, *Half A Man*, pp. 129–33; Johnson, *Along This Way*, pp. 175–76; Dyckoff, "A Negro City in New York," p. 954.

[37] Bardolph, *Negro Vanguard*, pp. 236–37; Butcher, *Negro in American Culture*, pp. 190–93; Johnson, *Black Manhattan*, pp. 118–19.

[38] Johnson, *Black Manhattan*, pp. 170–71; *New York Age*, January 17, 1891; July 11, 1912; February 6, 1913; *New York Tribune*, February 23, August 13, 1903.

[39] Butcher, *Negro in American Culture*, p. 68.

[40] *New York Times*, June 8, 16, 1914; *New York Age*, September 10, 1908; February 23, March 9, 1911; January 2, 9, October 30, 1913; June 15, 1916; May 3, 1919; May 1, 1920; Hartt, "I'd Like to Show

You Harlem," p. 357; Johnson, *Black Manhattan*, pp. 170–75.

[41] *New York Age*, November 28, 1912; September 12, 1913; June 1, 1916; May 31, 1919; Butcher, *Negro in American Culture*, p. 67; Hartt, "I'd Like to Show You Harlem," p. 334; Johnson, *Black Manhattan*, pp. 120–24, 179–80.

[42] See, for example, *New York Age*, February 20, 1908, and January 26, 1911.

[43] *Ibid.*, August 4, 18, 1910; March 2, May 18, November 16, 1911; September 12, December 19, 1912.

[44] *Ibid.*, February 23, 1911; May 22, 1913; October 1, 1914; October 19, 1916; March 6, 1920; *Crusader*, IV (February, 1921), 22, 24.

[45] *New York Age*, March 22, 1919; Butcher, *Negro in American Culture*, pp. 190–93; Johnson, *Black Manhattan*, pp. 175–79.

[46] *New York Globe*, August 18, 1883; *New York Age*, August 24, 1889 and February 28, 1891; Johnson, *Black Manhattan*, pp. 60–62.

[47] Johnson, *Black Manhattan*, pp. 63–65; *New York Age*, April 20, 1889; March 15, 1890; January 5, May 11, September 21, 1911; March 15, 1917; May 1, July 17, 1920.

[48] *New York Globe*, August 25, September 29, 1883; *New York Age*, June 3, 1909; August 7, 1913; January 8, 1914.

[49] R. R. Wright, Jr., "Social Work and the Influence of the Negro Church," *Annals of the American Academy of Political and Social Science*, XXX (November, 1907), 87; *New York Times*, November 24, 1901.

[50] *New York Times*, March 2, 1869, and March 13, 1871; *New York Freeman*, June 5, 1886; January 22, May 14, 1887; *New York Age*, March 8, 1890; Brooklyn *Eagle*, December 18, 1892, and January 10, 1896.

[51] *New York Age,* November 19, 1887; June 2, 1888; January 5, December 21, 1889; March 1, 8, July 5, 26, 1890; August 7, 1903; February 16, March 30, 1905; February 28, December 5, 1907; February 20, 1908; *Colored American Magazine,* I (September, 1900), 259.

[52] *New York Age,* December 20, 1890, and November 28, 1907.

[53] Butcher, *Negro in American Culture,* pp. 121, 162–63; Alain Locke, "The Negro's Contribution to American Art and Literature," *Annals of the American Academy of Political and Social Science,* CXL (November, 1928), 239–40; Brawley quote in Bardolph, *Negro Vanguard,* p. 26.

[54] Johnson, *Black Manhattan,* p. 263; also see Butcher, *Negro in American Culture,* pp. 125–26.

[55] *Selected Poems of Claude McKay* (New York, 1953), p. 23.

[56] *New York Age,* April 22, 1915, and September 7, 1918; *Crisis,* I (November, 1910), 6, and XIII (January, 1917), 150; Hartt, "I'd Like to Show You Harlem," 335; Martin, "Harlem Negro," p. 8; "Negro Society for Historical Research," Writers' Program (WPA) research paper, Schomburg Collection.

[57] *New York Age,* December 14, 1911.

[58] *New York Age,* October 8, 1908, and November 6, 1911; *Crusader,* V (November, 1921), 2; *Crisis,* II (August, 1911), inside back cover; New York *Dispatch,* January 7, 1921; Hartt, "I'd Like to Show You Harlem," p. 357.

[59] Hartt, "I'd Like to Show You Harlem," p. 335.

[60] Material on Garvey based on Edmund D. Cronon, *Black Moses: The Story of Marcus Garvey and the Universal Negro Improvement Association* (Madison, 1957).

[61] *New York Globe,* January 13, February 17, 1883; *New York Times,* February 24, 26, 1892; *New York Tribune,* April 11, December 15, 1879.

[62] T. Thomas Fortune, "Will the Afro-American Return to Africa?" *A.M.E. Church Review,* VIII (April, 1892), 389; *New York Globe,* July 28, August 4, 11, 1883; *New York Freeman,* January 15, 22, 1887; *New York Age,* February 8, 1912, and February 1, 8, 1919; *Crisis,* XVII (February, 1919), 173–76, and (May, 1919), 11.

[63] E. U. Essien-Udom, *Black Nationalism: A Search for an Identity in America* (Chicago, 1962), p. 54. Also see C. Eric Lincoln, *The Black Muslims in America* (New York, 1961), pp. 45–46.

[64] Rollin Lynde Hartt, "The Negro Moses and His Campaign to Lead the Black Millions into Their Promised Land," *Independent,* CV (February 26, 1921), 206.

[65] Quoted in August Meier, *Negro Thought in America, 1880–1915: Racial Ideologies in the Age of Booker T. Washington* (Ann Arbor, 1963), p. 262.

[66] Payne, "Negro in New York Prior to 1860," p. 60; Armistead Pride, "Register and History of Negro Newspapers in the United States, 1827–1950," unpublished Ph.D. dissertation, Northwestern University, 1951.

[67] Seth M. Scheiner, "Early Career of T. Thomas Fortune, 1879–1890," *Negro History Bulletin,* XXVII (April, 1964), 170–72.

[68] Between 1887 and 1910 the *Age* – one of the few newspapers for which complete circulation figures have been found – increased its circulation by only 1,500. N. W. Ayer and Sons, *American Newspaper Annual and Directory, 1887* (Philadelphia, 1887), p. 84 and *1910* (Philadelphia, 1910), p. 599.

[69] Frederick G. Detweiler, *The Negro Press in the United States* (Chicago, 1922), pp. 6, 61; Robert

T. Kerlin, *The Voice of the Negro, 1919* (New York, 1920), p. ix; Eugene Gordon, "The Negro Press," *Annals of the American Academy of Political and Social Science,* CLX (November, 1928), 253, 256; Hartt, "I'd Like to Show You Harlem," p. 335.

[70] *The New York Times,* November 24, 1901; Fenton Johnson, "Harlem By Day and Night," *Favorite Magazine,* IV (July, 1920), 363.

.5.

The Negro and the Wider Community

CONFLICT

ALTHOUGH MOST of the Negro's life was centered within the walls of his separate society, he did on occasion come into contact with the wider community. A large part of this confrontation resulted in conflict with the mores of white society. One manifestation of this conflict was the increase in Negro crime following the Civil War. Given the nature of the Negro's social and economic position in the city, wrote the New York *Post* in 1900, it was not surprising that lawlessness was a serious problem in the Negro community. To some degree this increase in crime was reflected in the police statistics of the day.[1] The figures, however, are open to serious question. First, they failed to indicate either the number of times a person was arrested or the nature of the crime. Second, many commentators claimed that the police more readily arrested Negroes because of an anti-Negro bias.[2] As Gunnar Myrdal has noted for a later period in the history of the Negro: "Negroes are more likely than whites to be arrested under any suspicious circumstances." Third, the number of criminal acts and their nature are not always reflected through arrest figures. Again, according to Myrdal, "those who come in contact with the law are generally only a selected sample of those who commit crimes." For example,

113

those violations of the law that frequently do not lead to arrest, such as white collar crime, are rarely committed by Negroes — "they commit the crimes which much more frequently result in apprehension and punishment." This, concludes Myrdal, "is a chief source of error when attempting to compare statistics on Negro and white crimes." Finally, criminal statistics of themselves provide no explanation for a high incidence of crime in the Negro community. It must be remembered that arrests occur more frequently among lower-class groups than in any other strata of society; and the size of the lower class is proportionately greater among Negroes than white groups. As another student of Negro life has concluded: "The data hitherto compiled . . . permit only one conclusion, namely, that the Negro appears to be arrested, convicted and committed to penal institutions more frequently than the white." Any other "assumption is untenable, for there are specific factors which seriously distort the arrest, convictions and commitment rates for Negroes without affecting these rates for whites in a similar manner." [3]

Despite the unreliability of criminal statistics, lawlessness among the city's Negro population caused consternation in the Negro as well as the white community. "The police courts of the city are furnishing food for serious comment," wrote the *New York Globe* in 1884, "in the large number of cases brought before them in which colored persons figure as delinquents and violators of the law." Writing in *Harper's* in 1900, a white reporter echoed the comments of the Negro newspaper when he observed that the Negro criminal element was becoming "alarmingly large." [4] A few months before this article appeared in *Harper's,* the New York *Post* contended that the city was "full of vicious and dangerous Negroes." And, in 1912, the Charity Organization bemoaned the "increase of shiftlessness and disorder among" New York's Negroes. Mary Ovington observed in 1919 that every street populated by Negroes had its disorderly element.[5]

Before and shortly after the turn of the twentieth century, Negro lawlessness centered in the Tenderloin area of the city. The Tenderloin, according to Jacob Riis, was a "black-and-tan" district inundated with Negro and white delinquents. Reformers condemned repeatedly the vice and corruption that permeated the district.[6] "Midnight fights, drunken orgies, and foul blasphemies," wrote the *Freeman,* dominated the night life of this neighborhood.

Disreputable Negroes frequented the Tenderloin's houses of prostitution, saloons, and gambling rooms.[7] They gambled in the "migrating" poolroom, the policy shop, and the faro bank. Occasionally an enterprising Negro opened an establishment that offered illicit sexual experience, gambling, and drinking under one roof. These "wide-open" places usually were run by Negroes who had won fame in boxing, horse racing, and other sports. Pickpockets plying their trade and drunken rowdies engaging in brawls even marred church picnics and excursions.[8]

As more and more young girls migrated from the South to New York City, prostitution increased as a problem in Negro neighborhoods. Unscrupulous employment agencies lured many girls north with promises of jobs that existed only in the so-called sporting houses. Unable to find jobs, and too often without parental guidance, many young girls resorted to prostitution for a livelihood. As early as 1879 George Sala, a foreign newsman on a visit to New York City, observed that there was a "very large proportion of female to male prisoners of African descent." In 1911 the *Age* reported that Harlem was becoming "infested" with the "dance-hall harlot and the diamond decked lover." At nights, the paper asserted, procurers and streetwalkers transacted their business on Harlem's streets. The Sons of North Carolina, in the same year, objected to the "immorality existing among girls" in certain sections of Brooklyn.[9]

Nor were law violators bothered to any great degree by the police. For some form of remuneration, many a law enforcement officer would disregard the illegal activities of the lawless. Negroes and whites censured the police for allowing crime to flourish. The *Herald* claimed in 1900 that the police permitted "depraved and vicious" Negroes to infest the Tenderloin. Crime was the result of the leniency "accorded all evil-doers, whatever their color" who had money to bribe law enforcement officials, asserted the *Post* in 1900. A Negro clergyman told the newspaper that crime was the "only field in which the color line" was not drawn.[10]

Nowhere in the city did Negro lawbreakers cause greater concern than among law-abiding Negroes — who were in the majority. Since most of the Negro transgressor's illegal operations occurred in the ghetto, the reputable Negro was the major victim of this lawlessness. His apartment was burgled; his person was robbed or assaulted; his children were exposed to the illegal activities of the Negro criminal. The actions of the licentious Negro, the law-abiding Negro believed, gave whites an unfavorable impression of the race. The "flashy" and "impudent" element, declared a Negro clergyman in 1883, did "more solid injury" to the race "than any other agency of evil." Negro leaders denounced the "swaggering, bumptious" Negro for bringing discredit to the race. In 1912 Mary Martel, a Negro columnist, counseled respectable Negroes to work toward the elimination of loitering, excessive noise, and crime in Negro neighborhoods. It was to their interest, she maintained, to eradicate the pernicious picture of their community created by the venal Negro.[11]

Many Negro leaders attributed the increase in Negro crime and antisocial behavior to the southern newcomer. In 1889 a meeting of Negroes at Cooper Union responded with "great applause" to a southern Negro clergyman's speech criticizing those undesirable Negroes who migrated north.

> You don't ever see the representative negro in New York. We get the nigger up here with a cigar in his mouth, with a gold-headed cane and a high silk hat, and it's doubtful if he's got enough money in his pocket to pay his room rent.[12]

In 1900 T. Thomas Fortune, editor of the *Age*, too, considered many southern residents of New York City a threat to law and order. This charge was seconded by Owen M. Walker, a southern Negro visiting the city in 1914, when he declared that the North was attracting the "weakest type" of southern Negro.[13] Both Booker T. Washington and W. E. B. Du Bois — who differed as to the best method for Negro advancement — agreed in 1901 that the lower type of Negro was coming to New York City. Du Bois, though, found that both the "competent and incompetent, the industrious and the lazy, the law-abiding and the criminal" came to New York City. The *Age* in 1907 saw only the "loud of mouth, flashy of clothes, obtrusive and uppish southern Negro" streaming into the city. The paper was even more outspoken in its criticism of the southern migrant in 1912. Many of the Negroes who came to New York from the South were "undesirable persons" as well as "criminally inclined" before they left the South, wrote the *Age*. By their disorderly behavior, the "few undesirables" brought down upon the entire Negro community the animosity and scorn of the city's whites.[14]

Convinced that the southern newcomer augmented the race's

criminal class, many New York Negroes attempted to discourage their southern kinsmen from journeying north. The *Age* in 1891 counseled southern Negroes to "shun" New York City unless they had "plenty of money or a position secured before coming here." Only "menial employment," and little of that, is offered the New York Negro, the paper cautioned. In the 1900s it warned the southerner of the "evil ways" of Gotham and advised him to "think carefully" before relocating in New York. It insisted that the South was the "natural home" of the Negro rather than the "slums of the great Northern cities." The "steady stream of new people from the Southern States," warned the Negro newspaper, had aggravated an already difficult situation.[15] Samuel Scottron, a successful Negro entrepreneur and a one-time member of the Brooklyn Board of Education, was dismayed by the complications caused by increased Negro migration to New York in the 1900s. He complained that newcomers were settling in New York "faster than they can be assimilated and adjusted to the surrounding conditions." [16] As Mary Ovington wrote in reviewing her work among the Negro population, the more established Negroes of the city viewed the influx of southern Negroes as a menace to their position. Some New York-born Negroes manifested their hostility toward southern newcomers by forming societies that restricted membership to Negroes born in the Empire State. For example, in 1884, a group of New York-born Negroes organized the Sons of New York. It appears that the members of the Society believed that their New York birth set them apart from Negroes born in the South, and, no doubt, they considered themselves superior to southern Negroes.[17]

Not only was the prospective migrant counseled to avoid coming to New York, but he was urged to remain on the farm. Whether out of self-interest or conviction, or both, the proponents of this position accepted Booker T. Washington's preference for the farm over the factory, for the country over the city, for the South over the North. Washington, on one occasion, urged the National League on Urban Conditions to assist those who had moved north to return to their southern homes.[18] In conformity with this position, the *Age* in the early 1900s claimed that the South was "the natural home of the Negro." It asserted that many of those who loitered on New York's streets had "left good homes and Christian surroundings in the South or the West before they came here and fell into evil ways." Another advocate of the rural ideal, the *Colored American Review*, insisted in 1915 that "the colored race thrives better in suburban and rural communities. The city, with its injustices, its temptations, . . . its unhealthy, poorly ventilated buildings, often prove too powerful a foe for the race to combat." Country life, the journal argued, contributed to better health and greater financial gain.[19] Hence, this group, through Booker T. Washington, accepted the Jeffersonian belief that God dwelled on the farm and the devil inhabited the city. These pro-rural urbanites looked, at least in part, to the simplicity of the rural past. With the evils of the city so clear in their minds, they considered the city a threat to morality and American ideals. Not unlike many white Americans at the turn of the twentieth century, these Negroes reproached the city for being the center of those foreign ways that threatened to corrupt American democracy.[20]

But not all Negroes adhered to the deification of rural life. When Negro migration reached a flood crest during World War I, even the *Age* advised Negroes to leave the South. It also implored Negro residents of the large northern cities to assist the newcomer. Still, the *Age* and other groups called for an orderly migration rather than an indiscriminate rush northward. The NAACP in 1920 encouraged its fellow Negroes to come north not "as aimless wanderers but after quiet investigation and careful location." The National Urban League called a National Conference on Migration in 1917 to ascertain methods by which southern Negroes could be assisted in their adjustment to their new homes. Shortly before the conference was held, another Negro newspaper, the New York *News*, asserted that it was the "moral and civic" duty of northern Negroes to help the southern migrant.[21]

Although many New York Negroes were quick to blame the southern newcomer for the rising Negro crime rate, they realized that other factors were responsible for the rise in antisocial acts. Compelled to live within a ghetto, the law-abiding Negro was given little choice in the selection of his neighbors. Where a white of sufficient means could flee to an area that contained a minimum of crime, the Negro, regardless of his financial or educational standing, was usually condemned to raise his children in neighborhoods filled with inferior housing and populated by disorderly persons. The Negro ghetto, therefore, brought together both the respectable and disreputable. Because of this situation, wrote the *Age* in 1908, it was next to impossible to "separate the hoodlum element from the respectable class of colored people." Furthermore, limited employment opportunities and low wages caused some Negroes to seek financial sustenance through illegal pursuits, for jobs that were opened to whites — even those who could not utter a word of English — were closed to Negroes. No doubt many southern newcomers came to the city unprepared for the rigors of urban life, but because of prejudice they encountered difficulty in finding employment.[22] The unstable nature of many Negro families, too, contributed to an increase in illegal activities among youths. A considerable number of Negro juveniles were raised in homes without the influence of a father. Parental controls were further reduced by the necessity of many mothers — married, widowed, or unmarried — to work. Still another factor was the long workday and workweek under which Negro parents labored in order to support their families.[23] In addition, according to Gunnar Myrdal in his study of the American Negro, "a poverty-stricken household, especially where there are not strong family traditions, weakens still further the family controls over the children"; and, "the proportion of lower class Negroes is so much greater" than in the white community. Consequently, the Negro youth resorted to the streets for companionship and recreation. The necessity to take in boarders to defray the rental expenses posted another potential threat to the family's stability and morality.[24] All of these problems were augmented by the fact that a majority of the Negro newcomers were in the young adult age bracket which accounted for a large proportion of the criminal class in white as well as Negro groups.[25]

Negro leaders also blamed the excessive consumption of alcoholic beverages for the high incidence of crime. In the nineteenth century reformers invariably associated excessive consumption of alcoholic beverages with poverty and crime. As one Negro educator remarked in 1905: "The whiskey shop attracts the dead game sport, the gambler . . . the licentious. It is a vice center and a swamp of moral lepers . . . the enemy to decency and morality." In the 1880s the *Globe* bemoaned the "frightful amount of lager beer, whiskey, and other intoxicants consumed by males and females, children and adults." The Negro paper urged its readers to "Stick to lemonade and ice cream." In 1886 the *Free-*

man, under the editorship of T. Thomas Fortune, called for the prohibition of the manufacture and sale of intoxicating beverages.[26] Because of Fortune's stand on prohibition and his hostility toward the Republican party, he was forced to resign the editorship in 1887. Under the editorial leadership of Fortune's brother, Emanuel, and Jerome Peterson the paper — now named the *Age* — rejected prohibition for a milder form of temperance.[27] From time to time in future years it was to denounce the "drink habit" as the "curse of the people of the country" and to allege that Negro crime was "stimulated and sustained by the curse of drink." [28]

This concern with the relation between crime and intemperance encouraged the creation of a number of temperance societies. In 1883 a "gospel temperance" meeting was held at the Siloam Presbyterian Church. Two years later, the Colored Mission reported that it gave "faithful instruction on the Temperance Question." At the same time, it formed a chapter of the Temperance League. The Prohibition Lecture Bureau conducted a campaign among Negroes in the 1880s. In 1890 the Colored Home organized a temperance club and the Shiloh Presbyterian Church held a meeting of the Women's Christian Temperance Union. One year later, a chapter of the W.C.T.U. was established at the Colored Mission.[29] During the 1890s and 1900s temperance received only occasional mention in the Negro press. The 1896 general conference of the African Methodist Episcopal Zion Church adopted a program to abolish the manufacture and sale of alcoholic beverages. It supported the W.C.T.U. and made it a "crime for any minister or member of the A.M.E. [Zion] Church to fight against temperance." Bishop W. B. Derrick said that the opening of saloons on Sunday was a "desecration of the Lord's Day." By 1908 there was a Negro chapter of the W.C.T.U. operating in Brooklyn.[30]

The campaign against drink as the mother of crime naturally disturbed Negro liquor dealers. In 1911 a number of Negro saloon-keepers organized the Negro Liquor Dealers Association of Greater New York to improve conditions in saloons, thereby hoping to gain greater public respect. But they discovered that it was difficult to counteract repeated charges that rowdyism centered in and about saloons. In light of such allegations, the *Age* in 1914 added its support to the rising national sentiment in favor of a prohibition amendment to the Constitution. But six years later, when the amendment neared adoption, the paper reversed its earlier position, fearing that prohibition would endanger those Negroes who relied on saloons for employment.[31]

Added to the problems discussed above was the inequitable treatment the Negro received at the hands of many of the city's policemen. As noted earlier in this chapter, the prejudiced element of the police force impaired the reliability of arrest statistics. Against a background of rising police hostility toward the Negro, the Negro community viewed the police as just another agency that sought to deprive them of their rights. This attitude, though, was not unique to New York. In other parts of the North and South, too, Negroes were not always accorded impartial justice. Many southern Negroes who came to New York brought with them their contempt for law enforcement agencies. In the South, according to Gunnar Myrdal, the Negro's major contact with the white community "is the policeman. He is the personification of white authority in the Negro community." Accordingly, wrote Robert R. Moton in 1929, Booker T. Washington's successor at Tuskegee, the southern policeman's maltreatment of the Negro led the Negro community to regard the police "not as an instrument of justice, but as an instrument of persecution." [32] The contemptuous attitude of many New York City policemen toward Negroes did little to change this attitude. Both white and Negro newspapers frequently denounced the police for their abuse of the city's Negro residents.[33] In 1907 the *Age* castigated the police force for persecuting Negroes more than any other group in New York. Negroes maintained that policemen were more inclined to arrest or use their billies on them than on whites. These officers of the law, it was alleged, thought nothing of invading Negro homes in violation of the constitutional protection against illegal search and seizure. "The sympathies of the police," concluded the *Age* in 1905, "have been unmistakably on the side of the white law breakers." A study made by the Public Education Association in 1913 supported these arguments; it reported that the city's policemen declared, "without mincing their words, that they considered the colored people worthless." [34] One incident that clearly illustrated the contempt in which many policemen held the New York Negro was the race riot of 1900.

On the night of August 15, 1900, there occurred a general assault on the Negroes of the Tenderloin district. Bad feeling between the white residents of the area, mostly Irish, had existed for a number of years. This animosity reached the breaking point after a Negro, Arthur J. Harris, killed a policeman on August 12 in the course of a scuffle. There were rumors that the police and some residents of the Tenderloin were planning to retaliate against the Negro population for Harris' action. With the city in the midst of a prolonged heat wave, there was the danger that a minor incident would precipitate a race riot. Against this background, it is impossible to determine with any degree of accuracy what single event actually started the outbreak. Once the violence erupted it developed into a general assault upon Negroes in the neighborhood; in the course of four hours of rioting, at least seventy Negroes were injured. During this period crowds went up and down the west Twenties and Thirties beating any Negro who happened to be in their path. Negroes were dragged from trolley cars and beaten by the mob.[35]

When the police arrived, they made a half-hearted effort to disperse the rioters. Before long, though, they not only disregarded the assaults upon Negroes but joined the rioters. A white observer remarked that "a squad of police marched up the street, and made a demonstration against every negro in sight." One Negro was dragged from a streetcar and beaten. Other observers accused the police of clubbing and kicking Negroes. No sooner had one law enforcement officer rescued a Negro from the crowd and placed him on a trolley car than another pulled him from the car and clubbed him to shouts of "shame" from the passengers. A Negro appealed to a policeman for help and "received a smash over the head with a nightstick in reply." In another case, a Negro woman asked a police officer to protect her from the mob. He replied: "Go to h—l, d—n you." Many Negroes vented their anger or contempt for the law by raining various objects on the police from their apartment windows; the law officers responded by firing their guns at the windows. It was only when the heat of the night was dampened by a sudden shower at three in the morning that the riot came to an end.

The severest condemnation of the police came as a result of an alleged beating of a Negro in a station house. A Negro bellboy, William J. Elliott, was arrested during the riot. When he arrived at the police station, he was taken to the cell area. A reporter, sitting near the front desk, heard someone yell: "Don't Murder me!" The newsman ran to the cell area and saw a Negro lying on the floor. In his news story, the journalist wrote that he had not seen the policemen actually kicking the man; however, he contended that he observed their feet moving in a kicking motion.

It appears that the police made little effort to arrest the white rioters. The *Tribune* reported that not a single white had been apprehended after three hours of rioting. Those persons who were arrested — mostly Negroes — were brought before Magistrate Cornell. The judge remarked that it was a "sad commentary upon yesterday's occurrences" that he had before him only "one white person — a small boy." He said that the white rioters had "acted like beasts, jumping on cars and attacking colored passengers indiscriminately." [36]

On August 16 and 17 there were occasional reports of clashes between whites and Negroes. In addition, according to press reports, many Negroes were arming themselves for self-protection. Most Negroes, however, preferred to remain within the safety of their homes or fled to the homes of friends in other sections of the city until passions had cooled. [37]

No sooner had the riot stopped than leading New York citizens, both Negro and white, condemned the actions of the police. Dean Richmond Babbitt, a white clergyman, called the police "municipal rioters and lawbreakers." He feared that the world would stand "aghast" at hearing of a police force that aided and abetted a mob that beat people who only were guilty of "having a black skin." The police, concluded the clergyman, "deliberately planned and conducted" the riot; these "blue-coated bullies" virtually led the mob. The *Post*, too, asserted that "evidence was not wanting . . . to show that one, if not the chief moving cause of the troubles, was a desire on the part of the police to avenge their colleague's murder on all the negroes in sight." The paper wrote that it had the statements of "disinterested observers" who reported "that the police tacitly encouraged the outbreak; some even went so far as to say that the police virtually led the hoodlums." The *Tribune* blamed the "severity" of the riot on the "unskillful and treacherous conduct of the police." Responsibility for the riot, charged the *Herald*, "must be traced directly and indirectly to the police." P. R. Cutyner, Negro minister of the Zion Methodist Episcopal Church, declared that the people of New York City had witnessed a "brutal spectacle" led by uniformed bullies. There was no attempt to seek out the guilty, declared the Negro clergyman, but merely to seek out a black face and "pounce upon him." T. Thomas Fortune asserted that it was time to find out how long the police were going to continue their abuse of Negroes.[38]

The blame for the riot atrocities, however, was not limited to the police. A general denunciation of the entire law enforcement machinery, the city government, and the local Democratic party followed. While many were shocked at the riot outrages, they did not refrain from using this as an opportunity to attack the city administration and Tammany Hall. It must be remembered that in the late 1890s and early 1900s New York City was in the midst of a campaign to eradicate corruption in the city government. Mainly through the efforts of Dr. Charles Parkhurst, the state legislature established the Lexow Committee in 1894 to investigate police corruption in the city and the Tenderloin in particular. This was followed five years later by the Mazet Committee's inquiry into the operation of New York City's government. After electing the reform-minded William L. Strong as mayor in 1894, Seth Low, former mayor of the city of Brooklyn, was unsuccessful in his bid for the mayor's office. Still, in light of the Mazet investigation in 1899, the reform group hoped to capture city hall in the election of 1901. Accordingly, the race riot of 1900 provided those seeking the elimination of corruption in government with further ammunition to use in their campaign against Tammany Hall.[39]

According to the *Tribune,* one of the leading proponents of reform, the lawless actions of the police could be attributed to the "abominable municipal government" that plagued New York City. In a cartoon the newspaper portrayed the Tammany Tiger dressed in a policeman's uniform and twirling a nightstick, while a Negro was lying on the ground with blood gushing from his head. The New York *Herald,* too, considered Tammany Hall responsible for the police outrages. Richard Croker, the boss of Tammany, was characterized as the real villain of the riots. The paper claimed that the riot was not anti-Negro, but illustrated the indifference of the police and the local Democratic party to crime. This was especially true in the area of the riot, where both black and white crime flourished. The *Post* repudiated a police force and a governmental system that "reeks throughout with corruption." There were insufficient inducements for policemen to be "sober and upright and merciful," for they needed only the right "political backing" to keep their jobs. A group of Democrats fighting the Tammany organization in the Ninth Assembly District censured the "malign and villain blow" delivered by the police force. Police chief William S. Devery was rebuked as a "ruffian," a man who encouraged prostitution, and a tool of Tammany. The police, one speaker told the insurgent group, not only abused Negroes and encouraged crime, but were being used to interfere with the primary elections in favor of the incumbents.[40]

Even Negro leaders joined in rebuking the city's Democratic party. The Reverend P. Butler Tompkins maintained that the police force was "one of the most corrupt organizations" in New York — it "has been in league with crime and criminals since the birth of its mother — Tammany Hall." Tammany, in turn was "the breeder of evil, the feeder of sin and crime." Negroes should rise up and "crush the head of this serpent." William Henry Brooks, Negro pastor of one of the leading Negro churches, St. Mark's Methodist Episcopal, and leader of the Negro protest movement against the police outrages, placed the responsibility for the riot at "Tammany's door." Negro criticism of the actions of the police during the riot was not restricted to those who opposed the local Democracy. A delegation of Negro Democrats called upon acting-Mayor Guggenheimer to register their protest against police abuse of Negroes. At the same time, though, the group reproached the Republican party for failing to guarantee the rights of Negroes throughout the nation and declared that Boss Croker was in their "hearts side by side with the immortal Lincoln." [41]

This tendency to use the riot as another weapon with which to castigate the Democratic machine, especially among white elements, was attested to by the attitude of the normally Democratic newspapers of the city. The Brooklyn *Eagle* rebuked the rioters and the police, but made no mention of Tammany Hall. Two Irish newspapers, supporters of the local Democracy, considered the race riot a disgrace, but failed to allude to either the charges against the police or the Democratic party.[42]

The *Sun* and the *Journal*, on the other hand, used the riots as an excuse to express a distaste for the Negro. The *Sun* wrote that the "abject inferiority of the colored population on the West Side in numbers, resources, influence, and prowess should make easy the avoidance of such a thing as a 'race riot.' " Allegations of police brutality were not stressed by the paper; in fact, they were referred to casually in a general article on the riot. The *Journal* devoted little space to the riot and made no mention of the charges against the police. Although it condemned the riot, it asserted that friction between Negroes and whites was a part of human nature. The paper concluded its editorial in Darwinian terms: "Nature aims to give the finest specimens control . . . knowing that those who combine superiority of muscle, brain, and cunning will come out on top." [43]

Negro leaders were not satisfied with merely expressing indignation at the police outrages, they decided to seek redress for their grievances. The leadership of the Negro protest movement fell to the Reverend William Henry Brooks, who in later years was to be a prominent member of both the NAACP and the Urban League. The Reverend Brooks wrote to leading Negroes urging them to join in demanding that the city take remedial action. He counseled the city's Negroes to secure justice through the courts instead of resorting to lawless retaliation: "We must be calm and law-abiding and we will win." Under his leadership, the Citizens' Protective League was organized to place before the city the Negro community's allegations. On September 12 the League held a protest meeting in Carnegie Hall; it also published a pamphlet containing some 78 acts of police brutality committed during the August riot. Two of the leading white civic organizations in New York City — the Society for the Prevention of Crime and City Vigilance League — joined the Negro group in calling for an investigation of the entire matter by Mayor Robert Van Wyck.[44] As one of its lawyers, the League obtained the services of Frank Moss. Moss had been one of Charles Parkhurst's followers as well as counsel to the Lexow and Mazet committees. During Mayor Strong's administration he was chairman of the Board of Police Commissioners.[45]

Rather than have his office conduct the investigation, Mayor Van Wyck instructed the Board of Police Commissioners to hold hearings. Before the Board began its investigation, the man who was to be chairman of the inquiry, Commissioner Bernard York, asserted that he disbelieved the charges of police brutality. He concluded that a policeman's billy and nightstick were to be used for controlling a mob and if a man was hit by a policeman with such a weapon it was "proof" that he was where he had "no business to be." The *Times* called this statement "folly" and "stupidity." [46]

Before the investigation began, a Grand Jury dismissed Negro complaints against the police because the Negroes were unable to identify those law officers who had committed the alleged assaults.[47] During the month of September, the Board of Police Commissioners held hearings on the charges of police brutality. Commissioner York refused to permit an attorney for the Negroes — William Ludlow — to cross-examine or elicit further information from witnesses. Frank Moss was allowed to make an occasional statement; but Commissioner York denied Moss's request to introduce evidence unless such material had been submitted to the Board for examination. Moss refused to follow this procedure. He contended that retaliatory steps would be taken against his witnesses if he followed the Board's ruling. The Brooklyn *Eagle* remarked that Commissioner York was "technically correct" in his method of investigation; however, his procedure prevented the "discovery of the truth." [48]

After a month of inquiries, the Board of Police Commissioners dismissed the charges against the police. Commissioner York stated that the allegations of police brutality were unfounded. No doubt, he remarked, some innocent people were hurt when the police attempted to quell the riot; however, the area of the disturbance required "extra vigilance." The measures employed by the police must be left to their "good judgment," he concluded. The *Times* termed York's decision "pure impudence"; the *Tribune* called the entire investigation a "whitewash." These developments were to figure in the municipal elections of 1901.[49]

In the two decades following the race riot of 1900, there was little change in the relations between the police and the Negro community. In 1901 the *Tribune* reported that a group of policemen chased a number of suspected Negro lawbreakers into their homes and "beat them on the head and bodies with their clubs." When a minor riot between whites and Negroes took place in 1905 on San Juan Hill, the police were once again accused of abusing Negro citizens. The *Age* held the police "largely responsible" for the outbreak. The *Post* as well as the anti-Negro *Sun* rebuked the police for their brutal actions.[50] A number of Negroes, however, extended their contempt for the police beyond verbal protests. It became common practice to rain bricks from roofs upon the representatives of the law.[51] The white press attributed to the lawless element of the Negro community a large portion of the responsibility for these clashes. The *Tribune* asserted in 1905 that too many Negroes looked on racial clashes as "legitimate objects of sport." But the Negro press and leadership held the police responsible for the Negro's contempt for law enforcement agencies. Accordingly, after the riot of 1905 Negroes recreated the Citizens' Protective League under the leadership of Philip A. Payton, Jr., and Samuel Scottron to protect the rights of the city's Negroes. Five years later the NAACP established the New York Vigilance Committee to investigate the outrages committed against the race.[52] Negroes held protest meetings and conferences with city officials to little avail, for conflicts between the police and Negroes continued down to and after 1920.[53] Negro organizations, therefore, served as vehicles to present the Negro's grievances to the public, hoping to appeal to the basic humanitarian instincts of an apathetic citizenry. Such was the case in 1917 when Negroes marched silently down Fifth Avenue protesting physical abuse inflicted upon Negroes in New York City and the nation.[54]

Even though many of the police officers involved in the 1900 riot were responsible for its excesses, they alone could not be blamed for its outbreak. A far more important factor was the tension between the Negro community and the adjoining Irish settlement. According to the *New York Times*, the majority of the rioters were Irish.[55] Antagonisms between the Irish and the Negro had existed since pre-Civil War days. Beginning with the massive influx of Irish into New York City in the 1840s, the Negro and the Irish battled for the same jobs. This rivalry soon turned to violence, culminating in the draft riots of 1863.[56] After the Civil War the discord extended into the area of housing and persisted in the competition for employment. The blame for precipitating these attacks must fall at the feet of a segment of the city's Irish. By way of reacting to these violent actions, the Negro press rebuked the Irish community. In 1865 the *Weekly Anglo African* charged that Irish policemen were "making very bad use of their power." The *New York Times*, four years later, gave further force to the charge that the Irish abused Negro residents of New York; the paper maintained that the Irish "fostered" prejudice against the black man and excluded Negroes from many of the labor unions of the city.[57] The complaints of Irish maltreatment of

Negroes continued throughout the remainder of the nineteenth century and into the twentieth century. Negro longshoremen, who had to traverse Irish neighborhoods on their way to and from work, were the victims of verbal and physical abuse.[58] More and more observers noted the contempt manifested by the Irish toward the Negro. In 1905 Mary Ovington charged that the Irish were "the most boisterously aggressive" toward the Negro. Samuel Scottron, writing on the occasion of a race riot in 1905, alleged that "with the single exception of the Irish-American," the Negro lived "in peace with everybody in the city of New York." [59]

Many members of the New York Negro colony, in condemning the anti-Negro attitudes and actions of the Irish, expressed their own contempt for the Sons of Erin. They complained that they were compelled to live near "the least desirable type of shiftless Irish." In 1905 the *Age* wrote that the Irish, "with their usual bigotry, grew sullen and menacing when the Afro-American moved in." It also maintained that the Irish members of the police force were recruited from the "coarsest and most ignorant individuals of the Irish race." [60] David Fulton, a Negro writing under the pseudonym of Jack Thorne in the early 1900s, asserted that the Irishman was the "very embodiment of discontent, the instigator of nearly all the troubles in the labor field, the inaugurator of political upheavals and race clashings." [61]

Animosity toward the Irish was only one aspect of a general expression of distrust and fear of foreign-born immigrants among a vocal element of the Negro community. To some Negroes the European newcomer represented a threat to the already limited employment and housing market of the New York Negro.[62] According to R. F. Hurley, a Negro clergyman writing in 1889, Negroes had to compete with foreigners for even substandard housing and menial jobs. A Negro newspaper columnist complained shortly thereafter that the government of the United States was too favorably disposed toward European immigrants, "and too badly neglected her own people." In 1913 a Negro social critic, James B. Clarke, observed that the "Negro's status in New York . . . would have been rapidly and permanently improved, industrially as well as in civic recognition had not the current of immigration" increased after the Civil War. To meet this foreign peril to the Negro's already precarious position, a Negro newspaper, the *New York Globe,* counseled its readers in 1883 to be reliable, honest, and efficient.[63] Other Negro spokesmen called for legislation that would reduce the tidal wave of foreign immigration to a trickle. The *New York Age* and James Weldon Johnson supported both the adoption of a literacy test requirement and a law establishing a quota system for future emigrants from foreign lands. "Speaking purely from a motive of self-interest," wrote Johnson in 1919, "the American Negro can say that the passing of a law restricting immigration for four years is a good thing," since it will provide Negroes a period free from foreign labor competition.[64]

Yet to reduce the Negro's attitude toward the foreign newcomer to one of mere hostility would be an oversimplification. The Irish, for example, earned both the support and animosity of Negroes; in fact, the same statement often contained scorn as well as praise. A racial stereotype, as John Higham has noted, "may express ambivalent emotions. It may blend affection and contempt." This conflict in Negro thought became more noticeable when Negroes could identify with a persecuted group. Thus, the Negro press continually supported the Irish in their fight for independence from England and denounced the anti-Semitic practices of tsarist Russia.[65] This ambivalent attitude of the Negro is particularly evident in regard to the Jewish immigrant. Not only could philo-Semitism and anti-Semitism be found in the thinking of the Negro community, but in the statements of a particular individual. While the Negro press could regret "that in this age of progress and light, so industrious, sober and intelligent a class as the Jews should have to be discriminated against," it also could contend that the press of the nation devoted too much space to condemning discrimination against Jews and not enough to advancing the cause of the underprivileged Negro. Accordingly, if Negroes could identify with the Jew's predicament — as they did when elements of the city's Irish population abused Negroes as well as Jews — they would condemn anti-Semitism. But once again such reactions were ambivalent. In the course of an article censuring those who persecuted Jews, the *Globe* argued that this was less important than anti-Negro measures. While the Jew owned stores and banks, the paper maintained, the Negro was handicapped in securing even the most menial employment.[66] This apparent paradox can be seen in the Negro's attitude toward the alleged business achievements of the Jewish community. Negroes both reviled and applauded the "cunning" of the successful Jewish businessman, whether foreign- or native-born. As one student of anti-Semitism has observed: "Seen in economic terms, the Jew represented both the capitalist virtues and the capitalist vices . . . the Jew stood for keenness and resourcefulness in trade. Yet keenness also meant cunning, and enterprise suggested avarice." [67] To some New York Negroes this demonstrated the ability of a minority group to overcome prejudice by virtue of financial success. To others it indicated that Jews for their own economic advancement persecuted Negroes.

In 1883 the *Globe* claimed that Jewish control of the southern money market oppressed the Negro laborers of that region. The *Age*, seconding this charge thirty years later, maintained that Jews and other aliens were "fast getting control of Southern merchandising, farming and banking interests." Nor, according to the paper, was the Jew's financial power limited to the South or even the United States — "as a money-lender he holds the purse strings of the world." "It is a peculiar race," the paper continued, it is "parasitical and predatory . . . preying upon and devouring the substance of others rather than creating and devouring the substance of itself. That is essentially the race characteristic of all parasites, all race fungi." What the Jew cannot win by merit, he will win by trickery. "As a salesman, as a moneylender," the *Age* concluded, "the disposition of the Jew is to take and to hold the long end and let the other man take and hold the short end of every proposition." For "it is the peculiarity of the Jew that if there is profit in anything he will discover it." Jessie Fortune, a Negro schoolteacher, after visiting the lower East Side in 1905, also maintained that Jews were preoccupied with financial accomplishments. She reported that the Jew's "sole aim" was to earn money. For this reason, she alleged, "all household duties are subservient to this purpose, so that as often as not, the dining room, parlor and sitting room serve as a tailor shop or work shop as the case may be." From her visit, Miss Fortune concluded that Jews, no matter what their occupations, made money. Some twenty years before the Negro schoolteacher's sojourn, a Negro newspaper columnist, who signed his name Colonel Hardscrabble, returned from a similar visit to the lower East Side. Hardscrabble reported that he was victimized by a "forked nose" Jewish merchant.[68]

These commentators accepted the stereotype of the Jew as a usurer, as a person motivated solely by materialistic concerns, as the power behind the financial world. But where others had created this myth of the Jewish tycoon to foster anti-Semitism, Negro leaders advised youths to pattern their lives after this legend. "If we are to be in elbow touch with other races, we must become like the despised Jew, the representative of business and money," advised a New York Negro lawyer in 1890. This position received a warm reception from the followers of Booker T. Washington, who maintained that economic success was a prerequisite for political and social advancement. Florence Williams, an ardent Washington supporter and a columnist for the *New York Age,* counseled her fellow Negroes in 1889 to imitate the great ambition of the Jewish people to place their "race upon a scale of absolute independence and domination in financial circles and to compel the world to acknowledge their business genius." She implored her readers to acquire "a little of the Jewish enterprise and spirit." Henry S. Creamer, a Negro writing in the *Age* in 1912, also praised the ability of the Jews in business. When Jews were denied access to a place, asserted Creamer, they bought the property. Consequently, he concluded, nothing was done in the United States with regard to finance "without our Jewish friend being consulted." [69] Praise of the Jew was not restricted to his alleged business acumen, but was extended to his supposed lawful habits, his group loyalty, and his "race" pride. "Jews are among the most moral and law-abiding citizens," maintained a Negro newspaper in 1880, it is "the exception when one of their number is found in any of our prisons." Twenty-five years later, the *Age* exhorted Negro girls to duplicate the "almost universal chastity" of Jewish girls; it urged Negro parents to "produce geniuses" comparable to leaders of the Jewish community; it implored all Negroes to "cultivate a lofty pride of race" similar to that of the Jewish people.[70]

Many Negro leaders, therefore, had accepted the stereotype of the Jewish propensity to business success not only to criticize the Hebrew, but to set him up as an example for their race to follow. This ambivalence was clearly evident in a series of cartoons carried in the *Age* during 1917 that showed a person with a long nose and speaking in a Yiddish dialect offering advice to a Negro youth on the best method of personal advancement.[71] To meet the occasion, then, anti-Semitism was intertwined with philo-Semitism, scorn was merged with praise, condemnation was united with commendation.

It must be noted that some Jews committed actions to encourage this paradox. In 1905, for example, a group of young Jews followed an elderly Negress down a street yelling after her "Nigger" and "Schwartze." Nor did the creation of a Negro stereotype by some Jews foster harmony between the two groups. In 1908 a group of Jewish property owners formed an association to exclude Negroes from a section of lower Harlem. The organization denied that it was motivated by racial prejudice, yet the Negro press made a point of noting its Jewish composition.[72] About one decade before the formation of this group of property owners, a recent Jewish immigrant to the city viewed all Negroes as unsanitary, violent, and criminally disposed:

> [The Negro] is unclean all vot he touches is unclean. Venn he fight and scream after his wifes and children, and cuts and hacks mit razors und knifes, I make fast mine doors und windows, und take mine wife und childrens to mine bruder's house, where we be noddings but white peoples.[73]

But, like the Negro's attitude toward the Jew, the Jewish community was not restricted to one position in its view of the Negro. Many Jews worked with such organizations as the NAACP to obtain equality for Negroes.[74]

Negro opposition to European immigration, however, went beyond economic motivations. Even the Negro's attitude toward the Jew was influenced more by the Negro's substandard position in society rather than any rivalry for housing or jobs. Jews and Negroes worked in different occupational fields. Until 1905, when Negroes entered Harlem, the two groups did not live near one another.[75] Before this date, there was only occasional mention of Jewish shopkeepers selling their wares in Negro neighborhoods — an alleged source of Negro-Jewish friction. Consequently, those Negro attitudes toward the Jew that were formulated before 1905 cannot be attributed merely to economic motives. The Negro's view of Jewish business success — whether scornful or laudatory — reflected his sense of insecurity, his marginal place in American society rather than employment or business competition. The Negro's substandard economic position can be ascribed to his inferior social and political status in American society — the arguments of the Booker T. Washington school notwithstanding — since finan-

cial success alone failed to bring first-class citizenship. For example, those Negroes who obtained a degree of affluence still experienced social and political discrimination in the wider community
(see chapters II, III and VII). Hence, New York City Negroes as
well as Negroes in other sections of the country were in a continual state of insecurity between 1880 and 1920. Social discontent
prevailed in Negro communities throughout the nation. Nativism,
which attracted elements of the white population in a state of
social unrest, had its appeal among Negroes. Along with their
burning desire to be freed of their second-class status, Negroes
fervently wanted to be part of the American dream. Like white
nativists, elements of the Negro community became what Gunnar
Myrdal has referred to as "exaggerated" Americans; they emerged
as strong advocates of 100 per cent Americanism. This attitude
was not limited to the Negro; it reflected what C. Vann Woodward has called the "powerful urge among minority groups to
abandon or disguise their distinguishing cultural traits and con-
form as quickly as possible to some national norm." [76] For many
Negroes, the national norm in the case of the European immigrant
was the attitude of the white nativist. Nativism gave the Negro a
way of proclaiming his loyalty to America, of saying to white
America that he was an American.

Some Negroes, not unlike white nativists, viewed the European newcomer as a danger to traditional patterns of law and
order. The "disturbers of public peace," declared Samuel Scottron
in 1905, were recruited from the ranks of European immigrants.
A decade and one-half earlier the *Age* charged that while Chinese
labor was barred from American shores, the "lazzaroni and ban-
ditti of Italy, the aged and helpless paupers of Ireland" were permitted entrance. "Wherever the Italians go," the paper wrote, "it
appears that a branch of the Mafia is set up." Henry C. Dotry, a
Negro writing in 1891, reported that the foreign-born element
contained a large proportion of diseased and "debased criminals."
The *Age* in 1909 even asserted that Negroes had copied the
"method of resisting the law from the foreign colonies in New
York." New York Negroes believed that the alleged disrespect
with which European immigrants held the law was responsible
for the race riot of 1900 and other abuses heaped upon the city's
Negro population.[77]

The European newcomer was not merely accused of a propensity to lawlessness, but with an inability to fit into the American democratic fabric. To both Negro and white nativists, the odd language of the European, his alien ideas and strange customs threatened to destroy American democracy. In the 1900s the *Age* contended that the crude foreigners entering the United States, "few of them speaking the English language," exhibited no understanding of a republican form of government. Instead, the paper alleged, the "Puritan civilization of New England and the cavalier civilization of the South, which laid the foundations of the Republic . . . are being replaced by a new citizenship, a new civilization," which will obliterate the Christian sabbath "for that of European license and the clamor for innovation of all sorts in the character and administration of the Government." Accordingly, the New York Negro press damned as "alien misfits" such new ideas of electoral procedure as the initiative, the referendum, and the recall. Again like the white nativist, the Negro viewed the urban political boss as well as the modern city as foreign innovations. It was alleged that the local political mogul supported by the immigrant vote had "Europeanized" the city. "American names are being rapidly overshadowed by European names" in New York City, wrote the *Age*. Disturbed by the Negro's insecure position in the city as opposed to the considerable influence of immigrant groups, the *Globe* in 1883 claimed that the Irish vote was not "always intelligently and honestly directed" — yet it made itself felt. The paper reviled political leaders for catering to the Irish and German vote.[78]

Negroes also maintained that Europe was sending its "socialistic labor" to America. In 1919 the *Age* reacted to a tenant rent strike in New York City, which a number of the foreign colonies of the city supported, as a bolshevik tactic. Contrary to the claims of Communist hunting committees, Negroes generally viewed with disfavor the tenets of bolshevism. With their strong religious heritage, their middle class ideals, their lack of a radical past, and their desire to be included within the American dream, the majority of New York Negroes rejected the overtures of Socialists and Communists and even the Back-to-Africa movement of Marcus Garvey.[79] During World War I, Negroes manifested their loyalty to the United States by taking great pride in the heroic exploits of all-Negro army units and the extensive sale of Liberty Bonds in Harlem. New York Negroes, therefore, attempted to compensate for their second-class position in American society by affirming their loyalty to the American system in the chauvinistic manner of the advocates of 100 per cent Americanism. As Samuel Scottron maintained in 1905: "The Negro has never known another flag . . . with all the strength of his soul, he is an American and only an American." [80]

Notes

[1] New York *Post*, August 18, 1900. For arrest statistics, see, for example, New York City Police Department, *Annual Report for 1870–1871* (New York, 1871), p. 26; *Annual Report for 1890* (New York, 1891), p. 36; *Annual Report for 1900* (New York, 1901), p. 38.

[2] *New York Age*, July 27, 1905, and June 4, 1914; New York *Post*, August 16, 18, 1900.

[3] Myrdal, *American Dilemma*, pp. 527, 966–79; Thorsten Sellin, "The Negro and the Problem of Law Observance and Administration in the Light of Social Research," in Charles S. Johnson, *The Negro in American Civilization: A Study of Negro Life and Race Relations in the Light of Social Research* (New York, 1930), p. 447.

[4] *New York Globe*, April 5, 1884; Speed, "The Negro in New York," p. 1250.

[5] New York *Post*, August 18, 1900; The Charity Organization, *Report for 1912*, p. 45; Ovington, "Gunpowder," p. 249, and *Half A Man*, p. 47.

[6] Riis, *How the Other Half Lives*, p. 150; Charles H. Parkhurst, *Our Fight With Tammany* (New York, 1895), *passim*. According to the *New York Tribune*, August 18, 1900, the Negroes of the Tenderloin were "to a considerable extent of depraved and vicious elements."

[7] *New York Globe*, August 18, 25, 1883; *New York Freeman*, June 19, 26, July 24, 1886; *New York Age*, August 14, 1913.

[8] *New York Freeman*, July 18, 1885, and July 17, 1886; New York *Post*, August 18, 1900; *New York Age*, April 6, 1911.

[9] *New York Age*, April 6, July 6, August 10, 1911; Frances A. Kellor, *Out of Work: A Study of Unemployment* (rev. ed., New York, 1915), pp. 227–28; National League on Urban Conditions Among Negroes, *Report for 1912*, p. 18, and *Report for 1913–1914 and 1914–1915*, p. 17; National League for the Protection of Colored Women, *Annual Report, 1910–1911* (New York, 1911), p. 6; White Rose Industrial Association, *Annual Report, 1911* (New York, 1912), p. 6; George Augustus Sala, *America Revisited: From the Bay of New York . . . to the Pacific* (2 vols., London, 1883), I, 761.

[10] New York *Herald*, August 17, 1900; New York *Post*, August 17, 18, 1900; Kennedy, *Negro Peasant Turns Cityward*, pp. 186–87.

[11] *New York Globe*, January 20, 1883; *New York Age*, September 14, 1911, and August 1, 1912. Also see *ibid.*, February 7, 1907, and June 9, 1910.

[12] *New York Times*, November 18, 1898.

[13] *New York Tribune*, August 17, 1900; *Milestones* (November, 1904), 7.

[14] *New York Times*, November 17, 1901; *New York Tribune*, April

4, 1901; *New York Age*, February 7, November 21, 1907.

[15] *New York Age*, September 5, 1891; February 14, April 4, 1907; July 16, 1908; June 24, 1909.

[16] *Ibid.*, May 14, 1908.

[17] Mary White Ovington, *The Walls Came Tumbling Down* (New York, 1947), p. 21; *New York Tribune*, January 27, 1889, and March 20, 1892.

[18] *New York Times*, April 20, 1914.

[19] *New York Age*, July 16, 1908, and June 24, 1909; *Colored American Review*, I (October 1, 1915), 13.

[20] Richard Hofstadter, *The Age of Reform: From Bryan to F. D. R.* (New York, 1955), pp. 173–84.

[21] *New York Age*, February 8, 15, 22, 1917; *Crisis*, XIX (January, 1920), 105; New York *News*, September 17, 1916; *Southern Workman*, LXVI (February, 1917), 72–73.

[22] *New York Age*, February 14, April 4, 1907, and July 30, 1908; Ovington, "Negro Home in New York," p. 25; Speed, "The Negro in New York," pp. 1249–50; Tucker, "Negro Craftsmen in New York," pp. 545–51.

[23] Blascoer, *Colored School Children*, pp. 103–14; Emerson, "Children of the Circle," p. 83; Federation of Churches, *Canvass No. 2*, pp. 90–92. The urbanization of the Negro family "has brought the most momentous change in the family life of the Negro since emancipation. . . . [It] has torn the Negro loose from his cultural moorings." E. Franklin Frazier, *The Negro Family in the United States* (Chicago, 1932), p. 484.

[24] Myrdal, *American Dilemma*, pp. 977–78; Federation of Churches, *Canvass No. 2*, p. 26; *New York Times*, November 24, 1901.

[25] *New York Times*, November 17, 1901; Kennedy, *Negro Peasant Turns Cityward*, pp. 122, 188; R. R. Wright, Jr., "The Migration of Negroes to the North," *Annals of the American Academy of Political and Social Science*, XXVII (June, 1906), 564.

[26] Robert H. Bremner, *From the Depths: The Discovery of Poverty in the United States* (New York, 1956), pp. 80–81; J. H. N. Waring, "Some Causes of Criminality Among Colored People," *Charities*, XV (October 7, 1905), 46; *New York Globe*, August 25, 1883, and May 24, June 21, 1884; *New York Freeman*, June 19, July 10, 24, August 21, October 23, 1886.

[27] *New York Freeman*, October 1, 8, 1887; *New York Age*, October 15, 22, 1887.

[28] *New York Age*, March 26, 1908; February 4, 1909; October 1, 1914.

[29] *New York Globe*, March 3, 1883; *New York Freeman*, April 27, June 19, 1886; *New York Age*, July 26, November 1, 1890; New York Colored Mission, *Report for 1885*, pp. 6, 10, 15.

[30] James T. Haley, ed., *Afro-American Encyclopaedia; or, the Thoughts, Doings, and Sayings of the Race* (Nashville, 1896), p. 189; *New York Age*, February 27, 1908, *New York Tribune*, January 14, 1902.

[31] *New York Age*, June 8, 1911; April 23, 1914; February 28, 1920.

[32] *American Dilemma*, pp. 530–45; Robert R. Moton, *What the Negro Thinks* (Garden City, New York, 1929), pp. 154–55; Kennedy, *Negro Peasant Turns Cityward*, pp. 186–87.

[33] New York *Post*, August 16, 18, 1900, and July 20, 1905; *New York Tribune*, December 26, 1901.

[34] *New York Age*, July 27, 1905; July 11, 1907; June 22, 1911; June 4, 1914; May 31, 1917; April 15, 1918; Blascoer, *Colored School Children*, pp. 23, 71; National League

on Urban Conditions Among Negroes, "Housing Conditions Among Negroes in Harlem," p. 25.

[35] The account of the riot is based on reports in the *New York Times,* August 16–18, 1900; *New York Tribune,* August 16–18, 1900; New York *Post,* August 16–18, 1900; New York *Herald,* August 16–17, 1900.

[36] *New York Tribune,* August 16, 17, 1900; *New York Times,* August 16–18, 1900; New York *Post,* August 16, 1900.

[37] *New York Tribune,* August 17, 18, 1900; *New York Times,* New York *Herald,* August 17, 1900.

[38] New York *Herald,* August 17, 21, 1900; New York *Post,* August 16, 20, 1900; *New York Times,* August 20, 1900; *New York Tribune,* August 17, 18, 20, 31, 1900.

[39] Charles Garrett, *The La Guardia Years: Machine and Reform Politics in New York City* (New Brunswick, 1961), pp. 38–40; Parkhurst, *Our Fight With Tammany,* pp. 240–52; Lincoln Steffens, *Autobiography* (New York, 1931), pp. 247–54.

[40] New York *Herald,* August 16, 17, 19–21, 1900; New York *Post,* August 16, 18, 1900; *New York Tribune,* August 19, 1900; *New York Times,* August 25, 1900.

[41] *New York Times,* August 20, 25, 27, 1900; *New York Tribune,* August 22, 1900.

[42] Brooklyn *Eagle,* August 16, 1900; *Irish-American,* August 25, 1900; *Irish World and American Industrial Liberator,* August 25, 1900.

[43] New York *Sun,* August 17, 18, 21, 1900; New York *Journal,* August 16, 17, 1900.

[44] *New York Times,* August 27, September 11, 13, 1900; New York *Herald,* August 21, 1900; Citizens' Protective League, *Story of the Riot* (New York, 1900). Also see postcards sent out by the Reverend Brooks, September 17, 1900, Citizens' Protective League folder in

Miscellaneous Letters and Papers, Schomburg Collection.

[45] *New York Times,* August 30, 1900; *Dictionary of American Biography* (22 vols., New York, 1928–1958), XIII, 279–80.

[46] *New York Times,* August 21, 26, 1900.

[47] *New York Tribune,* August 30, 1900.

[48] *Ibid.,* September 8, 10, 15, 20, 1900; Brooklyn *Eagle,* September 8, 1900; *New York Times,* September 20, 1900.

[49] *New York Tribune,* September 10, 1900; *New York Times,* October 5, 1900. For discussion of election of 1901, see chapter seven.

[50] *New York Tribune,* December 26, 1901; *New York Age,* July 13, 1905; New York *Post,* July 20, 1905; New York *Sun,* August 6, 1905.

[51] *New York Times,* July 14, 1903, and May 28, June 27, 1904; *New York Tribune,* July 13, August 16, 1903, and July 18, 1905; New York *Post,* July 20, 1905; New York *World,* July 16, 1905.

[52] *New York Age,* August 10, November 30, 1905; *New York Tribune,* December 27, 1905.

[53] *New York Age,* May 24, 1906; August 5, 1909; June 22, July 13, 1911; May 31, 1917; *New York Times,* May 27, 31, July 4, 1917, and March 26, July 20, 1919.

[54] *Crisis,* XIV (September, 1917), 241–44.

[55] *New York Times,* August 16, 1900. Also see New York *Herald,* August 17, 1900; Speed, "The Negro in New York," p. 1249.

[56] Ernst, *Immigrant Life in New York,* pp. 104–105; Florence E. Gibson, *The Attitudes of the New York Irish Toward State and National Affairs, 1848–1892* (New York, 1951), p. 142; Albon P. Man, "Labor Competition and the New York Draft Riots," *Journal of Negro History,* XXXVI (October, 1951), 377–402.

[57] *Weekly Anglo African,* August

19, 1865; *New York Times*, March 2, 1869.

[58] *New York Age*, July 20, 1905; *New York Daily News*, July 15, 1905; New York *Sun*, August 6, 1905; *New York Times*, July 26, 1905; *New York Tribune*, July 15, 1905; Ovington, *Half A Man*, p. 85.

[59] Ovington, "Negro Home in New York," pp. 29–30; *New York Age*, August 10, 1905.

[60] Emerson, "Children of the Circle," p. 82; *New York Age*, July 13, August 10, 1905. Also see *ibid.*, November 26, 1908, and September 2, 1909; New York *Sun*, August 6, 1905; *New York Times*, July 18, August 3, 1901, and August 22, September 27, 1903; *New York Tribune*, August 10, 1906.

[61] Thorne, *Eagle Clippings*, pp. 8–9.

[62] See chapters one and two for a discussion of this subject.

[63] *New York Age*, May 16, 1891; *New York Globe*, March 29, 1884; *New York Times*, April 14, 1889; James B. Clarke, "The Negro and the Immigrant in the Two Americas," *Annals of the American Academy of Political and Social Science*, XLIX (September, 1913), 34–35.

[64] *New York Age*, February 8, 1917; November 23, 1918; February 8, 1919.

[65] John Higham, "Anti-Semitism in the Gilded Age: A Reinterpretation," *Mississippi Valley Historical Review*, XLIII (March, 1957), 563; *New York Globe*, September 22, 1883; *New York Freeman*, January 30, February 27, April 3, 1886; *New York Age*, November 1, 1890.

[66] *New York Globe*, September 1, 1883; *New York Freeman*, July 23, 1887; *New York Age*, July 13, 1905.

[67] *New York Age*, February 8, April 11, July 11, 1912; *Colored American Review*, I (October 1, 1915), 2, 15; Higham, "Anti-Semi-

tism," p. 563; *New York Globe*, February 17, 1883.

[68] *New York Globe*, February 17, 1883; *New York Freeman*, November 27, 1886; *New York Age*, January 5, 1905; February 8, April 11, 1912; August 21, 1913.

[69] *New York Age*, March 16, 1889; March 1, 1890; July 11, 1912. For Washington position, see chapter three.

[70] *Suffragist*, January 8, 1880; *New York Age*, May 8, 1905; July 2, 1914; June 14, 1917.

[71] See, for example, *New York Age*, April 26, 1917.

[72] *Ibid.*, November 26, 1908; New York *Sun*, August 17, 1900.

[73] Edwin Emerson, Jr., "The Negro Ghetto," *Harper's Weekly*, XLI (January 9, 1897), 44.

[74] Among the Jewish members of the NAACP executive board were Jacob H. Schiff, Rev. Joseph Silverman, Henry Moskowitz, and Mrs. Max Morgenthau, Jr. See *Crisis*, I (November, 1910), 12–13.

[75] For residential pattern, see chapter one; for occupations held by Negroes, see chapter two, and for Jews, see Moses Rischin, *The Promised City: New York's Jews, 1870–1914* (Cambridge, 1962), chapters four and nine.

[76] Myrdal, *American Dilemma*, pp. 808–809, 952; C. Vann Woodward, *The Burden of Southern History* (Vintage ed., New York, 1961), pp. 13–14. Paul L. Murphy has applied a position similar to the one taken here to the 1920s: "To an Anthony Caminetti, the first person of Italian extraction to be elected to Congress . . . this [Red scare] was an opportunity to demonstrate that he, as well as others of his national origin, were fully 100 percent American." "Sources and Nature of Intolerance in the 1920's," *Journal of American History*, LI (June, 1964), 66.

[77] *New York Globe*, March 8,

1884; *New York Age,* November 1, 1890; May 16, 1891; May 25, 1905; August 5, 1909.

[78] *New York Globe,* February 16, 1884; *New York Age,* January 12, 1905; May 9, 1907; October 3, 1911; April 4, 1912.

[79] *New York Age,* May 16, 1891, and May 17, 1919; Spero and Harris, *Black Worker,* 398–404. For charges of communism among Negroes, see New York Legislature, Joint Com-

mittee Investigating Seditious Activities, *Revolutionary Radicalism: Its History, Purpose and Tactics* (4 vols., Albany, 1920), II, 1477–1519; *New York Times,* October 5, 1919; for Negro answer to these charges, see *New York Age,* February 8, August 9, 1919.

[80] *New York Age,* May 25, 1905; May 24, July 26, 1917; May 4, 11, July 20, 1918; National Urban League, *Report for 1917–1918,* p. 6.

.6.

The Negro and the Wider Community

COOPERATION

THE STORY of Negro-white relations was not restricted to conflict. Between 1865 and 1920 some members of the white community displayed increasing interest in the plight of the city's Negro settlement; they created organizations that attempted to improve the Negro's substandard socio-economic position. Such groups, though, were few in number before the late 1880s. In the two decades or so following the Civil War, northern Negroes received far less philanthropic assistance than their southern fellows. Aid to the needy was hampered by the failure of the Protestant churches to take cognizance of the problems of the urban resident — white and black alike. Since most Negroes were Protestants, this attitude had a detrimental effect on the Negro living in the city. It was not until the social gospel and progressive movements gained an important foothold in the United States in the late nineteenth century that whites contributed significant charitable assistance to the New York Negro.[1]

Before the Civil War, the Society of Friends conducted most of the charitable activities in behalf of the New York Negro. In 1836 three Quaker women, outraged at discovering that destitute Negro children were assigned to jails, established the Colored

Orphan Asylum on West Twelfth Street near Sixth Avenue. When these facilities proved to be inadequate, the directors of the Asylum found larger quarters on Fifth Avenue between Forty-third and Forty-fourth streets. After thirty years at the latter location, the orphanage was struck by tragedy: the participants in the draft riots of 1863 burned the Asylum to the ground. Fortunately, the children were led to safety by way of a back door. Temporary quarters were secured on Blackwell's Island until the Asylum was relocated farther uptown; and, finally, in 1905 a modern institution was opened in Riverdale. The Asylum's staff instituted a policy of assigning small groups of children to the care of an adult — the cottage system. To prepare the children "for useful citizenship," instruction was offered in spiritual matters, job training, and sports. So great was the demand to place Negro waifs under the care of the orphanage that the managers reported in 1881 that they were impelled to turn away many worthy children because of limited space. For all their interest in the orphaned Negro, the directors nevertheless considered the Negro inferior to the white. They embraced the nineteenth century attitude that misfortune was not attributable to environmental factors but to depravity, especially in the case of the Negro. In 1878 the directors spoke of the "peculiarities in the constitution of the colored people which are difficult to contend with." While the Negro children were "gentle and amenable to authority," they were deficient in "vigorous, independent thought and action." Because of this attitude, no doubt, the Asylum failed to employ a Negro as a member of its staff until 1917.[2]

In 1866 another home for Negro orphans — the Howard Colored Orphan Asylum — was opened in the city of Brooklyn. It sought to "shelter, protect, and educate the destitute of colored parentage, and to instruct said children in useful trades and occupations." It differed from the Colored Orphan Asylum in at least one important aspect — more than one-half of its board of directors was Negro.[3]

The Society of Friends also was instrumental in erecting a home for "the sick, aged, and destitute colored persons" of New York City. Opened in 1839, the Colored Home received support from both private gifts and the Commissioners of Public Charities. After a number of years in Manhattan, the operations of the Home were transferred to the more pastoral surroundings of the

Bronx. In 1882 the trustees changed the name of the Colored Home to the Lincoln Home and Hospital and initiated an out-patient dispensary as well as a training school for nurses.[4]

The most active philanthropic institution servicing the city's Negro community before the late 1880s was also a Quaker enter-prise — the New York Colored Mission. Founded as the African Sabbath School Association in 1865, it opened a school for Negro youngsters above a stable. Six years later the Association became the New York Colored Mission and located on West Thirtieth Street in the Tenderloin district. It declared that its primary purpose was the "religious, moral and social elevation of the Colored People." The Society of Friends as well as Negro min-isters held religious services in the Mission; during the warmer months these religious rites were conducted outdoors. Both chil-dren and adults attended the Sunday school and Bible classes. The Mission's staff launched a program to deal with the every-day problems of those Negroes who came under its protective wing. A nursery school was inaugurated so that Negro children could be removed from the "close, damp atmosphere of the apart-ments . . . while laundry work was carried on." Social workers, including a visiting nurse, went into Negro homes to help the sick, the underfed, and the poor. In 1883 the Mission obtained the services of a physician to minister to the health needs of its retinue of dependents. Troubled by the large body of Negro un-employed, it instituted an employment service to find jobs for those out of work. For young girls who came to the city without family, the Mission provided sleeping quarters as an alternative to the disreputable houses that attracted many of them. So that these and other young women might become better mothers and housewives, instruction in the latest homemaking techniques were offered. The needy could purchase inexpensive meals at the Mission's restaurant. Nor was the educational and social side of life neglected. Negroes could utilize the Mission's reading room and night school. Adults and adolescents attended Friday night social events. Through the Mission's boys' club, youths en-joyed athletic activities. By 1910 the Quaker organization claimed that it was servicing some 3,500 Negroes. With the emergence of other charitable agencies in the 1900s, the Mission cooperated with such non-church groups as the Urban League, the Charity Organization, and the Tribune Fresh Air Fund.[5]

Before the rise of secular societies, the Mission maintained a close relation with the New York City Mission and Tract Society. For a number of years preceding this alliance, the Tract Society had been working on its own among the city's Negroes. In 1866 it reported that New York's Negro population had "long been the object of our care" and meetings had "long been carried on among them." Also ministering to the Negro community in 1880 was a mission of the Scotch Presbyterian Church.[6]

Outside of the ventures of these agencies, little charitable work was made available to the city's Negro residents before the late 1880s. Change, however, was on the horizon. Within the Protestant church, those forces working for a more enlightened attitude emerged in the 1880s; and after 1895 they came to dominate "the most articulate sections of American Protestantism." Poverty was no longer regarded as a sign of depravity but as a manifestation of social ills. Where the Protestant clergy had been apathetic to the plight of the urban masses in earlier years, beginning in the 1880s they created a myriad of organizations that delved into the material as well as the spiritual life of the poor.[7] This point of view — the social gospel — affected the attitude of Protestant churches toward the Negro. During the 1880s, and to a greater degree in the 1890s, church affiliated groups became concerned with the position of the New York Negro. The New York Presbytery established a "colored" mission. The New York City Mission and Tract Society augmented its work among the Negro population by investigating the social condition of the Negro masses. In 1897 the Federation of Churches and Christian Workers, which was created in 1895 as "an interdenominational instrument for sociological investigation," completed a study of a Negro community on the West Side of Manhattan. As a result of its study, some concrete steps were taken to improve Negro living conditions.[8]

Negroes also benefited from the wider use of the institutional church. Where other religious charitable enterprises concerned themselves with only one or two aspects of life, the institutional church attempted to function as a blanket covering all facets of man's existence. Near the turn of the twentieth century, the Protestant Episcopal Mission Society opened St. Cyprian's Parish House and Chapel to administer to the Negroes of the San Juan

Hill district. St. Cyprian's was developed into the leading white-run institutional church working among New York's Negroes. Under its roof could be found classes teaching vocational skills. Those in need of jobs could utilize the Chapel's employment bureau. Recognizing that many mothers were not trained in the most satisfactory dietary and housekeeping techniques, the staff of St. Cyprian's gave instruction in homemaking. In line with this concern with dietary habits, a milk station was maintained where mothers could buy pasteurized milk at reasonable prices. In its soup kitchen, St. Cyprian's served meals to those who were short of funds. Nor did it restrict its activities to the confines of the parish house and chapel — the "friendly visitor," for example, was sent into the homes of many Negroes. To offset the less desirable diversions of the San Juan Hill neighborhood, recreational activities were conducted at the parish house. Like other religious groups, it sent many youngsters and their mothers on beach or country excursions.[9]

The desire to remove children from the sin and heat of city streets — the fresh air movement — was a major part of the programs of religious and secular charitable societies. The Memorial Baptist Church of Christ through its Fresh Air Department provided summer vacations in rural areas for a number of Negro mothers and their children. Another religious group, the Women's Auxiliary of the Cathedral of St. John the Divine, was concerned primarily with Negro youths. The Auxiliary maintained living quarters for employed females at its House for Working Girls. Also available at St. John's were sewing classes for girls and instruction in chair caning and shoe mending for boys.[10]

Concern for the plight of the Negro youth was reflected in the operations of the Young Men's and Young Women's Christian Associations. Where the Negro minister of St. Mark's Methodist Episcopal Church, H. M. Monroe, had complained in 1889 that the YMCA's of the city refused to admit Negroes to their programs, by the early 1900s a YMCA was serving the Negro neighborhood surrounding West Fifty-third Street. Within a few years, other branches for both girls and boys were opened in Harlem. In 1914 it was reported that the "Y" movement planned to spend $250,000 to expand its activities among New York's Negro settlement. The "Y" undertakings in Negro neighborhoods, moreover, were maintained on a segregated basis. Down to at least 1920 the YMCA and YWCA branches in New York City remained separate if not unequal.[11]

The Catholic Church, which had been administering to the needs of the urban masses well before the Protestant churches became involved in the problems of the city, instituted charitable enterprises for the benefit of New York's Negroes. Shortly after opening the first Catholic church in the city ministering to Negroes in 1883, St. Benedict the Moor, Catholics established a home for destitute colored children in Rye, New York. At St. Benedict's itself an active charitable program was undertaken. In addition, the Sisters of the Blessed Sacrament founded a school for Negro children.[12]

Despite the accomplishments of church organizations, both Protestant and Catholic, their achievements were few when compared to the extensive undertakings of secular agencies. Like church groups, secular associations mirrored the humanitarian influence of the social gospel movement. The settlement houses that catered to the residents of slum districts bore a striking resemblance to the institutional church. Serving on the boards of directors and the staffs of these organizations were clergymen as well as lay persons. Many social workers who considered themselves part of the rising progressive movement of the late nineteenth and early twentieth centuries were imbued with a strong sense of religious purpose. "For most Progressives," Carl Degler has remarked, "it was always clear that their fight was a moral one, a struggle of good against evil." As Jane Addams, the founder of Hull House in Chicago and a leading progressive, wrote: "the impulse to share the lives of the poor, the desire to make social service, irrespective of propaganda, express the spirit of Christ — an impulse as old as Christianity itself." [13]

Despite the commitment of a large part of the progressive movement to a moral mission, it is difficult to place those who assisted the New York Negro in a single category. Generally, they came from the middle class or higher; however, beyond this no generalization can be made as to their background except that they were a heterogenous group. Drawn to the cause of Negro assistance were the offspring of old native-born, Anglo-Saxon Protestant families and the children of immigrants, the person born with the proverbial golden spoon in the proverbial mouth and the self-made man, the so-called robber baron and the exponent of progressivism, as well as the advocate of socialism, the corporation lawyer, and the college professor. Although most of those who worked actively with Negroes — who gave their time, not just their money — were drawn from the progressive movement rather than the ranks of the "robber barons," the latter group still contributed many active participants and much needed financial assistance. Whether the men who made their fortunes by virtue of questionable business practices gave to Negro philanthropic enterprises because they suffered from guilt feelings or because they adhered to the social darwinist concept of charity as expounded by Andrew Carnegie, they did provide invaluable assistance to the cause.[14] Well before the rise of the social gospel or progressivism, the Carnegies and the Rockefellers had contributed to the advancement of Negro higher education in the South.[15] As for the urban progressives, they appear to have pushed into the background the racism that pervaded the progressive movement on the national level. Yet Lillian Wald, like Theodore Roosevelt, could not completely divorce from her thinking the usual Negro stereotypes. The Stillman House, created by Miss Wald to cater to the Negro community of San Juan Hill, devoted its story hours and drama classes to telling or performing Uncle Remus stories.[16] Despite this limitation, Lillian Wald and other social workers threw themselves into the struggle to improve the position of the urban masses whether Protestant or Jew, native-born or foreign-born, white or black.

The changed outlook of charitable agencies in regard to the Negro was reflected in the enterprises undertaken by the Children's Aid Society. Although the Society was created in the 1850s, it was not until the rise of progressivism that it became involved in the life of the Negro. In 1892 it opened on West Sixty-third Street the Henrietta Industrial School to afford greater educational opportunities for the Negro children of San Juan Hill. Seventeen years later the Society began the Henrietta Evening Trade School for Negro adults, especially those of West Indian background, at the same address. Instruction was given in dressmaking, homemaking, restaurant cooking, and janitorial work.[17]

In 1895 the New York Kindergarten Association, which had been founded five years earlier, launched the Free Kindergarten

Association for Colored Children — later known as the Mary F. Walton Free Kindergarten for Colored Children. The work of the Kindergarten went beyond caring for the young children of the Negro community. In the afternoon it opened its facilities to the older children of the neighborhood; social clubs for boys and girls were formed. Mothers could attend lectures on such topics as "Social and Sex Hygiene" and "Choice of Playmates," or take their children on excursions sponsored by the Kindergarten.[18]

Many prominent New York whites participated in the financing and programs of the Free Kindergarten. Jacob Riis helped the Negro school locate adequate quarters in the San Juan Hill district. On the parent body's board of directors was Dr. L. Emmett Holt. Descended from New England Puritan stock, Holt was one of the founders of the American Pediatric Society, a director of the Henry Street Settlement, and a member of the National Child Labor Committee. Also listed on the board of directors were Hamilton Mabie, who wrote for the *Outlook*; Richard Watson Gilder, son of a Methodist minister, assistant editor of *Scribner's Monthly*, political reformer, and chairman of the New York State Tenement House Committee of 1894; and Mrs. Joseph H. Choate whose husband was a member of such groups as the New England Society, the reform-minded Committee of Thirty, and the New York State Charities Aid Association. In addition to the descendants of the old gentry were the new rich or their immediate offspring — Morris Loeb, professor of chemistry in New York University and the son of Solomon Loeb of the investment firm of Kuhn, Loeb and Company; and the wife of one of the early directors of Standard Oil and a close affiliate of the "robber barons," Mrs. Walter Jennings. A latecomer to the Kindergarten Association, but destined to be one of the most influential whites working among New York's Negroes, was Mary White Ovington.[19]

Mary Ovington was born into a New England family with roots in the anti-slavery movement. Stirred by her maternal grandmother's description of the abolitionist struggle, young Mary developed compassion for the downtrodden. After attending private schools and Radcliffe College, she obtained a position as registrar in Pratt Institute, located in Brooklyn. There she was instrumental in launching the Greenpoint Settlement of the Pratt Institute Neighborship Association. Working in the Greenpoint

Settlement, Miss Ovington "saw unemployment, that nightmare that continues through the days and the months when a man is seeking work," she came into contact with labor organizers, and she sorrowed for those girls working long hours in factories. It was not until 1903, though, when she heard Booker T. Washington address the Social Reform Club that Miss Ovington became aware of the Negro's second-class position in society. In particular, she learned of the plight of the New York Negro. The picture portrayed for her was one of "ramshackle tenements, high infant mortality, and discrimination in employment." She left the meeting "with a realization that not only in Alabama but in our own New York we had a Negro problem."

Her concern for the Negro led Mary Ovington, in 1904, to obtain a fellowship to study the New York Negro through the influence of Mary Simkhovitch, director of Greenwich House and one of the leading social workers of the day. For the next seven years she delved into the past and present of the city's Negroes, publishing her findings in her first book, *Half A Man*. In the course of her investigation and in the years that followed, Mary Ovington lived among New York's Negroes. She was the only white person living in the Tuskegee, a model apartment house on West Sixty-third Street. In time she was to become involved in the work of many organizations seeking to improve the Negro's position. In 1905 she became a member of the auxiliary committee of the Free Kindergarten Association. Three years later she embarked on another enterprise in Brooklyn — the Lincoln Settlement Association. Striking at the poor living conditions of Brooklyn Negroes, the Association worked with the families of children attending its neighborhood house, day nursery, or kindergarten. During the second decade of the twentieth century, the Lincoln Settlement Association was to cooperate with the Urban League in attacking the social problems facing the New York Negro. In 1909 Mary Ovington organized the West End Workers' Association. Laboring among the Negro residents of San Juan Hill, its operations were similar to those of the Lincoln Settlement.

In her overall political orientation, Mary Ovington adhered to the principles of socialism. She wrote articles for the socialist journal, the *Masses*. In 1909 she joined with two other white Socialists, William Walling and Henry Moskowitz, in calling a national meeting that culminated in the formation of the NAACP.[20]

In 1902 a group of Negro mothers, unable to place their children in white nursery schools because of overcrowding or anti-Negro prejudices, instituted a program of assistance for the preschool Negro when they organized the Hope Day Nursery for Colored Children. Seeking to remove as many preschool children as possible from the small, poorly ventilated apartments of the tenements, they embarked on a program of activities in healthful surroundings. Mothers were encouraged to attend meetings, lectures, and discussions devoted to the question of child care.[21] Before long the Hope Day Nursery came under the tutelage of the Association of Day Nurseries of New York City. Playing a substantial role in helping the Negro group was Mrs. Arthur M. Dodge, president of the parent body. Mrs. Dodge's husband had inherited a prosperous lumber business from his father and engaged in various charitable pursuits. Another member of the Association was the wife of a leading New York physician and a professor of medicine, Mrs. Walter B. James. Also active in behalf of the white parent body was Mrs. Edward Berwind, whose husband was a self-made businessman. Born to immigrant parents, Berwind made his fortune in the coal mining industry and was an associate of J. P. Morgan. The wife of another man who rose from "rags to riches" was Mrs. Samuel Sloan. Sloan, an Irish immigrant, had achieved wealth as well as notoriety by virtue of his cutthroat railroad practices. Still another wife of a famous industrialist was Mrs. Solomon Guggenheim. Born to Swiss-Jewish immigrant parents, Solomon Guggenheim established a worldwide network of business investments. He was not only a patron of the arts, but had contributed a substantial sum to the building of an annex to the Mt. Sinai Hospital of New York.[22]

Four years after the creation of the Hope Day Nursery, Lillian Wald established a branch of the Henry Street Settlement — the Stillman House — in the San Juan Hill neighborhood. Shortly after arriving in New York City in 1893, Miss Wald opened the Henry Street Settlement in the lower East Side of Manhattan with the financial assistance of Jacob Schiff, a philanthropist and associate of Kuhn, Loeb and Company. Miss Wald's pioneer work among the urban poor earned for her a national reputation. While the Stillman House catered to the whites as well as the Negroes of San Juan Hill, Negroes were in the majority. Like the parent settlement house on the lower East Side, the Stillman House entered almost every aspect of urban life. A corps of nurses visited the homes of the needy; classes in vocational training were furnished for both juveniles and adults. Through its adult clubs, the Stillman staff hoped to encourage neighborhood pride. Those who came to Stillman's could avail themselves of the various educational facilities — a branch of the public library, classes in history, story and study hours, and dramatic classes. Negro youths also could partake in the activities of the athletic clubs, the playrooms, and the summer playground opened in cooperation with the Department of Parks and Playgrounds. During the summer months some children were sent to the more pastoral environs of upstate New York.[23] In 1909 Miss Wald established the Lincoln Day Nursery. Within a few years the Nursery was merged with the Stillman House into the Lincoln House.[24]

While Lillian Wald was living and working among the residents of the city's tenements, a small body of Negro and white women came together in 1897 to organize the White Rose Industrial Association in order to "check the evil of unscrupulous employment agents who deceive the unsuspecting girls desiring to come North." These women discovered that many employment agencies promised the girls lucrative jobs, but when they arrived in the city the girls found waiting for them instead jobs in houses of questionable reputation. The Association stationed an agent in Norfolk, Virginia, where many girls took steamboats to New York, to warn them of the hardships awaiting them in the North. For girls who were not discouraged from moving North or did not come in contact with the organization's southern representative, another worker was posted at New York's docks to meet the newcomers. The White Rose Association also opened a home on East Eighty-sixth Street where girls could stay until they found suitable employment and housing. In addition to housing facilities the Association maintained classes in sewing, cooking, and religious instruction. In 1905 the work of the organization was expanded when a small body of whites and Negroes formed the Association for the Protection of Negro Women. One year later, this little band of dedicated individuals extended its venture to other northern cities with the creation of the National League for the Protection of Colored Women. Using tactics similar to those of the White Rose Association, the National League investigated both the operational methods of employment agencies and the quality of lodgings available to young Negro women. Of the 44 agencies bringing Negro girls to the North, the League found that 17 were "doubtful and unsafe." To meet the perils facing the female migrant, it established six standing committees: travelers' aid, lodging house, education, employment, finance, and membership. It also prepared a list of recommended living quarters for young girls.[25]

Playing a prominent role in the formation of the National League for the Protection of Colored Women was one of the leading white reformers in New York City and the nation, Frances Kellor. Before coming to New York City in 1902 under a fellowship from the College Settlement of New York, Miss Kellor had studied at the University of Chicago and had conducted an investigation into southern prison conditions. Once in the city, she probed into the practices of employment agencies. Her findings were published in her first major book, *Out of Work* (1904). The exposures contained in this book, along with Miss Kellor's further investigations conducted under the auspices of the Inter-Municipal Research Committee, contributed to the passage of a state law regulating the operations of employment agencies. Her rise to prominence among New York reformers led Governor Charles Evans Hughes to appoint her to the Commission on Immigration. Once again her work was responsible for governmental action; this time a Bureau of Industries and Immigration with Miss Kellor as chief investigator was established.[26]

Other leading whites of New York City, too, took part in the work of the National League for the Protection of Colored Women. One was Mary E. Dreier who was the scion of wealthy parents. Most of Miss Dreier's philanthropic ventures were devoted to improving the position of the working girl. Between 1906 and 1915 she was President of the New York Women's Trade Union League of New York. During her tenure as president of that organization, she was also a member of the New York State Factory Investigating Commission. The wife of Haley Fiske, one-time president of the Metropolitan Life Insurance Company and father of that company's public housing program, was a member of the executive board. Many outstanding white residents of the city were listed among the National League's financial contributors. There was William Willcox, lawyer, associate of Jacob Riis, and Commissioner for Parks during the reform administration of Mayor Seth Low. In the last mentioned position, Willcox worked toward the full development of open air playgrounds. Another contributor was Edith Carpenter Macy, a staunch supporter of the Girl Scout movement. Her husband, Valentine E. Macy, was a member of the famed Macy family and an occasional reform candidate for political office. Still another donor was Robert C. Ogden of the John Wanamaker department stores and a trustee of two Negro colleges — Tuskegee and Hampton. From the investment house of Kuhn, Loeb and Company came Paul M. Warburg. The German-born Warburg earned a national reputation as a financier, and, in 1914, President Woodrow Wilson appointed him to the Federal Reserve Board.[27]

In addition to these whites, some of the city's foremost Negroes supported the League. Fred Moore, T. Thomas Fortune's successor as editor of the *Age*; Dr. William L. Bulkley, the leading Negro educator in the city of New York during the first decade of the twentieth century; Dr. Eugene P. Roberts, physician, department of health inspector, and member of many organizations endeavoring to improve the status of the Negro; the Reverend William H. Brooks, minister, organizer of the Citizens' Protective League, and later a member of both the NAACP and the Urban League. Negro participation in the undertakings of the National League for the Protection of Colored Women signified an important departure from the membership composition of earlier philanthropic organizations: for the first time, Negroes in any appreciable numbers shared responsibility for the operation of charitable agencies helping the more unfortunate members of their race.[28]

In 1906 this cooperative effort between Negroes and whites resulted in the creation of the Committee for Improving the Industrial Conditions of Negroes in New York. As its name connotes, this group endeavored to improve the economic status of the Negro. The Committee devised programs that it hoped would lead to wider employment opportunities, preparation for work in the skilled trades, improvement of neighborhood conditions, and extensive business investments. Through the efforts of one of its vice-chairmen, William L. Bulkley, the Board of Education opened night schools in Negro districts. Along with Dr. Bulkley,

other Negroes joined the organization's executive committee:
Charles W. Anderson, a leading politician, William H. Brooks,
Fred Moore, and Eugene P. Roberts. Nor was the white membership any less impressive. As chairman, the Committee selected
William Jay Schieffelin. Descended from a family of German
origin that traced its arrival in the New World to 1740, young
William entered his father's prosperous wholesale drug business
as a chemist. Driven by a desire to improve society, Schieffelin
participated in movements for honest government, decent working conditions, and better housing facilities. In 1896 he was appointed Civil Service Commissioner for the New York district.
In the next year, Schieffelin's fervent desire to see the end of
corruption brought him into the newly created Citizens' Union.
Also listed as members of the Committee for Improving the Industrial Conditions of Negroes in New York were such eminent
whites as Paul U. Kellogg, George McAneny, and Mary Ovington. Kellogg performed invaluable service for the Charity Organization such as directing, in association with Florence Kelley, the
widely known Pittsburgh survey of 1907–1908 into the living conditions of the laboring class. George McAneny battled for civil
service reform and improved housing. From 1910 to 1913 he
served as borough president of Manhattan.[29]

The Committee for Improving the Industrial Conditions of
Negroes not only named whites and Negroes to its various committees, it assumed a somewhat different approach to the Negro's economic problems than had its predecessors. Where earlier
philanthropic groups trained Negroes for the "usual" Negro occupations as seamstresses, washerwomen, janitors, servants, and
general laborers, the Committee prepared the race for positions
that were considered the exclusive province of whites. Where
the Committee's precursors made little or no mention of economic
discrimination, the Committee met the question head on. It considered the denial of equal economic opportunity a fatal blow to
the morale of the race. As a Negro youth told one of the Committee's vice-chairmen, Dr. Bulkley, in 1905: "Why should I finish
my course? What can a colored boy find to do?" [30]

The failure of organizations to unite their efforts, though,
debilitated the programs instituted by the Committee and its
forerunners. Outside of an occasional joint venture, the charitable
groups failed to join forces in their assault on the social evils fac-

ing Negroes. Their activities were a disjointed conglomeration of unrelated attempts to raise the living standards of the Negro population. To remedy this situation, Mrs. William H. Baldwin, the widow of the former president of the Long Island Railroad and a warm supporter of Booker T. Washington, called a meeting in the spring of 1910 of whites and Negroes interested in the New York Negro's plight. As a result of this gathering, the Committee on Urban Conditions Among Negroes was created. The new organization's primary purpose was to encourage greater cooperation between agencies laboring among the city's Negro residents. One year after its formation, the Committee on Urban Conditions Among Negroes merged with the Committee for Improving the Industrial Conditions of Negroes and the National League for the Protection of Colored Women into a new group, the National League on Urban Conditions Among Negroes (the Urban League).[31]

Selected as chairman of the new organization was E. R. A. Seligman, professor of economics in Columbia University, staunch defender of the Interstate Commerce Commission, proponent of honest government, advocate of a comprehensive conservation program, and a member of various social reform groups. Two of the vice-chairmen were Mrs. Baldwin and William Bulkley. As assistant treasurer the League chose L. Hollingsworth Wood, a Quaker and founder of the American Friends Service Committee. Later in his career, Wood was to be elected president of the Urban League. Among the members of the executive board and the finance committee were Felix Adler, founder of the Society for Ethical Culture, member of the Tenement House Commission, the Lexow Committee, and the National Child Labor Committee; Paul D. Craveth, a lawyer for Kuhn, Loeb and Company and son of the founder of the American Missionary Association and the first president of Fisk University; Mrs. Haley Fiske; Frances Kellor; and William Jay Schieffelin. Also listed as members of the policy-making bodies of the organization were prominent Negroes. Dr. Bulkley was chosen one of the vice-chairmen, Eugene Kinckle Jones began as field secretary and later became executive secretary, and George F. Haynes, who had earned a Ph.D. in sociology at Columbia University, was also appointed field secretary. Members of the various committees included William H. Brooks, Eugene P. Roberts, Fred Moore, R. R. Moton, and A.

Clayton Powell. Ironically, the Urban League included supporters of both the Du Bois and Washington groups.[32]

The Urban League cooperated from time to time with almost every group servicing the Negro community. It worked with the Charity Organization, the Children's Aid Society, the Henry Street Settlement, the Public Education Association, and even governmental agencies. The Charity Organization, which had conducted one of the earliest studies of Negro life in northern cities, sought to raise the living and health standards of the Negro community.[33] These cooperative ventures entered almost every aspect of city life save the question of civil rights which was left to the NAACP. As discussed in chapters one and two, the Urban League took an active part in improving neighborhood conditions and seeking new fields of employment for Negroes. Subcommittees were set up to find decent housing, to improve neighborhood conditions, to encourage a sense of neighborhood pride, to train Negroes for skilled occupations, and to find jobs for those who used its facilities. The League devoted a large portion of its efforts to laboring among the young people of the Negro community. Clubs for boys and girls were established; Big Brother and Big Sister units were set up to help youths on the verge of a life of crime. The League petitioned the city to open playgrounds and bathhouses in Harlem. In 1913 the basement of Public School 89, a predominantly Negro school, was opened as an afternoon playground. Within two years it was a full-fledged community center (Lenox Community Center) for young and old alike. Sporting events, dances, movies, and meetings of mothers were held at the school. In 1918, through the efforts of John Royall, a Negro political leader, and the Mutual Life Insurance Company, a vacant lot on 138th Street was converted into a playground. Local streets, too, were turned into play areas. In 1917 the city approved the erection of a bathhouse in Harlem. At the same time, the League sent youngsters to camp during the summer months. Using land donated by the Negro real estate firm of Nail and Parker, a boys' camp was erected at Verona, New Jersey. Cooperating with both the Negro Fresh Air Fund and the Tribune Fresh Air Fund, the Urban League sent a few Negro children on country vacations. In 1918 the Boys' Welfare Association was formed in Harlem to furnish recreational facilities for Negro youths. Still the League was not satisfied with these few gains; in 1920, then, it began a campaign to raise $10,000 to augment the operations of one of its affiliates, the North Harlem Community Service.[34]

Basic to the League's program for young people, naturally, was the desire to reduce juvenile crime. The work of the Big Brothers and Big Sisters, for example, was directed at those on the verge of lawlessness. The League's staff discovered that Negro youngsters who ran afoul of the law were denied adequate correctional facilities. Law-abiding and lawless Negroes faced the discriminatory ways of the wider community. The Public Education Association reported in 1913 that with few exceptions most private institutions for delinquent children, especially those for girls, barred their doors to Negro children. In 1913 the *Age* observed that public as well as private correctional institutions discriminated against the Negro juvenile lawbreaker. And, in 1912, Eugene Kinckle Jones wrote to Mayor William Gaynor that the present method of dealing with wayward Negro youths was unsatisfactory. Jones maintained that the children's court failed to investigate adequately the background of the youthful offender. He suggested that Negro probation officers be appointed, for they could achieve "a closer insight into the family life of colored homes . . . and as a consequence better results could be obtained." [35] Of particular concern to the Urban League and other Negro groups was the plight of the female offender. The Utopia Neighborhood Club, the Harlem Utilitarian Neighborhood Club, and the Conference of Organizations for the Assistance of Young Women — all subcommittees of the Urban League — called for the establishment of a separate correctional institution for wayward Negro girls. They held benefits to raise money to accomplish this purpose. In 1915 these efforts culminated in the opening of the Sojourner Truth House on West 131st Street. At about the same time, the Empire Friendly Shelter was located in Harlem as a "rescue home for unfortunate colored girls and women" and to provide a "proper environment for such young women to begin life anew." These facilities, though, only partially met the needs of the Negro community, for in 1919 members of the Urban League were still calling for additional facilities.[36]

For the Negro community, in general, the Urban League publicized the various services furnished by city and private agencies. In 1916, for example, it published a booklet, *What you need, Where to find it, How to use what you find.* This publication gave the location of local hospitals, clinics, milk stations, a Legal Aid Society branch, police stations, day and evening schools, playgrounds and recreation centers, and libraries.

Although many New York Negroes benefited from the facilities maintained by the Urban League and other philanthropic agencies, the resources of these organizations fell short of meeting the needs of a Negro population that had increased by more than 65 per cent between 1910 and 1920 and was still growing. As late as 1918, the Department of Health reported that Negro Harlem needed day nurseries, a Wassermann clinic, workers to visit the homes of Negro children, a park, more social, educational, and cultural centers, and wholesome amusements. But population growth was not the only impediment to effective charitable assistance. White and Negro commentators reported that many charitable groups refused to accommodate Negroes. On the whole, noted the *Outlook* in 1912, "little organized work in behalf of colored children" was practiced. It reported that of the 102 vacation schools operated by the Daily Vacation Bible Association in New York City during the summer of 1911, not one welcomed Negroes. Even the national director of the Bible School Association, R. G. Boville, admitted that too many "Christian philanthropists . . . appear to be indifferent to the aggravated need of the Negro." The *Age*, writing in a similar vein in 1913, observed that when Negroes attempted to obtain aid from many white charities they were told that no accommodations were available — the race received only the crumbs of charity. In the same year, a Public Education Association study maintained that the Women's Municipal League and the Women's Health Protective Association disregarded the plight of the Negro, while others gave only token service. The Tribune Fresh Air Fund, while cooperating with the Urban League, maintained a camp on Long Island for Negroes inferior to that provided whites.[37]

Those agencies working with Negroes also were hampered by a shortage of funds; they received far less financial support than that made available to organizations catering to whites. Moreover, the southern Negro received more philanthropic assistance than his northern counterpart. This preoccupation with the plight of the southern Negro disturbed the *Age*. The newspaper told those who were philanthropically inclined that "Charity should begin at home." Nor could needy Negroes rely to any great extent on their own race for assistance. Because of their limited resources they had to appeal to wealthy whites for aid. Unlike the Jewish immigrant, the Negro had no element of its citizenry comparable to the affluent German-Jewish community of the city to help him in his time of need.

Many of those organizations servicing the Negro community undermined their programs because of their failure to develop a dialogue with the Negro world. Frequently, their conception of the Negro was based on stereotypes. The Charity Organization, for example, claimed that the Negro was "more self-reliant in poverty than whites," that he was "slower to seek assistance and more eager to be independent again." Such a statement was a misplaced compliment and a misinterpretation of the Negro's attitude toward charity, for, as the Urban League so clearly indicated in its bulletins informing Negroes how to utilize almsgiving facilities, many Negroes did not even know how to seek charitable help. This was particularly so in the case of the southern newcomer. The anti-Negro attitude of many philanthropic enterprises, too, may have discouraged a sizable Negro element from appealing for benevolences. In addition, too many charitable societies failed to involve Negroes in their programs, thereby assuming a paternalistic attitude apart from the main body of Negro thinking. Negroes, on occasion, complained that they were given "limited representation on the managing boards and responsible working force" of charitable agencies. The Urban League attempted to alleviate this problem by providing qualified Negroes with fellowships for the study of social work.[38]

Also reducing the effectiveness of the coterie of almsgiving enterprises, including the Urban League, was the segregated nature of their operations. Perhaps these agencies viewed the Negro's social and economic problems worthy of separate treatment; still they encouraged the exclusion of the Negro from the wider community. With the exception of the Urban League and the Committee for Improving the Industrial Conditions of Negroes in New York, most charitable groups did little to widen the Negro's vistas, to expand his economic possibilities, to move him in the direction of first-class citizenship. At best, they gave the unemployed poor jobs at the bottom of the economic ladder, taught people how to keep clean homes in slums, took children off the street for part of the day and returned them to their small, crowded apartments at night and to the discrimination of the wider community in adulthood. They also trained mothers to be better homemakers but rarely worked toward the expansion of their budgets through higher paying employment for either themselves, their husbands, or their children. As indicated, the Urban League attempted to meet both sides of these problems; however, their success was dependent on the decline of prejudice among employers, landlords, and the white community at large. As of 1920, unfortunately, this had not occurred.

An important agency for the improvement of the Negro's position in society was education. Since more Negroes attended the public schools than any other educational institution, the kind of education they received there was of great importance to the future of the Negro community. In 1865 separate "colored" schools were available for the education of Negro children, but to judge from the records the results were not impressive. These educational institutions were the ultimate successors to the African Free School established by the Manumission Society in 1787. In 1834 the Manumission Society transferred the Negro schools to the Public School Society, and, in 1853, they became part of the city's school system.[39] The city, though, failed to devote adequate funds to educating Negro youths; while Negroes accounted for 1.6 per cent of the population of New York City, only 0.1 per cent of the 1859 school budget was used to educate Negroes. Between 1853 and 1864, however, a few Negroes entered schools reserved for white children. But as a result of the draft riots of 1863, the Common School Act of 1864 permitted local school authorities to provide separate but equal facilities for Negro children.[40]

In 1864 the inferior academic performance and poor attendance record of the "colored" schools gave rise to concern on the part of the members of the Board of Education. In that year, S. S. Randall, the Superintendent of Schools, reported that scholarship was "only fair"; attendance was "irregular"; and teacher qualifications were "not of the highest grade." He called for the replacement of the Negro teachers with white teachers of "superior" ability. Negro leaders agreed with Superintendent Randall's complaints as to Negro attendance, but disagreed with his proposal to replace the Negro teachers. In 1865 the principal of a New York "colored" school told the Annual Conference of the New York African Methodist Episcopal Church that the education of Negro children had been "sadly neglected by parents and guardians." The principal rebuked Negro elders for removing youngsters from school "for the most trifling and frivolous reason." Parents had taken their children from school "whenever a job for them became available." The *Weekly Anglo African,* in 1865, joined the Negro educator in criticizing the apathetic attitude of Negro parents toward education. It counseled mothers and fathers to "complete the freedom of our race by educating the present generation of children." However, the newspaper condemned Randall's plan to replace Negro teachers with white instructors. "We must have our own educators," the paper argued, "as well as our own education." Possibly, in reaction to the criticism of the Negro teacher, Charles L. Reason, principal of one of the "colored" schools and the leading Negro educator in the city, reorganized the "colored" Normal School.[41]

According to the Board of Education report for 1866, Negroes disregarded the advice of their leaders:

> It is to be regretted that the colored people have not fully understood the advantages they enjoy in the privileges of these schools, and it is with sorrow that your Committee have to report that they have not had the cordial co-operation of the parents and guardians of the colored children of this city in securing a larger and more regular attendance at the schools.

In an attempt to meet this situation, the Board of Education reorganized the "colored" schools in 1866. It removed these institutions from the control of local school boards and placed them under the direction of a five-man Committee on Colored Schools. Under the management of the local boards, the "colored" schools had been "wholly or in part neglected," the Board of Education reported. The new system, it contended, would result in "greater care" in teacher appointments. The "colored" schools were reorganized into five centers, dispersed throughout Manhattan. The Board reported that this arrangement was utilized to meet the "scattered" nature of the Negro population, which colonized in specific areas.[42]

For the remainder of the 1860s, the Superintendent of Schools continued to complain of the low rate of attendance at the "colored" schools. But in 1868 a Negro school building was opened at 155 Stanton Street in answer to the demands of the Negro population of that area.

During the 1870s Negro attendance at the "colored" schools remained below the Board's expectations. The city's educational leadership ascribed the cause of the high rate of truancy among Negro youths to their economic condition. In 1871 the Board of Education discovered that Negro parents had neither "fixed wages or steady employment."

> They are therefore subject to changes incidental to such mere temporary engagements, and their family arrangements are consequently liable to many vicissitudes. From these causes a large number of the children are called from school at a very early age, and are placed temporarily wherever their services will bring in a few dollars to aid in the support of themselves and their parents, without much regard to the bad effect of such a course upon the instruction of the children.

And, in 1873, it added:

> The poverty of so many of the parents, and their consequent need of the service of their children, as well as the long distance the latter have to go in order to attend the schools, so widely scattered as they are, render it impossible that the same regularity should exist in these schools as in others.[43]

A decline in enrollment in the "colored" schools after 1874 may be attributed to the fact that all of the city's schools were opened to Negro students under the provisions of the state Civil Rights Act of 1873. (The struggle to abolish segregated schools will be discussed in the next chapter.) By 1878 some 858 Negro children were enrolled in the "colored" schools and 159 others were in the predominantly white school houses of the city. Five years later, only 39 per cent of the enrolled Negro students of New York City attended the "colored" schools.[44]

The movement of the Negro population within the city provides another explanation for the poor enrollment at the separate Negro schools. The change in the Negro residence pattern was reflected in the closing of a number of the "colored" schools. Between 1872 and 1879, three of the six segregated schools were eliminated. The three remaining "colored" schools were located in the Greenwich Village neighborhood and the northern and southern portions of the Tenderloin district — areas that still had a sizable Negro population. These schools were closed when the Board of Education abolished the "colored" schools in 1884.[45]

Despite these changes in the school system, Negro leaders continued to be concerned about Negro truancy. In 1886 the *Freeman* observed that only 300 Negro children attended school while some 5,000 were "playing and loafing" in the streets. It suggested that the appointment of a Negro truant officer would solve the attendance problem. One year later, the paper blamed the low attendance and enrollment at Ward School 81, the successor to one of the "colored" schools, on the impression conveyed to Negro youngsters by their parents that "the tutor of his own race and color" was "totally incapable of instructing and advancing him." The low rate of enrollment at Ward School 81 was attested to in 1890 by the appeal of the Negro principal of the school for Negro newcomers to enroll their children in her school. Poor attendance remained a problem into the twentieth century. A study completed in 1913 by the Public Education Association reported that Negro truancy was still high. But the report noted that the deprivation the Negro faced at home and in the outside world was beyond the control of the Board of Education.[46]

The failure of Negroes to obtain jobs in other than the most menial fields led many Negro youths to question the value of an education. As early as 1818 the New York Mission Society reported that those Negroes trained in the schools of the city were compelled to spend their time "in idleness" despite their education. From this inactivity, concluded the Society, they acquire "those vicious habits which were calculated to render their previous education worse than useless." [47] William L. Bulkley made a similar observation almost a century later. What good was an education, the Negro educator asked rhetorically, when prejudiced whites denied Negroes employment in the fields for which they had been trained? Other factors worked toward a high truancy and drop-out rate among Negroes of school age. According to the Public Education Association report of 1913, those Negroes who came to the city from the South "had not had the school habit inculcated in them" because of the failure of southern school boards to provide adequate educational facilities for Negroes or because of the southern tradition of noncompulsory education. Furthermore, the report continued, since so many Negro parents lacked an education they could not help their children with their school assignments. The necessity of mothers to find employment also had a detrimental effect on the child. Too often, working parents could not insure their child's attendance at school and could not participate in school activities.[48]

The prejudice of many white teachers, noted a number of commentators, undermined a normal school-student relationship. Helena Titus Emerson reported in 1905 that the white teacher often discriminated against the Negro youngster. Negro students received "outrageous treatment" from teachers, alleged W. E. B. Du Bois in 1907. The Public Education Association observed similar attitudes. On occasion, white teachers protested the appointment of Negro instructors to schools with faculties composed entirely of whites.[49] Moreover, most Negro children — as will be seen in the next chapter — attended predominantly Negro schools despite the abolition of segregation in the city's schools.

Some advances in the quality of education offered Negro youths, however, were made. The man most responsible for these changes in the public school system was William L. Bulkley. As principal of a predominantly Negro school in the early 1900s, Dr. Bulkley improved not only the curriculum of that school but turned it into a virtual "social center." Frequent home visits and meetings with parents became a regular feature of the school program. Parents' meetings were not only devoted to discussing the educational problems of their children, but matters of concern to all Negroes. Dr. Bulkley delivered speeches at Negro churches, thereby establishing contact with those Negroes who did not use his school's facilities. Nor was the social side of life ignored — evening social events became a regular attraction at Dr. Bulkley's school. "It is here," wrote a white educator of the school, "that we see the effort being made to make the school a social centre for the parent and the child." Dr. Bulkley also developed an evening school program for working youths and adults. Classes were offered "to train men for larger industrial worth to themselves and to the community." Emphasis was placed on courses in bookkeeping, stenography, typewriting, electricity, carpentry, and preparation for civil service examinations. So successful was Dr. Bulkley's evening school that similar schools were opened for Negroes in Brooklyn and other sections of Manhattan.[50]

Yet, these efforts in and of themselves were at best only a step forward. Negroes still had to face the prejudice of the white community in seeking wider employment opportunities, better housing, and general equality. For without a change in the attitude of the white community, all the assistance of friendly whites and the efforts of Negroes in their own behalf would be for naught. As Alexis de Tocqueville observed some twenty years before the Civil War: "To induce whites to abandon the opinion they have conceived of the moral and intellectual inferiority of their former slaves, the Negroes must change; but as long as this opinion persists, they cannot change." [51]

Notes

[1] Aaron I. Abell, *The Urban Impact on American Protestantism, 1865–1900* (Cambridge, 1943), pp. 27–56; Robert H. Bremner, *From the Depths: the Discovery of Poverty in the United States* (New York, 1956), pp. 57–60; Franklin, *From Slavery to Freedom*, pp. 377–81; Henry F. May, *Protestant Churches and Industrial America* (New York, 1949), pp. 39–50.

[2] Association for the Benefit of Colored Children, *Annual Report, 1878* (New York, 1879), p. 5; Colored Orphan Asylum and Association for the Benefit of Colored Children, *Annual Report, 1881* (New York, 1882), p. 6; *From Cherry Street to Green Pastures: a History of the Colored Orphan Asylum at Riverdale-On-Hudson* (New York, 1936), pp. 1–28; "Mission Sketches," *Charities*, XV (October 7, 1905), 59–63; *Crisis*, XIII (March, 1917), 240; *Milestones*, II (May, 1910), 3–4.

[3] Howard Colored Orphan Asylum Society, *Annual Report, 1885* (Brooklyn, 1886), pp. 5, 21, 24; *Milestones*, II (May, 1910), 6–7.

[4] *New York Age*, March 30, 1889, and January 4, 1900; Colored Home, *Annual Report, 1865–1866* (New York, 1866), pp. 7, 24; *Annual Report, 1913* (New York,

1914), pp. 34–35; *Milestones*, II (May, 1910), 2–4; *New York Times*, May 2, 1867, and November 28, 1869.

[5] Blascoer, *Colored School Children*, pp. 172–73; *Milestones*, II (May, 1910), 5–6; New York Colored Mission, *Annual Report, 1871* (New York, 1872), pp. 4, 7; *Annual Report, 1872* (New York, 1873), pp. 4–5; *Annual Report, 1874* (New York, 1875), p. 4; *Annual Report, 1875* (New York, 1876), pp. 6–7; *Annual Report, 1877* (New York, 1878), p. 6; *Annual Report, 1879* (New York, 1880), pp. 6–8; *Annual Report, 1881* (New York, 1882), p. 7; *Annual Report, 1883* (New York, 1884), p. 7; *Annual Report, 1916* (New York, 1917), pp. 11–12.

[6] New York Colored Mission, *Annual Report, 1872*, p. 7; *Papers from the Records of the New York City Mission and Tract Society* (New York, 1866), p. 51; *Suffragist*, January 22, 1880.

[7] Abell, *Urban Impact*, pp. 5–7, 246; Bremner, *From the Depths*, pp. 124–26; May, *Protestant Churches*, pp. 202–203.

[8] Abell, *Urban Impact*, pp. 188–89; Federation of Churches, *Canvass No. 2*, pp. 21, 26, 85, 90–92; New York City Mission and Tract Society,

Annual Report, 1890, p. 142; "Seven Years of Social Exploration," *Federation*, III (June, 1903), 1–24.

⁹ *New York Age*, March 12, 1908, and August 3, 1916; Blascoer, *Colored School Children*, p. 176; *Milestones*, II (May, 1910), 8–9.

¹⁰ *New York Age*, May 4, 1911; Blascoer, *Colored School Children*, p. 176; *Milestones*, II (May, 1910), 7, 11.

¹¹ *New York Age*, October 30, 1913, and January 3, 1920; *Crisis*, VII (January, 1914), 130; *New York Times*, April 28, 1889; Blascoer, *Colored School Children*, p. 175; Cleveland Allen, "Work of the Y.M.C.A. of New York City," *Colored American Magazine*, XIV (May, 1908), 273–75; John Smith Brown, Jr., "The New York Branch of the Y.M.C.A.," *ibid.*, VII (June, 1904), 411; R. P. Hamlin, "Work of the Y.M.C.A. Among the Young Colored Men of Brooklyn, N. Y.," *ibid.*, XIV (June, 1908), 337–38.

¹² *New York Age*, November 2, 1889, and October 10, 1912; Blascoer, *Colored School Children*, pp. 60–61, 173. For an examination of Catholic charitable enterprises, see Aaron I. Abell, *American Catholicism and Social Action: a Search for Social Justice, 1865–1950* (New York, 1960), pp. 27–53.

¹³ Carl N. Degler, *Out of Our Past: the Forces that Shaped Modern America* (New York, 1959), p. 373; Jane Addams quoted in Charles A. and Mary R. Beard, *The Rise of American Civilization* (2 vols., New York, 1933), II, 421.

¹⁴ Joseph Fels, who made his fortune from the manufacture of soap products, promised "to spend the damnable money to wipe out the system by which I made it." Quoted in George E. Mowry, *The Era of Theodore Roosevelt, 1900–1912* (New York, 1958), p. 94. Andrew Carnegie, on the other hand, wrote that the "masses reap the principal benefit" from the fortunes gathered by the few. Rich men, too, "should be thankful for one inestimable boon. They have it in their power during their lives to busy themselves in organizing benefactions from which the masses of their fellows will derive lasting advantage, and thus dignify their own lives." *Gospel of Wealth and Other Timely Essays* (New York, 1901), pp. 13–14.

¹⁵ Franklin, *From Slavery to Freedom*, pp. 377–84.

¹⁶ For racism and the progressive movement, see Mowry, *Era of Theodore Roosevelt*, pp. 92–94; for Roosevelt's attitude toward the Negro, see Scheiner, "President Theodore Roosevelt and the Negro, 1901–1908," *Journal of Negro History*, XLVII (July, 1962), 169–82; and for Lillian Wald, see Blascoer, *Colored School Children*, pp. 174–75.

¹⁷ *Milestones*, II (May, 1910), 8.

¹⁸ *Ibid.; New York Age*, January 9, 1913; Blascoer, *Colored School Children*, pp. 173–74; Emerson, "Children of the Circle," pp. 81–82; Free Kindergarten Association for Colored Children, *Annual Report for 1905* (New York, 1905), pp. 1–2; *Annual Report for 1912* (New York, 1912), unpaged; *Annual Report for 1913* (New York, 1913), unpaged.

¹⁹ Emerson, "Children of the Circle," pp. 81–82; *Dictionary of American Biography* (22 vols., New York, 1928–1958), IV, 83–86; VII, 275–78; IX, 183–84; XI, 540–41; Roy Lubove, *The Progressives and the Slums: Tenement House Reform in New York City, 1890–1917* (Pittsburgh, 1962), pp. 89–90; *National Cyclopedia of American Biography* (54 vols., New York, 1891–1959), XXIV, 319; New York Free Kindergarten Association, *Annual Report, 1899–1900* (New York, 1900), p. 1.

²⁰ *New York Age*, January 9, 1913, and January 18, 1917; Blascoer, *Colored School Children*, pp.

24, 175; *Crisis*, V (February, 1913), 162–64; Free Kindergarten Association for Colored Children, *Annual Report for 1905*, p. 1; *Milestones*, II (May, 1910), 11; NAACP, *Branch Bulletin*, I (April, 1917), 40; Ovington, *Walls Came Tumbling Down*, chapters one and two; Ovington, "The White Brute," *Masses*, V (November, 1915), 17–18.

[21] Maude K. Griffin, "The Hope Day Nursery," *Colored American Magazine*, X (June, 1906), 397–400; *Milestones*, II (May, 1910), 9.

[22] Association of Day Nurseries of New York City, *Annual Report, 1912* (New York, 1912), p. 4; *DAB*, XVII, 213–14 and Supplement II, 37–38; Griffin, "Hope Day Nursery," 397; *National Cyclopedia of American Biography*, XV, 277–78; XXI, 26–27; XXXIX, 74–75; *New York Tribune*, May 30, 1902.

[23] *New York Age*, January 9, 1913; Blascoer, *Colored School Children*, pp. 174–75; *DAB*, Supplement II, 687–88.

[24] *New York Age*, May 4, 1911, and December 26, 1913; Blascoer, *Colored School Children*, p. 174.

[25] Blascoer, *Colored School Children*, p. 175; *Charities*, XIV (June 10, 1905), 825–26; *Milestones*, II (May, 1910), 8, 10; National League for the Protection of Colored Women, *Annual Report, 1910–1911*, pp. 2–6; White Rose Industrial Association, *Annual Report, 1911*, pp. 4–7.

[26] Frances A. Kellor, "Assisted Emigration from the South: the Women," *Charities*, XV (October 7, 1905), 15–17; *National Cyclopedia of American Biography*, XV, 248–49; E. M. Rhodes, "The Protection of Girls Who Travel: a National Movement," *Colored American Magazine*, XIII (August, 1907), 114–15.

[27] *DAB*, VI, 419–20; XII, 179; XIII, 641–42; XIX, 412–13; *National Cyclopedia of American Biography*, XIV, 382; i, 266; National League for the Protection of Colored Women, *Annual Report, 1910–1911*, p. 2.

[28] National League for the Protection of Colored Women, *Annual Report, 1910–1911*, p. 2; Clement Richardson, ed., *National Cyclopedia of the Colored Race* (Montgomery, 1919), p. 226; *Who's Who in Colored America* (6 vols., Yonkers, 1927–1950), II, 313.

[29] *New York Age*, May 17, July 12, 1906; May 14, 1908; May 25, 1909; Bremner, *From the Depths*, pp. 54–56; *Colored American Magazine*, XIII (September, 1907), 210; "Work of the Committee for Improving the Industrial Conditions of Negroes in New York," *ibid.*, XII (June, 1907), 459–64; Lubove, *Progressives and the Slums*, pp. 238–39; *National Cyclopedia of American Biography*, XLIV, 52–53; *Who's Who in America, 1952–1953* (Chicago, 1953), p. 1321.

[30] *New York Age*, May 17, 1906; May 14, 1908; May 25, 1909; William L. Bulkley, "The School as a Social Center," *Charities*, XV (October 7, 1905), 76.

[31] *Crisis*, VIII (September, 1914), 243–44; *DAB*, I, 548–49; National League for the Protection of Colored Women, *Annual Report, 1910–1911*, p. 7; National League on Urban Conditions Among Negroes, *Report for 1910–1911*, pp. 4–6.

[32] *DAB*, Supplement I, 13–14; Supplement II, 130–31, 606–609; National League on Urban Conditions Among Negroes, *Report for 1910–1911*, p. 3, and *Report for 1915–1916*, p. 3; National Urban League, *Report for 1917–1918* (New York, 1918), p. 1; Wood obit. in *New York Times*, July 23, 1956.

[33] Brooklyn Urban League for Social Service Among Negroes, *Annual Report, 1919* (New York, 1919), pp. 4–7; National League on Urban Conditions Among Negroes, *Report for 1915–1916*, pp. 15–16; *Report for 1916–1917*, pp. 11–12; and *What*

you need, Where to find it, How to use what you find (New York, 1916), pp. 4–5. For the work of Charity Organization among Negroes, see, for example, *New York Age,* June 29, 1905, and December 29, 1917; "The Negro in the Cities of the North," *Charities,* XV (October 7, 1905), 1–96.

[34] National League on Urban Conditions Among Negroes, *Report for 1910–1911,* pp. 15–16; *Report for 1911–1912,* pp. 25–26; *Report for 1913–1914 and 1914–1915,* p. 19; *Report for 1915–1916,* pp. 9, 13; *New York Age,* February 20, 1913; July 9, 1914; August 5, 1915; February 22, 1917; January 17, 1920; *New York Times,* June 22, 1920.

[35] Blascoer, *Colored School Children,* pp. 28–32; National League on Urban Conditions Among Negroes, *Report for 1911–1912,* pp. 25–26, and *Report for 1912–1913,* pp. 15–16; *New York Age,* June 12, July 25, 1913; Eugene Kinckle Jones to Mayor William J. Gaynor, October 26, 1912, Gaynor Papers, New York City Municipal Archives.

[36] *New York Age,* September 5, 1912; June 12, July 25, 1913; September 28, October 19, 1916; April 19, 1919; *Crisis,* VIII (September, 1914), 244; National League on Urban Conditions Among Negroes, *Report for 1913–1914 and 1914–1915,* pp. 18–19, and *What you need,* p. 8; New York City Department of Health, *Everybody's Chronicle,* I (August, 1915), 1. Closely related to the Urban League's activities in behalf of youths was its campaign to ameliorate the unsanitary and unhealthful conditions that pervaded many areas of Negro life. It cooperated with the Health Department, for instance, in distributing literature advising Negroes on proper health habits and in maintaining milk stations. It joined with the Association for the Prevention of Heart Disease in studying the incidence of heart disease among Negro children. *New York Age,* April 8, 1915, and February 22, 1917; National League on Urban Conditions Among Negroes, *Report for 1916–1917,* p. 11; New York City Department of Health, *Weekly Bulletin,* VI (April 7, 1917), 105; *Survey,* XXXVII (December 30, 1916), 37, and XLIV (June 12, 1920), 381.

[37] *New York Age,* September 4, 1913, and March 2, 1918; Blascoer, *Colored School Children,* pp. 34–38; *Outlook,* CI (June 29, 1912), 458.

[38] *New York Age,* March 6, June 26, September 4, 1913; May 18, 1916; March 6, 1920; Franklin, *From Slavery to Freedom,* pp. 377–82; National League on Urban Conditions Among Negroes, "Social Service Fellowships for 1917–1918," *Bulletin,* VI (October, 1916), unpaged; *Report for 1913–1914 and 1914–1915,* p. 13; *Report for 1916–1917,* p. 9.

[39] Charles C. Andrews, *History of the New York African Free Schools* (New York, 1830), p. 7; Hirsch, "The Negro and New York," pp. 426–31; New York City Board of Education, *Annual Report for 1884* (New York, 1885), p. 52. (Hereafter cited as B.E., *Report.*)

[40] Hirsch, "The Negro and New York," p. 427; *New York State Statutes At Large, 1864* (Albany, 1864), p. 357; *New York Tribune,* August 24, 1899.

[41] B.E., *Report for 1864* (New York, 1865), Appendix, p. 16, and *Report for 1865* (New York, 1866), Appendix, p. 35; African Methodist Episcopal Church, *Minutes of the New York Annual Conference of 1865* (New York, 1865), pp. 26–28; *Weekly Anglo African,* August 12, 19, 1865.

[42] B.E., *Report for 1866* (New York, 1867), pp. 12–13, 100; *Report for 1868* (New York, 1869),

Appendix, unpaged; *Report of Committee on Colored Schools for 1866* (New York, 1866), p. 4.

[43] B.E., *Report for 1869* (New York, 1870), p. 180–81; *Report for 1871* (New York, 1872), p. 43; *Report for 1873* (New York, 1874), p. 34; *Directory for 1868* (New York, 1869), p. 138.

[44] B.E., *Report for 1871–1879, passim; Journal for 1878* (New York, 1879), p. 816; *New York Statutes At Large, 1873* (Albany, 1873), pp. 583–84.

[45] B.E., *Directory for 1881* (New York, 1882), pp. 167–69; *Journal for 1872* (New York, 1873), pp. 396, 656–57; *Journal for 1875* (New York, 1876), p. 244; *Journal for 1883* (New York, 1884), pp. 370–71; *Report for 1878* (New York, 1879), p. 87.

[46] *New York Freeman,* September 11, 1886; *New York Age,* April 5, 1890; Blascoer, *Colored School Children,* p. 18.

[47] Quoted in Arnett G. Lindsay, "The Economic Condition of the Negroes of New York Prior to 1861," *Journal of Negro History,* VI (April, 1921), p. 142.

[48] Blascoer, *Colored School Children,* pp. 13–14, 16–21; Bulkley, "The Industrial Condition of the Negro in New York City," p. 592; "The School as a Social Center," p. 76.

[49] *New York Age,* October 3, 1907, and July 22, 1909; *New York Times,* May 8, 1901; *New York Tribune,* December 28, 1899; Blascoer, *Colored School Children,* pp. 13–14, 16–21; Emerson, "Children of the Circle," p. 83; Ovington, *Half A Man,* p. 18.

[50] *New York Age,* April 6, 1905; May 14, 1908; May 25, 1909; Blascoer, *Colored School Children,* pp. 13–14; Bulkley, "The School as a Social Center," p. 77; *Colored American Magazine,* XIII (August, 1907), 95; National League on Urban Conditions Among Negroes, *What you need,* pp. 4–5.

[51] Quoted in Charles E. Silberman, *Crisis in Black and White* (New York, 1964), p. 13.

.7.

Politics and the Struggle for Equality

DOWN to the present day the Negro's political position has borne a close relation to his struggle for equality. "Negroes have so many odds directed against them and suffer so many injustices," wrote Gunnar Myrdal in 1944, that "it is only natural that when Negroes come to think at all about social and political problems they think nearly exclusively about their own problems." A similar observation was made by Ralph Bunche in a paper prepared for the Myrdal study:

> When the Negro views any matter of broad governmental policy, he ordinarily weighs it not as an American citizen, but as a Negro American. His first queries will always be: "How will it effect 'Negroes'?" "Will it be so administered as to embrace Negroes fairly?" [1]

At least since the Civil War, Negro voters have interpreted a candidate or party's stand on the issue of equality for the Negro as the determining factor in their voting habits; the civil rights issue has been the litmus paper test for candidates hoping to attract the Negro vote. Accordingly, after the Civil War Negroes, in general, allied with the Republican party, the party that had brought down the peculiar institution of slavery. In New York this loyalty to Republicanism was furthered by the party's support of extending the franchise to Negroes on an equal basis with whites.

Following the adoption of a new state constitution in 1821, property qualifications for all prospective New York voters except the Negro disappeared. Negroes who wished to exercise the franchise were required to own a freehold valued at $250. Down to the Civil War attempts to give New York Negroes the vote on an equal basis with whites ended in failure. In 1846 and 1860 the voters of the state rejected proposals for according Negroes voting equality.[2] With the end of the Civil War and the approach of a constitutional convention in 1867 controlled by the Republican party, the New York Negro's chances of receiving an equal vote waxed brighter. Early in the convention the delegates split up into three groups: Democrats who contended that the Negro should not receive voting equality because he was the white man's inferior; those Democrats who were willing to allow the Negro the vote if a majority of the white voters approved the change; and the majority of Republicans who wished to accord Negroes voting equality and opposed a separate referendum on this question. The Republicans believed that the entire constitution with the voting change included should be submitted to the voters.[3]

According to the proponents of the first position, granting the Negro the vote would endanger the democratic system. A Brooklyn Democrat, Henry C. Murphy, argued that extending the ballot to the black man "will confound the races and tend to destroy the fair fabric of democratic institutions, which has been erected by the capacity of the white race." It is "morally and socially wrong," for "political equality . . . will lead to . . . social equality with the white race." Another delegate from New York City, Stephen I. Colahan, contended that "The negro race is a physically discolored and mentally inferior one, dependent, helpless and lazy." Possibly at some future date, Colahan continued, "when the negro can be learned at least in the objects of our government, then I may be willing to extend him the ballot"; but until such time granting equal suffrage to the Negro "would of necessity injure my country and affect my race." Another New York City delegate, Magnus Gross, also asserted that it would "require long and careful training" to make the predominant "animal propensities" of the Negro "subservient to a well-balanced mind and strong moral sense." Abraham B. Conger of Rockland contended that Negroes "cannot maintain good health or a vigorous constitution, or live to old age in this climate of the State of New York." "Frankness," "kindness," and "humanity" requires the intelligent whites of this state to tell Negroes that "'you are destined, by the laws of nature, over which we have no control, to be sojourners in this State.'" And, continued Conger, if the Negro is given political equality he will flock to New York in great numbers. If this happens, "You give him a grave. . . . You offer him liberty and political rights . . . liberty to die." [4]

Where this first group of Democrats resorted to unrestrained attacks on the Negro, a second faction was more reserved in its criticisms of the Negro. Smith M. Weed, a Clinton Democrat, was more optimistic about the Negro's chances of becoming a voter, but "until he is educated, he is not competent to perform the duties of a citizen." However, he concluded, the question of the Negro's ability to be a good citizen had nothing to do with the "real issue" — the right of voters to decide if they wished to accord political equality to the Negro. On the basis of voter rejection of proposals to remove property qualifications for Negroes in 1846 and 1860, Weed and his supporters believed that this change also would be rejected. The Republicans, on the other hand, agreed that the question should be submitted to the voters for approval, but as part of the entire constitution not as a separate question. Patrick Corbett of Onondaga accused the Democrats of using anti-Negro sentiment for political advantage: "Hatred for the negro for the last thirty years has been the political capital of the party." Another Republican argued against the innate inferiority of Negroes. It was "the degradation which slavery brought upon the race" that prevented Negroes from developing their full capacities. Anyone who argues that there are anatomical differences between whites and blacks, concluded Corbett, "is a quack." As still another delegate, Martin I. Townsend of Rensselaer, argued, the Negro was created by the same God that gave life to the white man. Townsend attributed the differences between the races to "worldly circumstances." Despite these arguments, most Republicans spent little time in advancing the theory that all men were created equal — something it appears that many doubted — but to quieting fears that political equality would lead to either a mingling of the races or Negro domination. Townsend contended that there was no danger of intermarriage "by a man who respects his blood." Horace Greeley maintained that the citizens of the state "can afford to be just — nay generous — because we cannot pretend to be afraid of Blacks," since they shun the northern regions of the country.

> I have no doubt that, under the beneficent rule of freedom, they will gradually gravitate toward the tropics, where they belong. They will go there because it is their nature to go there; and they will become still fewer here in proportion to our whole population.[5]

As the convention progressed, however, many Republicans switched from their earlier opposition to a separate vote on the question of abolishing property requirements for prospective Negro voters. Even without the suffrage issue opposition to the constitution was mounting; Republicans, therefore, became convinced that the inclusion of the suffrage change would insure the defeat of the constitution. Thus, the majority of the delegates agreed to submit the change in voting requirements to a separate voter referendum.[6]

In the meantime, the Republicans discovered another way of granting Negroes the franchise free of property requirements. On a strict party vote, and before the state constitution was sent to the electorate for approval, the Republican controlled state legislature ratified the Fifteenth Amendment in 1869. When the proposal to abolish property qualifications for the Negro was put before the voters, however, it was defeated 282,403 to 249,802. There was one encouraging sign: some 47 per cent of the voters declared in favor of equal voting rights for Negroes, whereas only 28 per cent had done so in 1846 and 37 per cent in 1860. Thus, the wishes of the state legislature and a majority of the electorate came into conflict. But when the voters returned a Democratic majority to the state legislature in 1869, the new body proceeded to rescind its predecessor's approval of the Fifteenth Amendment. The Democrats argued that those who proposed the Amendment were contemptuous of the people and "of the right of the State to regulate the elective franchise." It was not until three-fourths of the states ratified the Fifteenth Amendment in March of 1870 that New York Negroes secured the franchise on an equal basis with whites.[7]

Once the vote was obtained, the vast majority of Negroes found little reason to support the Democratic party — the party that had defended slavery, the party that sought to deny them equal voting rights. When New York Democrats, in later years, attempted to appeal to Negro voters they would have to work against this heritage and the anti-Negro actions of their southern counterparts. As will be seen, even when the Republican party deserted the Negro after 1877, most Negroes saw no suitable alternative in the Democracy.

Viewing the acquisition of the vote as a "Heaven-sent bene-faction," the mass of New York Negroes supported the prophet sent from above, the Republican party. So intense was this loy-alty that those Negroes who dared to support the Democracy were regarded as infidels. "This Convention," resolved a meeting of Negroes in Poughkeepsie in 1870, "will discountenance any person or persons who has or will continue to vote the Democratic ticket" and will "consider them an enemy to our race forever." In 1871 a group of pro-Republican Negroes asserted that an alli-ance between Negroes and Democrats would be "disgraceful as would be a copartnership with the Southern Kuklux." [8] Naturally, Negroes voted and campaigned for Republican candidates. Meet-ings were held to affirm Negro support for the presidential candi-dacies of Ulysses S. Grant in 1872 and Rutherford B. Hayes in 1876.[9]

In the two decades following the Civil War, the city's Negro residents experienced other gains than those in connection with the franchise. In 1873 the state legislature passed a law forbidding the exclusion of any person because of race or color from "full and equal enjoyment of any accommodation, advantage, facility, or privilege furnished" by public conveyances, innkeepers, theaters, public schools, licensed owners of public establishments, and other places of public amusement. It also expunged from previous statutes the word "white." In 1881 another act spelled out more clearly the term "licensed owners." Included in this category were hotels, inns, taverns, and restaurants.[10] Although these laws for-bade discrimination in most areas of public life, the Negro, as will be seen later in this chapter, still endured subtle evasions of the law. He was overcharged, given poor service, or was provided with poor facilities at many restaurants, hotels, and theaters. It was often extremely difficult to prove that poor service at a public place was in reality discrimination.

Evasion of the civil rights laws, however, was next to impossible in public transportation. (Where a reserved room or seat was desired, it was a different story.) Before the Civil War public conveyances in New York City had adopted a policy of segregation. Under this practice Negroes were restricted to cars with signs reading "Colored People Allowed in this Car." In 1855 this practice received a setback. A Negro woman who was denied access to a "white" railway car brought a suit for damages against the railway company. The judge ruled that she had a right to travel in the car; the jury found in favor of the woman. But one year later another judge ruled that a railway could exclude a Negro from a "white" car if admitting the Negro to that car would hurt business. Segregation on public conveyances persisted down to and after the Civil War. George Rose, a foreign traveler visiting the city in 1868, reported that Negroes feared ejection from public trolley cars; however, as a result of the state legislature's action in 1873, another visitor to New York in 1886, John Kirkwood, observed that Negroes were treated with "respect" on public conveyances.[11] Negroes also made gains in areas not covered by the civil rights laws. In 1871 the *New York Times* reported that a Negro served on a Manhattan jury. A decade later, John F. Quarles was the first Negro lawyer admitted to the New York bar. In 1881 Negroes were selected for service on a coroner's jury.[12]

During the 1880s Manhattan's Board of Education abandoned its policy of maintaining a segregated school system. Prior to the Civil War years, Negroes had been permitted to enter the predominantly white schools of the city; however, as a result of the draft riots of 1863 this practice was abandoned in 1864. By virtue of the Civil Rights Act of 1873 the city's Board of Education allowed Negro children to reenter schools other than those for Negro students. Consequently, attendance at the separate Negro schools declined, but they continued to operate without any proposal being made for their complete abolition until the late 1870s.

In 1878 Commissioner Ferdinand Traud of the Board of Education introduced a resolution to abolish the "colored" schools as "contrary to the spirit, if not in direct violation" of the act of 1873 that gave all persons use of public school facilities. In addition, he asserted that the separate Negro schools were an unnecessary financial burden. The Committee on Colored Schools rejected the Traud resolution. It argued that the Negroes of the city were opposed to the abolition of the "colored" schools, for if they wished these institutions to be closed they merely had to send their children to the predominantly white schools of the city. Although it appears that the Committee's argument had validity, a Negro newspaper in 1880 called for the termination of the separate Negro schools. It declared that New York City must stop the practice of using "the color of a child's skin" as an excuse "for separation in education matters."

In 1882 the question of closing the "colored" schools was raised by Commissioner Jacob Schiff of the Board of Education. Schiff contended that the "abolishment of social and race prejudice" was one "of the underlying purposes of a public school system." He argued that the "maintenance of separate schools for different races" perpetuated race prejudice. Like Commissioner Traud, Schiff reported that the "colored" schools were a needless expense.[13]

The Negro community met the Schiff resolution with mixed reactions. Rufus Perry, a Negro cleric, speaking before a meeting of Negro citizens at Chickering Hall, praised the abolition of the "colored" schools — the "relics of barbarism." However, he opposed any action that would deprive the Negro teachers at these schools of their jobs. Perry's fears for the teachers appeared to be justified when one of the three remaining "colored" schools was closed in 1883 with no provision for maintaining its Negro instructors. The Negro community was faced with a dilemma: on the one hand, they wanted integrated schools, and, on the other, they wished to protect the jobs of the Negro teachers. While those persons attending the Chickering Hall meeting adopted a resolution urging the Board of Education to retain the Negro teachers and merely to change the name of the "colored" schools to "ward" schools, the Globe urged the Board to reexamine the teachers and then reappoint them on the basis of merit. Most Negroes rejected the Globe's argument. It was not that they opposed integration, it was their desire to avoid an all-white teaching staff in the city.

A committee of New York City Negroes, under the leadership of Bishop W. B. Derrick and the educator, Charles L. Reason, persuaded the Board of Education to delay its plan to close the "colored" schools for one year. At the same time, the committee appealed to the state legislature to enact the Chickering Hall resolution. In 1884 the legislature passed a law that provided protection for the jobs of the Negro teachers; the act stated that no teacher could be removed except as provided by law. Three years later, a New York Supreme Court ruled that an attempt by the New York City Board of Education to discharge three Negro teachers on the basis of a decline in attendance at the former "colored" schools — now called ward schools — was a violation of the act of 1884.[14]

The only result of the Board's action was to change the name of the "colored" schools to ward schools 80 and 81 and to adopt a policy eschewing segregated schools. The superintendent of schools declared in 1884 that the Board made no distinction between Negro and white children. In practice, though, this policy did not work toward the integration of the schools — Negro children were usually limited to a few schoolhouses that were predominantly Negro. In 1896 the *Tribune Monthly* reported that "in spite of all assertions to the contrary" Negro children had difficulty "getting into many of" New York City's public schools. A study of the city school system in 1913 reported that while Negroes were enrolled in almost every school in Manhattan, some 60 per cent of these students attended five of the 64 schools investigated and 72 per cent attended nine schools. By 1920 this practice was still very much in existence. It appears, however, that the residential pattern rather than any policy of the Board of Education was responsible for the predominantly Negro schools.[15]

Following the abolition of the "colored" schools, the Board of Education pursued a policy of appointing Negro teachers to schools with a majority of white students as well as those with a high percentage of Negroes. When a group of white teachers protested the assignment of a Negro teacher to its all-white faculty in 1901, Superintendent of Schools Jasper replied that he looked only for "efficiency and merit" in a teacher. Any instructor who manifested disrespect toward the Negro teacher would be discharged, he warned. Five years later, the *Age* applauded the increase in the number of Negro teachers in predominantly white schools. When William L. Bulkley was appointed principal of a school with an overwhelming white student body, the all-white faculty of the school protested to the Board of Education. The Board rejected the protest.[16]

Other areas that were to become part of Greater New York in 1898 lagged behind Manhattan in abolishing their separate schools for Negro children. Even though Mayor Seth Low of Brooklyn had appointed a Negro to the Board of Education in 1882, Philip A. White, the city still denied Negroes unrestricted admission to all-white schools. When Negroes appealed to the courts for redress under the Civil Rights Act of 1873, none was forthcoming. In 1883 the Court of Appeals, the highest court of the state, denied the petition of a Negro mother to compel an all-white Brooklyn school to admit her child. The Court held that the Civil Rights Act of 1873 had not repealed the provision of the Common School Act of 1864 allowing local school authorities to maintain separate schools for Negro children so long as they offered equal instructional facilities. "We cannot say why the establishment of separate institutions for the education and benefit of different races," argued the New York Court thirteen years before Plessy v. Ferguson, "should be held any more to imply the inferiority of one race than that of the other." Chief Justice William C. Ruger, speaking for majority of the court, continued along this line of thought:

> A natural distinction exists between these races which was not created, neither can it be abrogated by law, and legislation which recognizes this distinction and provides for the peculiar wants or conditions of the particular race can in no just sense be called a discrimination against such race or an abridgment of its civil rights.

In a dissenting opinion, George F. Danforth argued that the Fourteenth Amendment prohibited such legislation as the Common School Act of 1864, which "either implies legal inferiority in civil society . . . and which if permitted, would, in the end, subject them while citizens to the degrading condition of an enslaved race." Furthermore, in obvious disagreement with the majority, Justice Danforth asserted that "all previous limitation on account of color . . . ceased with the enactment of" the act of 1873.

In reaction to this decision, Philip A. White introduced a resolution that all Brooklyn schools be opened to Negroes. It was promptly passed by the Brooklyn Board of Education. Yet, separate Negro schools persisted in sections of Brooklyn until 1894.[17]

The state legislature, however, still refused to outlaw segregation in the schools of the state. In 1894 it reenacted the Common School Act of 1864. On the basis of this law, the Borough of Queens retained a segregated school system. In 1899 Mrs. Cisco, a Negro, attempted unsuccessfully to enroll her children in the white schools of Jamaica. The separate Negro schools grew out of neighborhood patterns, contended the borough's president of the Board of Education, not any policy of the school board. The Appellate Division of the state court system upheld the right of a local school district to maintain separate educational facilities for Negroes. Relying on King v. Gallagher, the five-judge court ruled unanimously that Negroes may be denied admission to white schools so long as the school district afforded educational opportunities for Negroes in conformity with the Consolidated School Law of 1894. From the Negro's point of view this decision had its favorable side, for the state legislature in 1900 adopted a law abolishing segregated schools throughout the state.[18]

Despite the gains Negroes had achieved in the schools, the courts, the transportation facilities, and the public places of New York City, they suffered many violations of their rights.[19] In addition, the position of the southern Negro had deteriorated. Following the Compromise of 1877, the Republican party turned its back on the southern Negro. This policy was continued and extended during President Chester A. Arthur's term in office (1881–1885) when the President worked with Independent Democrats in the South rather than with white and Negro Republicans. Negroes became disillusioned with the Republican party, believing that the Grand Old Party had surrendered the southern Negro to the Democratic heirs of the slaveocracy. This impression was buttressed in 1883 when the United States Supreme Court, composed mainly of Republicans, declared the Civil Rights Act of 1875 unconstitutional. Negroes in New York City and other sections of the nation reacted bitterly to this decision as well as violations of Negro rights in the South.[20]

In 1879 a group of New York City Negroes condemned the outrages committed against the southern Negro. A protest meeting of approximately 1,500 Negroes at a local church criticized the invalidation of the Civil Rights Act. The press carried statements denouncing the Court's action.[21] A number of Negroes in both the North and South questioned the Republican party's fellowship for the Negro. In New York City, T. Thomas Fortune, who had begun his career as a Republican, led the rebellion against the party that had broken the bonds of slavery. "Our faith in the Republican party," wrote Fortune in 1883, "hangs by the frailest thread." He suggested that Negroes would find it to their benefit to vote for Democrats. Using his newspaper, the *Globe* and its successor, the *Freeman,* as well as other journals, Fortune castigated the Republican party. Questioning Republican devotion to equal rights, he accused members of the party of using the Negro "in their transit from mediocrity and obscurity to fortune and fame." Where southern slaveholders had employed "the lash and brutal power of ownership" to control Negroes, the Republican party relied on "the hopes and fears" of the race. Under the rule of Reconstruction governments, according to Fortune, the South became a "squeezed lemon, and a hell for colored people." The young journalist illustrated these statements with his own experience in Florida, where "mercenary" men "deceived the colored people, and . . . sold them out to the enemy for a paltry mess of pottage." This type of Republican, who had "forgotten the principles for which Sumner contended, and for which Lincoln died," now dominated the party throughout the nation. Republicanism, declared Fortune, had "degenerated into an ignoble scramble for place and power." [22]

As a result of his disenchantment with the Republican party, Fortune advanced the candidacy of certain Democrats. While he still condemned the "Bourbon Democrats," he praised "independent" and "progressive" Democrats. In the election of 1884, Fortune supported the Democratic candidate for the presidency, Grover Cleveland. [23] According to the newspaper editor, those Negroes who worked in behalf of James G. Blaine's candidacy were "flunkies." Even these lackeys, asserted Fortune, were not expected to make themselves at home in the New York headquarters of the Republican party. After Cleveland's victory, the New York journalist praised the President for his desire to have the Democratic party "grow more broad, liberal, and tolerant" in matters affecting Negroes. In the New York mayoralty election of 1886, Fortune urged Negro voters to support Abraham Hewitt, the victorious Democratic candidate, who was opposed by Theodore Roosevelt and Henry George.

Fortune's actions during 1887 and 1888 also exhibit a definite tendency to campaign for Democratic rather than Republican candidates. He opposed the candidacy of U. S. Grant's son, Frederick Grant, for Secretary of State of New York. When Grant lost, Fortune declared gleefully: "Perhaps I helped to kill him with my little hatchet." In 1888 Fortune supported Cleveland and asserted that the Republican party had had its day. He claimed also that the city's Democratic newspapers had been more impartial "in the employment of colored talent and in quoting colored newspapers." Fortune announced that the Democratic party was no longer the slaveocracy of antebellum days.[24]

Despite his support of Cleveland, Fortune refused to ally himself completely with the Democracy. The party's southern wing was still a thorn that scratched his conscience. In 1886 he denounced the New York Democratic organization for running the worst governed city in the nation. In January of 1887 Fortune's newspaper, the *Freeman*, portrayed Roscoe Conkling as a man of "abilities" and "honesty" in a period of "extravagance and dishonesty." Fortune, though, believed that both major parties were "rotten to the core." In line with this position, he urged Negro voters to practice political independence, to think "less of 'the party' and more of themselves." For myself, he wrote, "I shall unburden my mind not as a Republican or a Democrat but as a colored man." To implement this philosophy of independence, the newspaper editor urged Negroes as early as 1883 to form their own nonpartisan organization. It remained with them alone to secure their rights, for the white man was "a cunning fellow" who was disinterested in the plight of the Negro.[25]

In 1887 Fortune advanced a formal plan for such an independent organization, the Afro-American League. Response to this proposal varied from enthusiastic support to opposition on practical grounds. Although local chapters of the League were organized, a national unit was not launched until 1890.[26] Fortune's proposals appear to have received a cool reception because of his unconventional political beliefs and unorthodox personality traits. Not only did Fortune's support of the Democracy irritate many Negro leaders, his own unique version of Marxism alienated others. He rebuked "industrial slavery" as being more "irresponsible" than all other forms of slavery. Seeing the national struggle in terms of capital versus labor, he repudiated the Republican party as a "money power." Negroes as well as whites were victimized by the "land owners and money lenders." While Fortune would later desert this position and ally himself with the philosophy of Booker T. Washington, in the 1880s his beliefs angered many Negroes who wanted their fellow Negroes to share in both the American capitalistic and democratic systems. Nor did Fortune's diatribe against the clergy win for him many friends. As one reviewer wrote of his *Black and White:* Fortune must have been in a "terrible bad bilious condition, or like Carlyle extremely dyspeptic when he indicted the clergy." Moreover, Fortune's tendency to be impulsive or to go off on unpopular causes (or from the journalist's point of view, to be independent) alienated many potential allies and was in later years a serious annoyance to his close friend Booker T. Washington. One prominent Negro, the journalist Edward E. Cooper, considered Fortune a "queer fellow" and a "mystery." Alexander Crummell, an eminent Negro clergyman and intellectual, described Fortune in 1897 as "a pitiful creature — for years wriggling in and wriggling out — fr[om] one fanatical theory to another . . . always carried away with a prodigious estimate of himself and his own personal importance." Crummell compared the journalist to one of Dryden's wives who in the "space of one revolving moon, is poet, fiddler, ruffian and baffoon [*sic*]." Many Negroes considered Fortune's conversion to the prohibition cause in 1887 further proof of his instability. It is ironic that within another decade and one-half Fortune would be referred to as "drunken Tom Fortune." And one reason for the friction between Booker Washington and the editor of the *Age* in the 1900s was the latter's excessive drinking.[27]

Fortune's support of prohibition as well as his repudiation of the Republican party in favor of nonpartisanship generated a battle for control of the *Freeman.* New York's Negro Republicans condemned Fortune's political views. William H. Johnson, the Negro Republican state committeeman-at-large, charged that the *Freeman* under Fortune's pen failed to reflect Negro opinion. He described the newspaper's editor as an "intelligent and aggressive citizen of independent proclivities" who ran "a very breezy newspaper." Under great pressure, Fortune resigned as editor of the *Freeman* on October 8, 1887, and turned its reins over to his brother, Emanuel, and Jerome Peterson. He admitted that his point of view, while containing "new ideas of thought and action," failed to represent the thinking of the Negro majority. The new editors, who changed the name of the paper to the *Age,* announced that they would follow a "strictly" Republican policy.

Negro Republicans were quick to express their approval of the *Freeman*'s replacement. Jacob H. Simms, president of the Republican Union and Protective Club of the City and County of New York, welcomed the appearance of a "straightout Republican paper." [28]

Along with Peterson and Emanuel Fortune, most of New York City's Negroes in the 1880s supported the Republican party. As early as 1871, the city had at least eight Negro Republican clubs with a membership in excess of 3,200. During the next fifteen years the Grand Old Party created more Negro groups. By 1884 some 35 Negro Republican organizations were in operation. On the other side of the political fence, the Democratic party failed to obtain substantial support from the city's Negro voters before 1898. In 1871 a group of Negro Democrats formed the Griffin Excelsior Guards; however, it appears that this group was unsuccessful since no mention was made of it in the years that followed. New York City's Democrats, no doubt, realized that Negroes still considered the Democracy their enemy. Tammany Hall's ability to win elections by large majorities in the two decades that followed the Civil War minimized the value of the Negro vote on the local level. This fact was attested to by the *Age* in 1887, when it reported that it would require "a good revulsion of public feeling to overcome the usual Democratic majorities rolled up on Manhattan Island." [29]

In the presidential election of 1888, New York's Democratic party made its first concerted effort to attract a Negro following. Since Grover Cleveland had captured the electoral vote of New York State in 1884 by only 1,109 ballots, the Negro vote of the state took on importance. Democrats realized that if they could acquire the support of a substantial portion of the approximately 25,000 Negro voters in the Empire State, they would enhance the chances of a Cleveland victory in the election of 1888. Thus, while the Negro vote was not important to Democratic candidates within New York City, it was significant in a statewide election. [30]

In appealing for Negro support, the state Democratic leaders utilized the New York State Cleveland League which had been created in 1884. The directors of the League wasted no time in campaigning for the Negro vote of New York City. J. C. Matthews, the Negro chairman of the League, an Albany lawyer and former Republican, joined with T. McCants Stewart, the leading Negro Democrat in the city, in organizing three Negro Democratic assembly district clubs. Born in Charleston, South Carolina in 1854, Stewart attended Howard University and received a law degree from the University of South Carolina. After coming to New York City, he was admitted to the bar in 1885. As a lawyer, he was considered a "skilled and eloquent advocate." Between 1891 and 1895 Stewart served on the Brooklyn Board of Education. In addition to his interest in politics, he frequently traveled to Liberia and later in his career became an associate justice of the Supreme Court of Liberia.

By putting all their votes in the Republican basket, Stewart believed that Negroes had encouraged both Democratic and Republican indifference to their plight. Only if Negroes would divide their support between the parties on such issues as the tariff, silver, and civil service as well as civil rights would they receive the recognition they deserved.[31] For these views, Stewart was condemned by many leading Negroes such as Frederick Douglass and Emanuel Fortune. Fortune averred that he could understand why a Negro might support the prohibitionists but never the Democrats. For this reason, he insisted, the votes Stewart would carry into the Democratic camp would be "so infinitesimal that it will require a microscope to find" them.[32]

Despite Emanuel Fortune's contention, the Democratic campaign to court Negro voters created consternation at Republican headquarters. As the Age noted in August of 1888, the Democrats were "dead set" in their desire to win a sizable portion of New York's Negro vote. Consequently, a host of Negro Republican organizations was formed to meet the Democratic challenge. Where there were only 35 such groups in 1884, by election time of 1888 there were at least 200 Negro Republican clubs in the city.[33] Negro leaders took to the campaign trail in support of Benjamin Harrison's presidential candidacy. The Negro clergyman and Republican politician W. B. Derrick, for example, made over 100 speeches in behalf of the Republican cause. In one speech, he criticized Negroes who even thought of voting for a Democrat. "Every colored voter in the North who so far forgets himself as to vote a Democratic ticket," he warned, is "selling his own damnation and blighting the hopes of his people in the oppressed South." [34]

Although Grover Cleveland lost both the presidential election and the electoral vote of New York State, his party had come to realize the importance of the Negro vote in the Empire State. In 1889 the Democrats organized the Colored Citizens Chapin Club in New York City under the leadership of T. McCants Stewart.[35]

While the majority of Negroes, it appears, remained Republicans in the election of 1888, the Negro assembly district clubs of the G.O.P. were plagued by intraparty squabbles. These organizations divided over the best method of securing patronage from the white leadership of the party. In 1888 the split within the various Negro Republican organizations led to the appointment of Bishop W. B. Derrick as arbitrator. He was able to secure a temporary halt to the quarrels. In 1889, however, the disputes again flared up. Like the disagreements of 1888, most of the conflicts involved the question of political patronage. The officers of Negro clubs were criticized for their failure to secure adequate political appointments for Negro Republicans. The insurgents charged that Negroes voted for the party at the polls; yet when the spoils of victory were being distributed the race was disregarded. According to another cleric in politics, Negroes gave undivided support to Republicans on election day; therefore, they deserved "better recognition" in the distribution of the spoils. Republicans must "stop juggling with the Negro question," cautioned the *Age*, if they wanted to win the presidential election of 1892.[36]

The frequent squabbles among Negro Republicans were also a reflection of the desire of individual Negroes to achieve recognition within the Negro community. Since Negroes were barred from opportunities available to whites of equal ability, political leadership, like religious service, was a path along which many Negroes could rise in status. Consequently, many Negro politicians who criticized those in positions of power were merely playing the role of the "outs" seeking to become the "ins." No doubt the frequent internecine battles hurt the status of the Negro leadership class and prevented Negroes from obtaining a greater degree of political recognition, yet this point can be overemphasized. It must be remembered that the New York Negro community had not as yet become a significant enough proportion of the population to be a determining factor in most elections. When Negroes did receive some measure of political recognition, as in the election of 1888, it was in response to the importance that their vote carried.[37] Nor was political squabbling a Negro phenomenon; factionalism was a persistent feature of New York City politics. As James Q. Wilson has written: "Negro politics in northern cities is a reflection of the politics of the cities as a whole." Opposition to the Negro Republican incumbents of the city, though, may have gone beyond mere self-interest. The fact that whites selected their political leaders annoyed Negroes. "The white wardheelers," the *Freeman* wrote ruefully in 1885, "have controlled our votes ever since the war." [38] Thus, all of these factors worked toward friction within Negro political organizations.

These intraparty disputes continued before and after the election for members of the New York State Legislature in 1889; but it appears that Negro Republicans gave their overwhelming support to the party at the polls. At a "Grand Mass Meeting," Negroes were implored to save their city and state by voting the Republican ticket. The *Age* told its readers to vote against the Democratic party, the party that drew "upon the liquor dealer fraternity for a majority of its candidates." For the first time, Republican candidates from districts with a large Negro population advertised in the Negro press. The *Age* claimed that the Negro vote in the Eleventh Assembly District was responsible for the 300-vote victory of State Senator Lispenard Stewart. Despite Stewart's victory, as well as the return of T. Thomas Fortune to the Republican party and the editorship of the *Age*, there was dissatisfaction with the large number of Democratic victories.[39]

Negro discontent with the treatment accorded them by the political parties and the abuses heaped upon them in the South caused Fortune's plan for a nonpartisan Negro organization, the Afro-American League, to gain wider acceptance. The journalist's desertion of prohibition and the Democratic party made him more palatable to those Negro Republicans who had repudiated him earlier. Where Fortune had castigated the Republican party in previous years, in 1889 he was saying that "only the mercenary Negro" would "be found in the future on the Democratic side of the fence." Nevertheless Fortune retained a degree of political independence; above all, he considered himself a "race man and not a party man." [40] According to Fortune's plan, the Afro-Ameri-

can League was to be a confederation of local chapters. Brooklyn
Negroes formed the first branch of the League in October of 1889.
One month later, a chapter was established in Manhattan. Similar
groups were organized in other areas of the nation.[41] As a result
of these successes, Fortune called for a national convention to
meet in Chicago on January 15, 1890.

Fortune opened the convention by telling the delegates that
they were "here to-day to emphasize the fact that the past condition of dependence and helplessness upon men who have used us
for selfish and unholy purposes . . . must be reversed." Negroes
are tired of being "used by one party as an issue and by another
as a stepping stone to place and power." He maintained that only
through independent action could Negroes improve their status,
for the political parties cared not "a fig for the Afro-American."
The race, Fortune continued, had "served parties long enough
without benefit to the race. It is now time for the parties to serve
us some, if they desire our support." He implored the delegates
to "stand for race, and not for this party or that party." In the
future "We shall labor as one man, inspired with one holy purpose, to wage relentless opposition to all men who would degrade
our manhood and who would defraud us of the benefits of citizenship."

Fortune counseled his audience to fight disfranchisement,
mob rule, "the penitentiary system of the South," segregation, and
discrimination. To put these plans into effect, he urged the League
to establish a series of committees and bureaus. An Afro-American
Bank to "concentrate" the earnings of the race was one feature of
his plan. In line with the philosophy of Booker T. Washington,
Fortune advocated the creation of a bureau of technical and industrial education. He contended that the race needed more artisans, educated farmers, and laborers than "educated lawyers, doctors and loafers on the street corners." To assist the race in the
purchase of goods at lower prices and to stimulate business investment, he suggested the establishment of a bureau of cooperative
industry. Fortune also proposed the creation of a committee on
legislation to work toward political equality for the race. Fortune's program, therefore, contained elements of the philosophy of
W. E. B. Du Bois as well as Booker T. Washington.[42]

During the months that followed the Chicago convention,
New York members of the League expanded their organizational

activities. Alexander Walters, a Negro clergyman, was elected chairman of the New York City branch of the League. A New York State chapter was organized with T. McCants Stewart as its legal adviser. Brooklyn Negroes formed another branch of the League to add to the one created in 1889.[43]

Despite these gains, the mass of Negroes throughout the nation failed to support the League. Many sections of the white press condemned the organization as an attempt at class warfare and as unrepresentative of the mass of "decent" Negroes. The *Chicago Tribune* labeled Fortune "a tricky New York coon" who was in reality "a Democratic decoy duck." The League, however, was doomed to failure; after a brief flurry of support Fortune announced in 1893 the League's demise. Fortune's proclivity to independence may have been a factor in the League's failure. In selecting a president, the delegates by-passed Fortune and elected the more stable and orthodox J. C. Price. Yet, this alone could not account for the organization's failure; as Emma Lou Thornbrough has noted, the League "lacked vitality and failed to attract mass support." Moreover, Negroes still indicated their desire to rely on the Republican party for protection.[44]

New York Negroes still expressed disappointment with Republicanism on both the national and local level. In general, they supported the Federal Elections Bill (the Lodge Bill), and when it was defeated they expressed disappointment.[45] The persistent failure of New York Republicans to reward loyal Negroes with jobs rankled the *Age*. The discriminatory practices of a number of political clubs angered the city's Negroes. For example, in 1890 the picture of Jacob H. Simms, Negro leader of the United Republican Association of the Eleventh Assembly District, was destroyed by white members of the club. Negroes also experienced discrimination at public places despite the state civil rights laws of 1873 and 1881. Because of the color of his skin, T. McCants Stewart was denied access to his reserved stateroom in 1886 on a boat he was traveling on from New York City to Albany. In 1890 a Brooklyn restaurant rebuffed the request of two Negro stenographers to sit at a front table. In the same year, a midtown hotel bar refused to serve T. Thomas Fortune. Negroes, despite constant attempts, were unable to obtain positions as policemen in the city. And, in 1886, a benefit of the Grand Army of the Republic restricted Negroes to a particular section of a Brooklyn theater because of "public sentiment." [46]

It is not surprising, then, that when State Assemblyman Hamilton Fish, a Republican, introduced a bill to protect the "civil and public rights" of the state's citizens "against discrimination on account of race, color, or religion," the Negro population called for its passage. In light of the frequent violations of the civil rights acts of 1873 and 1881, Negroes wanted a law that would provide for the revocation of the licenses of public places that discriminated on the basis of color. When the bill failed to pass Negroes could express only disappointment. Even though the Republican party alone could not be blamed for the defeat of the Fish Bill, Negroes could not help but manifest further disillusionment with the Grand Old Party.[47] Yet, as the *Age* noted sorrowfully, the Negro had no other choice. Support of the Democratic party appeared out of the question. An alliance with the Democracy was a "folly," wrote Fortune in 1892, for even though Cleveland was a good man he could "never be greater than his party." Three years earlier, the newspaperman asserted that Negroes can expect nothing from the Democratic party "but malignant opposition to their manhood and citizen's rights," for the Democracy was as "incapable of changing its policy as the leopard his spots." Fortune's paper, also in 1889, described the Democratic party as "the party of retrogression and cussedness"; it was no more than the "rankest nest of political crookedness anywhere to be found in the United States outside of the South." [48]

Nor could the Negro press find comfort in third party movements. When the Republican party allied with the People's Municipal League in supporting Francis W. Scott for mayor in 1890, the *Age* charged that this put the G.O.P. in a "state of hilarious confusion." The New York Republican party was "deficient in the needful qualities of successful leadership." Looking at reform Republicans — the Mugwumps — it discovered persons seeking to disfranchise "the masses of voters of all races" through ballot reform. No doubt the Liberal Republican arguments for the end of Reconstruction in the 1870s left Negroes with bitter memories of reform Republicans since many of them were now Mugwumps. The *Age* even counseled southern Negroes to avoid joining the socialistic Farmers' Alliance: "We warn Afro-Americans everywhere to be cautious of committing themselves to the support of the Farmers' Alliance and its revolutionary purposes and aims." Similarly, it viewed contemptuously what it considered to be the anti-individualistic doctrines of Socialists such as Edward Bellamy.[49] Negroes believed they had only one place to turn — the Republican party. The Negro leadership suppressed its misgivings and followed the G.O.P. in supporting the Fusion candidate for mayor, Francis W. Scott, who lost the election to the Democrat, Hugh Grant. Republican candidates for federal and local offices continued to receive Negro support at the ballot box.[50]

Yet, Negro disillusionment with the Republican party accounted for some minor defections to the Democracy in the election of 1890. The Brooklyn *Eagle* reported that while a majority of the metropolitan area's Negro citizens "still identified with Republicanism the proportion inclining to association with the Democracy is augmenting every year." The newspaper asserted that this change had occurred to a greater degree on the local level than in national elections.[51] Negroes may have found it easier to give vent to their anger against local Republicans for what they considered the national party's desertion of the southern Negro. Whatever the reason, the New York Democracy pursued the Negro vote. During 1891 a group of young Negroes organized a Democratic club. Leading Negroes, such as T. McCants Stewart, addressed Negro meetings in support of Democratic candidates. In the presidential election of 1892, the Democracy revived the Cleveland League. The League counseled Negroes to vote for the Democracy — the party of the future. It accused Republicans of living "in the past" and of clinging to "the glories and shames" of former years. On the other hand, the Democratic party looked to "the glory of the future," the leadership of the League asserted. Its members were praised for their abandonment of Republicanism and for seeing a "better, more hopeful light" in the Democracy. Realizing that their southern counterparts limited their appeal, they advanced the argument that it was to the Negro's best interest to divide his vote.[52]

During the last seven years of the nineteenth century, Democrats continued their campaign for the Negro vote. In 1895 the party suffered a serious loss when T. McCants Stewart switched his loyalty to Republicanism. Believing that the party was so hampered by its southern wing, Stewart concluded that support of the Democracy was a waste of time. At the same time, Negro Republicans still expressed disappointment with their treatment by the white leadership of their party. In 1895 Negroes protested their exclusion from the Blaine Republican Club of the Eleventh Assembly District. One of the white leaders of the club, John Sabine Smith, reported that this action had alienated the 1,000 Negro voters of the district. One year later, Brooklyn Negro Republicans complained that the party had denied them "proper recognition." But any mass Negro desertion from Republicanism was offset when the Republican leadership of the state legislature obtained passage of a law that entitled all persons:

> To full and equal accommodation, advantages, facilities, and privileges of inns, restaurants, hotels, eating houses, barber shops, theaters . . . public conveyances . . . and all other places of public accommodation or amusement, subject only to the conditions and limitations established by law and applicable to all citizens.

Violators of the law (the Malby Act) were subject to a fine ranging from $100 to $500, or imprisonment for thirty to ninety days. An important difference from previous civil rights laws was that under the Malby Act the aggrieved party could collect damages up to $500. It was also more specific in its definition of a place of public accommodation.[53]

The *Times* characterized the law as "featherheaded legislation." The paper contended that this piece of legislation attempted to "establish a social relation which a law higher than all civil statutes" declared "to be forever impossible." Negroes were "growing lazier and more untrustworthy from year to year." The newspaper referred to the section giving the injured party the right to sue for damages an attempt "to enable Negroes to blackmail the keepers of restaurants and hotels." White hotel and restaurant owners joined the *Times* in voicing their objections to the new law. They organized the New York City Hotel-Keepers Association to petition the legislature for repeal of the Malby Act. In Huntington, Long Island a number of barbers converted their shops into "private clubs" to evade the provisions of the law.[54]

According to the *Times*, Negro leaders were divided as to the values of the Malby Act; however, in the years that followed a number of Negroes attempted to exercise their rights under this law. Most Negroes, though, failed to do so. Many owners of public places responded to the law with subtle methods of evading its provisions. In restaurants and saloons Negroes were overcharged to discourage their patronage. A Broadway theater restricted Negroes to a particular section of the house. In 1901 the *Tribune* reported that Negroes were denied service at the better restaurants and were prevented from purchasing tickets to the best known theaters. W. E. B. Du Bois, writing for the *Times* in the same year, asserted that the Negro "found public opinion determined to 'keep him in his place.'" [55]

While Negroes were fighting to attain equal access to public facilities, an open revolt occurred in the ranks of Manhattan's Negro Republicans in 1897. The insurgent movement was led by the Colored Republican County Organization. James O. Wright, one of the leaders of this group, contended that the party's state leadership had disregarded his organization. He argued also that the appointment of Lemuel E. Quigg as leader of all Manhattan Republican organizations was an insult to the Negro members of the party. Quigg's "every act and effort" had been "to the detriment of the success of the Colored Republican County Organization" which represented "the sentiment of colored Republicans of the city," Wright alleged. The insurgent group believed that Boss Tom Platt, who had appointed Quigg, was responsible for denying to Negro Republicans "their share of patronage." A particular grievance was leveled by Wright against District Attorney W. M. K. Olcott of Manhattan. According to Wright, the District Attorney was guilty of "offensive, disgusting, and outrageous treatment of men endorsed by" Negroes for positions in his office. The Manhattan insurgents received support from a similar group in Brooklyn — the Independent League of Colored Republicans. The League threatened the Negro Republican leadership that it would nominate its own candidate for the city council if Olcott received renomination. [56] Present in this factional fight were three persistent elements of Negro intraparty struggles: the desire of the "outs" to become the "ins," disappointment with the Negro's share of the Republican spoils, and the intense resentment many Negroes felt toward the appointment of their political leaders by the white power structure.

Where previously most Negro threats had been disregarded by the white leadership, this time the insurgent Negroes caused consternation at Republican headquarters; within five days a compromise plan was formulated. The recent gains made by Democrats among the Negro electorate contributed to this turnabout. Negro Republicans were promised positions not only in District Attorney Olcott's department, but in the offices of the sheriff, the county clerk, and the mayor. In addition, a position for a Negro was created on the executive committee of the county Republican organization.

Although this compromise was accepted by the officers of the Negro Republican organization, Wright and his group of insurgents were dissatisfied and refused to support the party's mayoralty candidate, Benjamin F. Tracy, in the election of 1897. Wright reported that his group and the majority of the city's Negro clergymen were endorsing the candidacy of Seth Low, the Fusion choice. He implied that those Negroes who would back Tracy were concerned only with private gain and not with bettering the plight of their fellow Negroes. While the regular Negro Republican organization and the Negro press were averse to joining with the fusionists, most of the Negro clergy advocated the election of Fusion candidates in the 1890s. Shortly after the insurgent rejection of Tracy's candidacy, a Colored Men's Auxiliary of the Citizens' Union was organized to support Seth Low. It claimed that two-thirds of the city's Negro voters were behind the Fusion candidate; notwithstanding, the Democrat, Robert Van Wyck, won the election.[57]

As dissension divided Negro Republicans, Democrats were attempting to procure a larger share of the city's Negro vote. In the 1890s the Chapin Club campaigned in Negro districts for Democratic candidates. Early in 1898 the leader of Tammany Hall, Richard Croker, appointed Edward E. Lee, chief bellhop at the Murray Hotel, to the chairmanship of the United Colored Democracy. Here was another case of the white leadership rather than the Negro rank and file selecting a leader of a Negro organization; for this reason, no doubt, Lee earned the name the "black Croker." This paternalistic attitude of white political leaders is illustrated by a statement reputed to have been made by Boss Croker:

Your people [the Negro] are a poor people. Tammany Hall is a poor man's organization. The colored man rightly belongs in

Tammany Hall. I'll start you off by appointing a leader. . . .
And although your vote is only 10 per cent I will place a
colored man in every department of the city government.

Lee accordingly claimed that Tammany had given "the colored
people fully $30,000 worth of patronage." At the same time Rufus
L. Perry, Jr., a Negro lawyer and later a convert to Judaism, organized the Afro-American Democratic Association. In August of
1898 the Negro National Democratic League met at the clubhouse
of the United Colored Democracy. This meeting, no doubt, was
called to impress on New York City's Negro voters that their race
was taking part in the national affairs of the party.[58]

These actions of Tammany Hall caused Republican circles to
take steps to meet the Democratic challenge. All factions within
the Negro section of the G.O.P. united to meet the Democratic
threat. The Republican cause was helped by the statements of
their gubernatorial candidate of 1898, Theodore Roosevelt, prais-
ing Negro soldiers who had fought in the Spanish-American War.
No doubt Roosevelt's remarks and the actions taken by southern
Democrats against Negroes brought the Negro clergy and other
sections of the Negro community to his side. Shortly before election day, sixteen of New York City's Negro clergymen issued a
statement attacking the Democracy.

Colored men of New York: The condition of the South is
desperate. The Democratic party is without an issue. They have
adopted as an issue of the present campaign the false cry of
Negro domination.
Colored men of New York, remember that when you vote
for Tammany you vote for the party of Tillman, you vote for
the party that has taken away the right of suffrage from our
brethren in the South.[59]

Tammany Hall, which began 1898 with high hopes of securing a sizable portion of the city's Negro vote, was discouraged by
its failure to attract Negro voters. Only one Negro minister supported the Democratic ticket. Tammany also was disheartened by
an enthusiastic parade of Negro Republicans in the Twenty-fifth
Assembly District. Yet the Democrats looked hopefully toward
obtaining a larger share of the city's Negro electorate in the presidential election of 1900. This prospect was shattered by the race
riot of that year. As has already been pointed out in chapter five,
the leading Negroes of the city, along with many of the white

newspapers, blamed Tammany for the alleged brutality of the police. The *Post* reported that many Negro Democrats were deserting the party.[60]

Negro hostility toward Tammany was carried into the mayoralty campaign of 1901. The *Tribune* announced that the city's Negro citizens had begun "a crusade against Tammany Hall." It reported that the Negro clergy was leading this movement. The ministers urged Negroes to cast their votes in support of Seth Low for mayor and against the party responsible for the riot of 1900 — Tammany. One of the leaders of the movement, Bishop W. B. Derrick, counseled Negroes that they could refute the charge that they were "friends of vice and intemperance" by voting the Fusion ticket. He asserted that Tammany Hall was a "sinful organization composed of men filled with iniquity." Negroes must defend their homes "by redeeming New York" from "degradation and shame," Bishop Derrick concluded. The cry of "remember the riots" was rampant in Negro neighborhoods. It appears that the greater number of Negroes cast their votes for the victorious Seth Low.[61]

In the election of 1903 a group of Negroes led by the insurgent Negro Republican James O. Wright supported Low for reelection, but the victor was George B. McClellan, the Democratic candidate. No mention was made in the press of the position of other Negroes.[62] In 1905 Negroes joined the campaigns of the three leading candidates. The *Age* advised Negroes to vote for William H. Ivins, the Republican candidate. It reported that many Negroes were "sick and tired of the Fusion business." The United Colored Democracy conducted a spirited campaign to reelect McClellan. Negro Democratic clubs were formed in four of the city's five boroughs. Tammany announced that Mayor McClellan had appointed more Negroes to public office than both Mayors Strong and Low — a claim that the Republican *Age* sustained. William Randolph Hearst, the choice of the Municipal Ownership League, received the endorsement of the Colored Men's Municipal League and the Colored Voters for the League Ticket. On election day, according to the *Age*, many Negroes deserted the Republican party and cast their votes for the victorious McClellan. Negro animosity toward Tammany because of the race riot of 1900 obviously had waned.[63]

With the increase in the size of the city's Negro population and the concentration of that citizenry in specific districts, the Negro vote assumed greater importance. In those areas containing a significant Negro electorate, Negro voters often determined the outcome of elections for such offices as alderman, assemblyman, or district leader. In 1906 areas with a large Negro population experienced a number of heated battles for control of the local Republican district organization. One of these elections occurred in the Thirteenth Assembly District where one of the candidates for the district's leadership — John H. Farrell — was accused of condoning anti-Negro activities. The United Colored Republicans alleged that Farrell's followers had assaulted the Negro partisans of his opponent, John J. Hahn. Farrell also was accused of being a Democrat and having declared that he could buy "niggers" for "$1 a head!" Hahn won the election by 100 votes, and it appears that the Negro vote was the decisive factor in his victory. However, most of the other candidates who received Negro support lost. In one leadership race the *Age* contended that the split in the Negro vote resulted in the defeat of the candidate it favored.

Negro discontent with their small allotment of patronage from the Republican party was a factor in these leadership races. This sentiment was reflected in the election of the officers of the Negro district clubs. Some protested that their leaders were responsible for their failure to secure adequate Negro membership on the county committee and at the state convention. They also condemned their exclusion from the executive committee of the Ninth Assembly District which had a large Negro element.[64]

The apparent success of Democratic appeals to Negro voters during the general elections of 1906 caused the *Age* to remark that the "Afro-American vote" was "no longer a Republican unit." Democrats increased the size of their vote in districts with a large percentage of Negroes. After the election, President Theodore Roosevelt's discharge of about 160 Negro soldiers for "shooting up" the town of Brownsville, Texas, augmented discontent among Negro Republicans. They not only considered the evidence against the soldiers inconclusive, but they believed that the President failed to give the soldiers a fair hearing. In 1907 the *Age* asserted that the actions of Presidents Roosevelt, McKinley, and Hayes proved that the G.O.P. had "abandoned" the Negro.[65]

Although many of New York's City's Negroes had transferred

their allegiance to the Democratic party, the majority still remained loyal to Republicanism. It must be noted once again that southern Democrats continued to violate the rights of the Negro. Those Negroes who continued to vote Republican believed that the solution to their problem was the selection of candidates favorable to Negro equality. The severest criticisms of Roosevelt's action in the Brownsville matter came from members of his own party. Senator Joseph B. Foraker of Ohio was the President's strongest critic. While Ohio Negroes urged the nomination of Foraker for the presidency in 1908, New York Negroes advocated the selection of Charles Evans Hughes.[66] William Howard Taft was not popular among Negroes because of his association with Roosevelt in the discharge of Negro troops. However, as a result of some hard work by Booker T. Washington, many of the nation's Negro newspapers came out in support of Taft.[67]

After Taft's nomination by the Republicans, a number of New York's Negro Republicans endorsed the Democratic candidacy of William Jennings Bryan. Bishop Alexander Walters departed from his earlier allegiance to Republicanism. The Cosmopolitan Club, a Negro group, counseled Negroes to vote for the "Great Commoner." However, a statement attributed to Bryan asserting that Negro disfranchisement was justified must have cost him many Negro votes. The *New York Age*, which was now under the complete control of Taft's ardent admirer, Booker T. Washington, publicized Bryan's alleged remarks.

[Bryan] yearns over the oppressed Filipino; his heart bleeds for the poor and downtrodden everywhere, yet when it comes to equal treatment for the black man of his own country, all he has to say is that "the white men of the South are determined that the Negro shall be disfranchised everywhere it is necessary to prevent the recurrence of the horrors of carpetbag rule."

The *Age* insisted that a vote for a Democrat was a vote "to retard the progress of the race." Republican clubs as well as the *Age* used every weapon within their power to advance the cause of Republicanism. In an appeal for the Negro vote of the city, Taft appeared at one of the city's Negro churches less than two weeks before election day.[68]

Once the election was over, Negro Republicans again claimed that they were denied an equitable share of the spoils of victory. According to the *Age* in 1909, Negroes had received no benefits for their support of the Republican and Fusion parties. Edward E. Lee, the leader of the United Colored Democracy, asserted in the same year that Tammany had given the Negro a role in city politics "not heretofore attained by them." In 1910 the *Age* contended that Republicans had accorded the Negro a "dirty deal" in connection with patronage. Even though it considered itself a "Republican institution," it announced its disappointment with both the party and President Taft. This was evidenced in the local and national elections of 1910; according to the *Crisis,* not since emancipation had so many "colored voters cast the Democratic ticket." The journal attributed this rise in the Democratic vote to the Brownsville affray, the duplicity of the Republican party, Taft's hostility toward the Negro, and the more "hospitable attitude" of Democrats. Since most Negroes felt that they could not ally with the Democratic party, they turned to organizations independent of political parties to manifest their identity and grievances. To more and more Negroes, nonpartisan groups appeared to be the answer to their problems.[69]

New York's Negroes joined with Negroes throughout the nation during the first decade of the twentieth century to establish organizations independent of political parties in an attempt to attain equality for the race. While industrial associations expanded their activities and new ones were formed during the ten-year period, those groups that stressed civil rights became the dominant voice in Negro life. Disfranchisement, segregation, and lynchings in the South, as well as the more subtle forms of discrimination in the North, brought forth the wrath of Negro leaders. They condemned both major political parties for their failure to provide in practice what the Constitution guaranteed in theory. As each violation of Negro rights occurred — whether it was a lynching in the South or a race riot in the North — Negro appeals for independent action multiplied. Between 1898 and 1910 T. Thomas Fortune's proposal for a nonpartisan Negro organization gained greater currency among Negro leaders. The problem of the first decade of the twentieth century was to establish a workable national body of this sort.

In 1898 Fortune's Afro-American League was resurrected as the National Afro-American Council. Fortune, while granting that such an organization was needed, doubted that it would receive mass support. Meeting in Rochester, New York, in September of 1898, the delegates offered Fortune the presidency of the Council. When the journalist declined this overture, the group turned to Bishop Alexander Walters of New York City. Walters was born in Bardstown, Kentucky, in 1858, but left that city while still in his teens to study theology under private tutors in Indianapolis, Indiana. At the age of twenty he returned to Kentucky to conduct religious revival work among the Negroes of that state. Soon he was assigned as pastor to various churches extending as far west as San Francisco. In 1887 he settled in New York City as pastor of the African Methodist Episcopal Zion Church; five years later, he was ordained a bishop of that church. At the time of the creation of the Afro-American Council he was a Republican and a Washington supporter, but in 1908 he switched his allegiance to the Democracy and the anti-Washington forces. For both vice-president and chairman of the executive committee, the Council selected Fortune.

The Council was a strange amalgamation of the philosophies of Washington and Du Bois. On the organization's executive board were Du Bois, the head of the Business Bureau; Charles W. Anderson, Negro politician, frequent Republican appointee to office, and a strong ally of Booker T. Washington; Alexander Walters, while still a Washingtonian was showing signs of independence; and T. Thomas Fortune, the erratic journalist and at the time staunch supporter of Washington. The paradoxical nature of the Council's leadership was reflected in the organization's statement of objectives. On the one hand, it called for further forward strides in the areas of industrial education and business enterprise; and, on the other hand, it signaled for an all-out struggle for political equality and encouraged more Negroes to pursue a college and university education. But from its very creation, the Council's program was impaired by its failure to attract the support of the Negro majority and the persistent struggles for control of the organization between the Washington and Du Bois groups. The Council served as an arena of battle for the two forces. As Emma Lou Thornbrough has written: "The history of the Afro-American Council . . . was inextricably linked with the fight over Washington as a race leader." It also had to battle the Niagara Movement, organized in 1905 by the college educated cohorts of Du Bois, for mass support. In this regard neither organization was successful. While Washington enjoyed occasional periods of control over the Council, in 1907 it was virtually captured by the Du Bois group and in 1908 it disappeared from the scene with its president, Alexander Walters, moving over to the Du Bois camp.[70]

As the Du Bois-Washington forces struggled for control of the Afro-American Council, other nonpartisan Negro groups were being formed in New York City. Most of these organizations adhered to the Du Bois position of civil rights first; the Washington point of view was definitely on the wane. As a result of the race riot of 1900 New York City's Negro community organized the Citizens' Protective League. Although the League was concerned only with the immediate problem of police protection, its public statements expressed demands for the improvement of the Negro's status. Except for a brief period in 1905, the League was inactive after the election of 1901. In 1903 the New York Conference Committee on Negro Suffrage was formed to agitate for the end of Negro disfranchisement in the South. Meetings were held in New York City and New Jersey both to denounce violations of Negro rights and to create a national organization to counter these usurpations. In May of 1903 the Fannie Jackson Coppin Human Rights Association of Brooklyn summoned a state convention of Negro women to "assist those" who were "fighting against the disfranchisement of the Negroes of the South." One month later, a meeting of Negro men and women of New York, New Jersey, and the New England states drafted a resolution that appealed for a national convention of Negroes. In 1906 the Negro Independent Political League was launched to encourage the race to "stand upon a political basis and occupy a political position" independent of the political parties of the city.[71]

Most of these organizations were established with the purpose of eventually expanding into a national unit. This wish appeared to be realized when the Niagara Movement came into existence in 1905, but it too ended in failure. The Niagara Movement never enjoyed a following of consequence among New York Negroes. The Brownsville affray of 1906 did stimulate protest activities in the city and the nation. The Constitution League, the first Negro protest organization to bring whites and blacks under the same roof, furthermore, stole the Niagara Movement's limited thunder when it took the lead in condemning President

Roosevelt's action. Established by John Milholland, a white manufacturer of pneumatic tubes and a future member of the NAACP, it brought into its fold such Negro opponents of Booker T. Washington as Monroe Trotter, the Boston newspaperman, and Reverdy Ransom, a New York City clergyman. The League conducted its own investigation into the Brownsville affair and found that there was no basis for Roosevelt's dismissal of the soldiers. Yet it too enjoyed only a brief life.[72]

Negro advocates of equal rights, and now sympathetic whites, met with difficulty in forging a workable national organization. Even so, these groups engendered an important change in Negro political life — they brought under their wings Negroes of all political persuasions. They pointed up the persistent theme in the history of the American Negro: that when the issue of Negro rights was at stake political labels had little meaning. Because of the discrimination piled upon the Negro by the wider community, the Negro was black before he was a Democrat or a Republican or a Socialist. In the early 1900s, as overt violations of Negro rights increased, as political parties continued to avoid the so-called Negro question, as the Negro developed a larger, more erudite, and race conscious leadership class, and as more whites were convinced of the justice of the Negro's cause, the more likely it was that a successful independent Negro protest organization would emerge. What was needed was one culminating incident, one final action. In 1906 Brownsville appeared to be the answer; but because of Washington's undermining of those groups which opposed his policy of alleged conciliation, and because of the inability or unwillingness of the various civil rights groups to unite, no organization came forward to assume national leadership. Finally, in 1908 occurred that ultimate incident, that final event, that culmination of indecency that "shocked the sensibilities of many whites" and brought home to Negro civil rights leaders the folly of petty bickerings.[73]

This event was the Springfield, Illinois, race riot. Race riots had occurred before; however, this riot took place in the city in which Abraham Lincoln was buried and the city that was preparing to celebrate the centennial of the Great Emancipator's birth. As the St. Louis *Post Dispatch* editorialized: "It was one of the worst . . . race riots that ever disgraced the country, and the disgrace is the more humiliating in that the outrages were perpetrated under the very shadow of Lincoln's tomb." As a result, a few prominent whites issued a call for a national conference in Springfield on Lincoln's Birthday in 1909 to consider the question of discrimination against the Negro. Present at the conference were William English Walling, co-founder of the National Women's Trade Union League and an advocate of socialism; Henry Moskowitz, defender of reform causes concerned with working conditions, sanitation, and honest government; Oswald Garrison Villard, publisher of the New York *Post* and the *Nation*; John Dewey, the famous philosopher and educator; Jane Addams, social worker and founder of Hull House in Chicago; William Dean Howells, the noted novelist; Mary White Ovington; and John Milholland. This coterie of reformers laid the foundation for the launching of a nonpartisan organization composed of Negroes and whites, the National Association for the Advancement of Colored People.[74] When the NAACP was formally organized in 1910, other leading whites joined the association. Selected as president was the lawyer, Moorfield Storey, who had served as Charles Sumner's assistant. Storey also had been a Mugwump and a member of the Anti-Imperialist League. Other officers of the organization were Walling, Milholland, Villard, and Frances Blascoer who had conducted social work enterprises among the Negroes of New York City. The members of the general and executive committees included Florence Kelley, an associate of Lillian Wald and Jane Addams and a reformer in her own right; Jacob Schiff, a partner of Kuhn, Loeb and Company and a financial supporter of the Henry Street Settlement, the National Child Labor Committee, and Tuskegee Institute; the Rev. Joseph Silverman, rabbi of Temple Emanu-El in New York City; Dr. Stephen S. Wise, a Jewish clergyman and close associate of Lillian Wald; and Clarence Darrow, the famous criminal lawyer. Other members of these committees were John Dewey, Henry Moskowitz, Mary Ovington, E. R. A. Seligman, and Lillian Wald, as well as such prominent Negroes as William H. Brooks, William L. Bulkley, W. E. B. Du Bois, A. Clayton Powell, and Alexander Walters. New Yorkers constituted more than one-half of the executive and general committees. Although whites comprised the vast majority of the officers and top committee assignments of the NAACP, Negroes performed most of the work. "The interracial character of the N.A.A.C.P.," August Meier has observed, "was fundamental to its success, for it gave the agitation for Negro rights a wider audience, better financial support, and the prestige of names of well-known whites." While the organization's appeal to the masses was and still is limited, it has served as a sounding board for the Negro's feelings of frustration.[75]

In 1911 the NAACP organized the New York Vigilance Committee to be located "in the heart of the colored district where all cases of injustice and discrimination could be brought with the least inconvenience to all concerned." Selected as chairman of the group was Gilchrist Stewart — Negro businessman, graduate of Tuskegee Institute, and the Constitution League's chief investigator of the Brownsville incident. The secretary-treasurer was Joel E. Spingarn, poet and literary critic. After receiving his Ph.D. from Columbia University, he taught comparative literature at that institution. In 1911 he underwent the honor, if not the novel distinction, of being discharged by the University's president, Nicholas Murray Butler. A reformer who ran for Congress in 1908, Spingarn supported Roosevelt's Progressive party in 1912. In 1930 he was elected president of the NAACP.[76]

In the course of the second decade of the twentieth century, the NAACP and other sources of Negro leadership condemned the discriminatory practices imposed upon New York's Negroes. Although the Negroes of the city never suffered the outrageous treatment that was directed at their southern fellows, wrote Spingarn in 1912, they still had to face "the most galling conditions." As the *Tribune* had noted a decade earlier, the Negro endured discrimination in "the most cosmopolitan of American cities." The Negro could neither "get a comfortable room in a fashionable hotel . . . or a good seat in a well known theatre," the paper averred. The harassment that Negroes experienced caused the *Age* to remark in 1910 that New York Negroes should not be preoccupied with Jim Crow life in the South, but should devote their attention to discrimination in New York. Negroes, for example, accounted for only 1 per cent of the city's municipal employees in 1910. Even though there were Negro members of the Brooklyn police force in that year, no Negro as yet had been added to Manhattan's force. Finally, in 1911 the first Negro policeman, Samuel J. Battle, was appointed to that borough's law enforcement agency. Although Mayor Gaynor and Police Commissioner Waldo urged more Negroes to become policemen, only five Negroes were members of the force by 1918. But in the same year, the *Age* contended that Negroes were excluded from public transportation employment above the rank of porter. Moreover, as noted in chapter two, Negroes were barred from many areas of private employment. Despite the Malby Act and its precursors, Negroes still encountered difficulty in gaining entrance to places of public accommodation. They were excluded from many of the better restaurants, theaters, and movie houses of the city. Or, when a Negro was given service at some public place, he found that he paid higher prices than white customers. One Negro clergyman in 1913 summarized the effect that discrimination had upon the Negro when he wrote that it was next to impossible for Negroes "to get many of the ordinary conveniences . . . of life." Prejudice also manifested itself in the city's hospitals. According to a study made by the Urban League in 1912, most hospitals in the city discriminated against Negro doctors and nurses. In 1916 a group of Negro physicians protested to the city regarding its inferior status in the hospitals of New York. Prejudice went beyond the professional staff, it filtered down (or up) to the Negro patient. In 1913 the NAACP accused Harlem Hospital of "gross ill treatment and neglect of colored patients." Negroes as late as 1912 still contended that they were discriminated against in the selection of jury panels. And in 1913 the State Boxing Commission prohibited bouts between Negro and white pugilists.[77]

Negro groups such as the NAACP did more than describe these positions. While the NAACP maintained a nonpartisan position, it was not averse to supporting or opposing political parties or candidates on the basis of their position on the so-called Negro question. The first presidential election that involved the NAACP was that of 1912. Certain members of the NAACP favored the Progressive party's candidate, Theodore Roosevelt. The majority, though, were suspicious of the Rough Rider because of his action in the Brownsville affair and his close friendship with Booker T. Washington during his presidential administration. When Roosevelt decided to seat lily-white delegations at the Progressive convention and described the southern Negro as ignorant and incapable of self-leadership, many members of the NAACP turned their backs on his candidacy. While such friends of the Negro as Jane Addams, Henry Moskowitz, and Joel Spingarn endorsed the

Progressive candidate, they accused him of drawing a "race dead-line." [78] Negro disillusionment with Roosevelt was summarized by Reverdy C. Ransom, who had been an early supporter of Roosevelt for the Republican nomination in 1912. He reported to a Negro audience that Roosevelt's position had struck him "like the stupefying stroke of a brutal blow. . . . I felt like one feels when he is returning from the cemetery after having buried a cherished friend." Roosevelt had "summoned us to the barren sand hills of his Armageddon to battle for his white mudgod . . . we behold the heaps of the slain . . . the eight million defense-less Negroes." The *Age* charged Roosevelt with having forced upon the Progressive party the views of southern racists.[79]

Leading members of the NAACP, such as W. E. B. Du Bois and Oswald Garrison Villard, now turned to the Democratic candidate, Woodrow Wilson. While they were disturbed by Wilson's southern birth, his alleged exclusion of Negro students from Princeton during his presidency at that institution, and his timid statements on according the Negro equal treatment, they still came out in favor of the Democratic candidate. "On the whole, we do not believe that Woodrow Wilson admires Negroes," wrote Du Bois, but he "is a cultivated scholar and he has brains." Wilson would treat Negroes "and their interests with farsighted fairness," the editor of the *Crisis* hypothesized. Also working in behalf of Wilson's candidacy was the National Colored Democratic League led by Alexander Walters. Walters played up the old T. McCants Stewart argument of dividing the Negro vote — our "political ills have largely come through the solidarity of the Negro vote." If the Negro would divide his vote, Walters suggested, the southern white man would not fear Negro domination. Walters also pub-licized a letter he had received from Wilson regarding the Negro's struggle for equality. As advertised in the *Age*, Wilson proclaimed in the letter that it was his "earnest wish to see justice done to the colored people in every matter; and not mere grudging jus-tice, but justice executed with liberality and cordial good feel-ing." [80]

Wilson by no means received unanimous support from the Negro community; in fact, those members of the NAACP who backed the Democratic choice may have done so because of Washington's adherence to the candidacy of William Howard Taft. As early as 1911, the *Age*, a proponent of the Washington position, referred to the then Governor of New Jersey as one of those "gifted . . . stubborn enemies to the progress of the colored race." The paper accused Wilson of treating Negroes as "foreigners and outcasts" during his governorship. Once Wilson was nominated, the *Age* increased its criticisms of the Democratic candidate. It played up his southern birth and what it considered his general hostility for the Negro. No "self-respecting" Negro, the paper averred, could support Wilson "without proving a traitor to himself and to his race." As to its choice, the newspaper wrote that no president "has been bolder and more outspoken against race prejudice than President Taft." For those Negroes who had misgivings concerning the incumbent, the *Age* reminded them of Republican contributions to the betterment of the race. Negroes were "born in the Republican house," it was the party that had given unswerving devotion to the Negro. Throughout the city rallies were held in support of Taft's candidacy. Yet Taft ran third in the nation, and it appears that along with the victor he finished behind Roosevelt among Negro voters.[81]

When Woodrow Wilson assumed the presidency, the worst fears of Negroes were realized. Various governmental departments were segregated, scores of Negro governmental employees were either discharged or were demoted to lesser positions, and Wilson failed to appoint Negroes in any appreciable number to political office. Negroes of both the Washington and Du Bois camps wrote Wilson protesting his Negro policy. Negro Republicans as well as Democrats expressed their dismay. The NAACP wrote Wilson that Negroes "desire a 'New Freedom,' too." [82]

In New York City, Tammany Hall seized on Wilson's actions to attack the independent Democrat and Fusion candidate for mayor in 1913, John Puroy Mitchel, as a "Woodrow Wilson-anti-Tammany Democrat." It emphasized certain similarities in the backgrounds of the two men. Like Wilson, Tammany maintained, Mitchel had a strong southern heritage — his father and two uncles fought on the Confederate side in the Civil War. Wilson's treatment of the Negro was labeled "traitorous, un-American, unjust, undemocratic and hypocritical." Any man who supported this brand of democracy, and Mitchel in particular, "ought to damn him eternally in the eyes of the Colored voter." The old-line Democrats accused Wilson and Mitchel of seeking the destruction of "the greatest and fairest political organization in the country for the Colored voter, the organization that has been his consistent and unfailing friend for many years — Tammany Hall." In seeking Negro votes for the Tammany candidate, Edward McCall, the "regular" organization claimed that where the Fusion administrations of Strong, Low, and Gaynor gave the Negro less than $5,000 a year in patronage, Tammany had given $600,000 a year. To further McCall's campaign for Negro votes the Independent Colored Voters Association was formed to buttress the work of the United Colored Democracy.[83]

Despite the attempt to associate Mitchel with Wilson in the mind of the Negro electorate, most Negroes supported the Fusion candidate. Mitchel informed the Negro community that he regarded segregation as "abhorrent to American institutions and American law." He defended Wilson, saying that the President was making an honest effort in the direction of equality despite the opposition of a reactionary Senate. He promised that he would appoint persons to governmental positions without regard to race or color. Although most Negroes appear to have subscribed to Mitchel's candidacy for mayor, they refused to endorse his running mate for comptroller. As the *Age* noted, all party lines were disregarded in the 1913 elections.[84] This was illustrated by Negro support of the Progressive party. But the party hurt its chances of receiving substantial Negro backing when it failed to nominate any Negro for elective office. Consequently, a group of Negroes broke with the Progressives and formed the Civil Club. The Club immediately nominated John M. Royall, a Negro, for alderman from a district with a large Negro population. Negroes were told that if they voted for Royall as a unit they would make their vote a "potent and influencing factor in our civic and political welfares." Negro leaders almost to a man united behind the Negro candidate. E. E. Lee, a Democrat, as well as Gilchrist Stewart, a Republican, endorsed Royall's candidacy. Royall campaigned on issues of deep concern to New York Negroes — better neighborhood conditions and wider employment of Negroes in city jobs. Even though Royall lost, the *Age* maintained that he secured 85 per cent of the Negro vote. As yet, the Negro vote had not assumed sufficient proportion in any New York district to elect a Negro candidate without white support. The NAACP believed that the method of drawing district lines accounted for the failure of Negroes to succeed to elective office. "It looks as though the Republicans of New York would prefer to gerrymander colored Harlem," the *Crisis* alleged in 1916, "so as to distribute it in Democratic districts rather than to risk the election of a colored member to the Legislature." [85]

As the presidential election of 1916 approached, Wilson's chances of winning a sizable portion of the Negro vote appeared unlikely. Wilson had done nothing to abate Negro disappointment with his racial policy; he only augmented Negro resentment toward his administration when he sent the marines into Haiti and appointed a white minister to the Negro republic. Negroes had come to consider the ambassadorship to Haiti a Negro prerogative. When informed that he might even lose the Negro vote he had won in 1912, Wilson responded angrily: "If the colored people made a mistake in voting for me, they ought to correct it." Similarly, he treated Negro protests with almost complete contempt. T. Thomas Fortune, now writing for the *Colored American Review*, considered Wilson the exemplification of the southern racist. James Weldon Johnson condemned Wilson not only for his Negro policy, but because he had brought the nation more than once "to the brink of war," because he had conducted a "petty and dishonorable war" against Mexico, and because his foreign policy, in general, had been one of "timidity, indecision, inaction, and cowardice." This discontent spread into the Democratic camp. A Negro Democrat, Ralph E. Langston, who had supported Wilson in 1912, switched his allegiance to Charles Evans Hughes. Wilson had treated the Negro "most shabbily," asserted Langston, and the race would show "that the Negro strikes back at his enemies the same as other self-respecting races." According to the *Age*, Negro Democrats were working harder for the Democratic gubernatorial candidate, Samuel Seabury, than Wilson. Accordingly, Negro support for Wilson in the election of 1916 was inconsequential.[86]

The Republicans wasted no time in capitalizing on Negro resentment toward Wilson. Negro support for Wilson was a "political folly and race-suicide," his actions had "shown that the Democratic party cannot be trusted to deal fairly" with the Negro, read a Negro Republican advertisement in the *Crisis*. Four more years of Wilson, the Republican campaign tract continued, would mean the "complete elimination of the Negro from American politics." The Negro's only alternative, the Republican advertisement concluded, was to vote for a "man of highest character and of absolute sincerity in his devotion to the cause of liberty, justice and humanity" — Charles Evans Hughes. Where Wilson at best vacillated on the problems facing the Negro, Hughes announced his adherence to "equal and exact justice to all . . . for the maintenance of the rights of all citizens regardless of color." The *Age* praised Hughes as not just a man of words but of deeds. Hughes and Fairbanks Colored Leagues appeared throughout the nation. To bring the Negro leadership into closer communication with the party, the G.O.P. created a Colored Advisory Committee. Despite strong Negro support, Hughes failed to win the election.[87]

Although the Negro's struggle for equality on the national level received a severe blow as a result of Wilson's Negro policy, in New York Negroes recorded a number of significant gains. In 1913 the state legislature enacted another law (the Levy Act) prohibiting discrimination in areas of public life. It was declared illegal for owners of public accommodations, resorts, or amusement facilities to "directly or indirectly refuse, withhold from or deny" access to those facilities on the basis of race, color, or creed. If an employee denied a person use of such places for the reasons mentioned, it was "presumptive evidence" that he was acting for his employer. Before the passage of this act, many employers had claimed that employees who discriminated against Negroes were acting contrary to the management's policy. It was also declared illegal to advertise that a public place restricted its clientele to persons of a particular race or religion. This was a special grievance of the Jewish community. It appears that the Levy Act was enacted in response to the urgings of Jews as well as Negroes. The violator of this law was subject to a fine ranging from $100 to $500 or imprisonment for a period from 30 to 90 days. In addition, the aggrieved party could sue for damages not in excess of $500. Under this piece of legislation, a few Negroes brought successful suits. For instance, a Negro took action against a Manhattan theater that compelled Negroes to sit in the balcony. The Negro was awarded $100 in damages and the theater abandoned its policy of segregation.[88]

The law received a setback when the Court of Appeals ruled in 1918 that the Levy Act did not apply to saloons. The state legislature reacted quickly to correct this flaw. Two years before this alteration in the Levy Act, the ban on mixed boxing exhibitions was rescinded.[89]

In the mayoralty election of 1917, Negroes generally expressed satisfaction with the Mitchel administration. When Negroes had asked for the elimination of certain obnoxious scenes from the movie "The Birth of a Nation" in 1915, Mitchel honored their request. He also had recommended the appointment of Negro interns to Harlem Hospital and had approved an appropriation for a public bathhouse in Harlem. In 1917 he appointed a Negro, Dr. Eugene P. Roberts, to the Board of Education.[90] Thus, it is not surprising that Mitchel received strong backing from Negro New York. Despite Tammany's attempts to portray Mitchel as anti-Negro, Negro leaders announced that they admired the Mayor's "frank talk." Mayor Mitchel won the respect of many Negroes when he held a conference with prominent New York Negroes to discuss their grievances. Consequently, when Mitchel advertised in the Negro press that he had made the police the servant of the people, "to Help, and not to Hurt," the Negro voter could not but agree. Despite overwhelming Negro support for the incumbent, the election went to his opponent, John Hylan.[91]

Even though Negroes had lost a friend in city hall, the new mayor could not overlook the interests of a population that had been enlarged as a result of the tide of newcomers rushing to the city from the South. In 1918 Bellevue Hospital agreed to add Negro interns to its staff, and, a year later, the New York City Board of Magistrates appointed the first Negro court attendant. When Mayor Hylan was asked what he would do if such anti-Negro organizations as the Ku Klux Klan attempted to operate in the city, he responded that he was "unalterably opposed to any organization which" sought "to capitalize or promote racial hatred." Under his administration, he asserted in 1921, the "civic rights and privileges of colored citizens have been fully and impartially recognized by the city." The Mayor concluded that he was "unalterably opposed to distinctions on account of race, creed or color, through either governmental agencies or any other agency." [92]

The growth in the Negro population of the city also earned for the race places on the Republican ticket in 1917. One of the candidates, Edward A. Johnson, was elected to the state assembly; another, James C. Thomas, was defeated for the post of alderman. The *Age* blamed Thomas' defeat not on whites, but Negroes who voted for either the Democratic or Socialist candidates. The fact that the Republican party nominated Negroes for public office before the Democracy helped to maintain the Negro's alliance with that party. While Thomas was winning election to the state assembly in 1918, Johnson was defeated. The following year the Republican party made a deal: it set aside Thomas' district, the Twenty-first Assembly District, as a Negro province and turned Johnson's district, the Nineteenth, back to white control. The other parties recognized Negro predominance in the Twenty-first by also nominating Negro candidates for the assembly. Despite this gain, Negro Republicans were annoyed with the Thomas-Johnson deal and the failure of their party to give them what they considered a decent share of the patronage in the city and the state.[93]

Negro demands for equality were stimulated by the war to make the world "safe for democracy." Although this is a "bit of high-sounding phraseology," wrote James Weldon Johnson during the war years, those who are mouthing it "are advertising the article, making it a household word." It is time for Negroes to insist that the "aims and ideals of America" be extended to them. "The war, indeed," Richard Bardolph has written, "greatly strengthened the Negroes' . . . determination to achieve fuller participation in American life." [94] Negroes had served both on the battlefield and in the defense plant to help win the war and work toward the brave new world. More than ever before they were unlikely to accept second-class citizenship; but white America was not so inclined. Lynchings rather than disappearing increased in the South, race riots directed against the Negro, especially in the North, increased in number and ferocity, and the less violent and more subtle forms of discrimination were still very much present. Even though the NAACP and other groups protested against such atrocities, redress was not forthcoming.[95] Against this background, the Negro community of New York and the rest of the nation made fertile ground for those who were advancing quick solutions to the Negro's problems. As James Weldon Johnson wrote in 1930, looking back on the immediate period following the war:

> Eight months after the armistice, with black men back fresh from the front, there broke the Red Summer of 1919, and the

mingled emotions of the race were bitterness, despair, and anger. There developed an attitude of cynicism that was a characteristic foreign to the Negro. There developed also a spirit of defiance born of desperation. These sentiments and reactions found varying degrees of expression in the Negro publications throughout the country; but Harlem became the centre where they were formulated and voiced to the Negroes of America and the world. Radicalism in Harlem, which had declined as the war approached, burst out anew. But it was something different from the formal radicalism of pre-war days; it was a radicalism motivated by a fierce race consciousness.

Thus when Marcus Garvey called for a return to Africa, black America gave him a warm reception. Negro Socialists and Communists based their appeals on the same background. Sterling Spero and Abram Harris have written that the rise of "left-wing" sentiment among Negroes following World War I "bore the earmarks of economic unrest and social dissatisfaction for which the inertia of the labor movement and American race psychology were responsible." [96]

Yet communism and socialism, despite the charges of state and federal investigating committees, never attracted a large Negro following.[97] This can be seen in the campaigns for election to the state assembly. In 1918 the Socialist candidate in the Nineteenth Assembly District received only 9 per cent of the vote in opposing two other candidates — one Negro and one white. When the Socialist was the only Negro in the race a year later his percentage rose to only 12 per cent; and in 1920 the Socialist choice, once again the only Negro in the assembly campaign, captured a mere 11 per cent of the vote. Similarly, in the contest for assemblyman from the Twenty-first Assembly District, the best showing made by the Socialist party was in 1919 when its candidate was opposed by two Negroes.[98] Negroes, despite all the insults they received at the hands of white America, still wanted to be part of the American capitalistic system.

With the approach of the presidential election of 1920, the Negro vote of New York took on added importance. As a result of the great influx of Negroes to the city during the war years, the *Age* estimated that the Negro electorate had increased by 45 per cent. Democratic prospects of attracting a substantial Negro following in the fall elections had been damaged seriously by Wilson's Negro policy. In addition to Wilson's early actions, he had fallen into further disfavor with the Negro community because of his failure to issue promptly a proclamation condemning lynchings or mob assaults committed against the Negro. The *Age* severely criticized the Democratic ticket of James M. Cox and Franklin D. Roosevelt. It alleged that Roosevelt had assisted Wilson in the execution of his segregation and Haitian policies.[99]

Warren G. Harding, the Republican presidential candidate, appealed directly for Negro votes. His reference to the Wilson administration's "rape" of Haiti won cheers from the Negro press. Throughout the campaign, the *Age* carried the following statement of Harding in bold letters in a prominent section of the paper:

> I would not be fitted to be President of the United States if I did not tell you in the South precisely the same thing I would say in the North. I want you to know that I believe in equality before the law . . . You cannot give one right to a white man and deny the same right to a black man.

Harding also maintained that "the federal government should stamp out lynching." The Republican vice-presidential candidate, Calvin Coolidge, seconded these remarks when he asserted that Negroes "should be defended from lynching, and . . . be freely granted equal opportunity." By virtue of Wilson's failure to support the Negro in his struggle for equality and the continued outrages piled upon Negroes in the Democratic South, the Republican party could once again look forward to strong Negro support at the polls.[100] In spite of Negro disappointment with the limited efforts on the part of the Republican party to secure equality for the race throughout the nation, Republicanism in 1920 still attracted a large majority of the city's Negro voters. The southern Democracy had remained the albatross about the neck of New York's Democratic party. It was not until the New Deal of the 1930s that the Democracy turned its minority vote among Negroes into a majority.

As for equal rights, New York's Negroes had made significant, if limited, strides forward since the Civil War. School segregation was outlawed, but de facto segregation took its place. Negroes were granted equal rights in public places, but the use of subtle discrimination too often devitalized these rights. Negroes were elected to public office, but from predominantly Negro districts. By 1920 New York society had accorded the Negro certain legal protections, yet, at the same time, many elements of that society had invented techniques for evading those very laws.

Notes

[1] Myrdal, *American Dilemma*, pp. 783, 785.

[2] Litwack, *North of Slavery*, pp. 88–91; Gilbert T. Stephenson, *Race Distinctions in American Law* (New York, 1910), p. 283.

[3] For debates, see *Proceedings and Debates of the Constitutional Convention of the State of New York, 1867–1868* (5 vols., Albany, 1868), I, 236–551; V, 3875–96.

[4] *Ibid.*, I, 236–37, 310–11, 317, 388.

[5] *Ibid.*, I, 240–41, 258, 329–30, 514.

[6] *Ibid.*, V, 3875–91; *New York Times*, December 8, 1869.

[7] *New York Times*, March 18, April 15, September 23, December 8, 1869, and January 6, April 22, 1870; Stephenson, *Race Distinctions*, p. 283.

[8] *New York Times*, September 24, 1870, and March 13, April 16, 1871.

[9] *Ibid.*, March 13, 1871; August 16, 27, October 4, 1872; July 27, 1876.

[10] *New York Statutes At Large, 1873*, pp. 583–84; *Laws of New York, 1881* (Albany, 1881), I, 541.

[11] Johnson, *Black Manhattan*, p. 46; Kirkwood, *Autumn Holiday*, p. 30; Litwack, *North of Slavery*, pp. 111–12; George Rose, *The Great Country; or, Impressions of America* (London, 1868), p. 28.

[12] *New York Times*, December 14, 1871; May 14, 1880; January 12, 1881.

[13] B.E., *Journal for 1878* (New York, 1879), pp. 816–19, and *Journal for 1882* (New York, 1883), p. 361; *Suffragist*, February 26, 1880.

[14] B.E., *Journal for 1883*, pp. 294–95, 370–71, 557; *Journal for 1884* (New York, 1885), p. 433; *Journal for 1887* (New York, 1888), pp. 199, 202, 215; *New York Globe*, January 27, 1883, and April 5, May 3, 1884; *New York Sun*, February 13, 1883; *New York Times*, February 13, 1883.

[15] Blascoer, *Colored School Children*, pp. 11–12; B.E., *Annual Report of the Superintendent, 1884* (New York, 1884), pp. 52–53; Dyckoff, "A Negro City in New York," p. 954; Hartt, "I'd Like to Show You Harlem," p. 357; *Tribune Monthly* (March, 1896), 51.

[16] *New York Age*, April 5, 1906, and July 22, 1909; *New York Times*, May 8, 1901. On the subject of the teacher protest against Dr. Bulkley, the *Hebrew Standard* wrote that the teachers "have set a very bad example of race-prejudice and should by no means be allowed to have their own way in this matter." Such discrimination is a "wanton and malicious attempt to introduce the race question into our public schools." Quoted in *ibid.*, July 22, 1909. For similar incidents, see *New York Tribune*, December 28, 1899; Ovington, *Half A Man*, p. 18.

[17] *New York Globe*, December 15, 22, 1883; *New York Tribune*, August 24, 1899; People ex. rel. King v. Gallagher, 93 New York 438–66 (1883); Brooklyn Board of Education, *Proceedings for 1894* (New York, 1895), p. 522.

[18] *New York Tribune*, August 23, 24, September 7, 1899; *Laws of New York, 1894* (Albany, 1894), II, 1288 and *1900* (Albany, 1900), II, 1173: People ex. rel. Cisco v. School Board of the Borough of Queens, N.Y.C., 61 New York Supplement 330–33 (1899).

[19] For specific incidents, see *New York Freeman*, June 19, December 18, 1886; *New York Age*, July 5, 7, 1890; *New York Times*, October 2, 1890, and November 6, 7, 1891.

[20] Vincent P. DeSantis, *Republicans Face the Southern Question* (Baltimore, 1959), pp. 173–77; DeSantis "The Republican Party and the Southern Negro, 1877–1897," *Journal of Negro History* (April, 1960), 73–82; Stanley P. Hirshon, *Farewell to the Bloody Shirt* (Bloomington, Ind., 1962), pp. 101–105; Rayford W. Logan, *The Negro in American Life and Thought: the Nadir, 1877–1901* (New York, 1954), pp. 45–46.

[21] *New York Globe*, October 25, November 3, 1883; *New York Tribune*, March 18, 1879.

[22] *New York Globe*, October 20, 25, 1883; T. Thomas Fortune, *Black and White: Land, Labor, and Politics in the South* (New York, 1884), pp. 111, 126; Fortune, *Negro in Politics*, pp. 18, 21–22, 35–36; Fortune, "The Democratic Return to Power," *A.M.E. Church Review*, I (January, 1885), 220.

[23] Fortune, *Black and White*, p. 127; Fortune, *Negro in Politics*, p. 52; Fortune, "Democratic Return to Power," p. 220. Fortune, however, failed to obtain the full support of his newspaper in his rejection of the Republican party. On November 3, 1883, for example, the *Globe* asserted that Negroes would "do well" to support Republicans. Also on July 19, 1884, the paper urged the nomination of Blaine as the Republican presidential candidate. This controversy within the editorial board may have prompted Fortune to discard the *Globe* and to establish in its place the *Freeman*. See John T. Morris, "The History and Development of Negro Journalism," *A.M.E. Church Review*, VI (January, 1890), 313.

[24] *New York Freeman*, January 27, 1883, and October 23, 1886; *New York Age*, November 12, 1887; January 28, 1888; August 31, 1889; Fortune, *Negro in Politics*, pp. 45, 52.

[25] *New York Globe*, February 3, September 1, 1883; *New York Freeman*, October 23, 1886, and January 15, June 4, 1887; Fortune, *Black and White*, pp. 127, 131; Fortune, *Negro in Politics*, pp. 12, 61.

[26] *New York Globe*, September 1, 1883; *New York Freeman*, June 4, 1887. For response to Fortune's proposal, see Emma Lou Thornbrough, "The National Afro-American League, 1887–1908," *Journal of Southern History*, XXVII (November, 1961), 496–98.

[27] *New York Globe*, February 17, March 10, 1883; *New York Freeman*, March 20, 1886; Fortune, *Black and White, passim*; *Republican Greeting to 25,000 Free and Loyal Colored Voters of the State of New York, 1887–1888* (Albany, 1888), p. 6; T. McCants Stewart, Review of *Black and White*, *A.M.E. Church Review*, I (January, 1885), 193; Edward E. Cooper to John E. Bruce, June 30, 1899, Alexander Crummell to Bruce, September 27, 1897, Bruce to Crummell, November 6, 1897, John E. Bruce Papers, Schomburg Collection. For Fortune's association with Washington, see Thornbrough, "More Light on Booker T. Washington and the *New York Age*," *Journal of Negro History*, XLIII (January, 1958), 34–49.

[28] *New York Freeman*, October 8, 1887; *New York Age*, October 15, 1887; *Republican Greeting to 25,000*, pp. 6, 15.

[29] *New York Age*, November 12, 1887, and October 27, 1888; *New York Times*, March 13, April 16, 1871.

[30] *New York Age*, August 25, 1888. Estimate of the size of New York State Negro electorate given in

Republican Greeting to 25,000, p. 3.

[31] T. McCants Stewart, *The Afro-American in Politics: An Address at a Meeting of Colored Citizens . . . October 27, 1891* (October, 1891), p. 5; New York State Cleveland League, *Proceedings of the Convention of 1892* (Brooklyn, 1892), pp. 2, 8; *New York Globe*, April 4, 1883; *New York Age*, November 19, 1887, and August 18, 25, September 29, October 13, 1888. For biographical information on Stewart, see *ibid.*, November 5, 1887; July 27, 1889; March 16, 1911; John Puroy Mitchel, "The Public Schools of New York," *Crisis*, XIV (July, 1917), 132; and for Matthews, see Meier, *Negro Thought*, pp. 29–30.

[32] *New York Age*, October 22, November 12, 1887.

[33] *Ibid.*, August 11, September 29, October 27, 1888. Among these organizations were the Harrison and Morton Political and Literary Association of the Seventeenth Assembly District, the Colored Republican League of the Eleventh A. D., the Lincoln Club of the Seventeenth A. D., the Harrison and Morton Campaign Club of the Nineteenth A. D. *Ibid.*, July 7, August 4, 11, 25, October 13, 27, 1888.

[34] *Ibid.*, October 20, November 10, 1888.

[35] *Brooklyn Eagle*, October 28, 1891; Stewart, *Afro-American in Politics*, p. 5.

[36] *New York Age*, August 4, September 8, 29, 1888, and March 9, 30, October 5, November 9, 23, 1889.

[37] Leslie Fishel, "The Negro in Northern Politics, 1870–1900," *Mississippi Valley Historical Review*, XLII (December, 1955), 476, has not given sufficient emphasis to this point in blaming the "Lack of organization, absence of discipline, bitter jealousy and its consequent feuding"

of "Negro political units in almost all northern states" for the Negro's second-class position in northern politics.

[38] James Q. Wilson, *Negro Politics: the Search for Leadership* (Glencoe, Ill., 1960), pp. 23–24; *New York Freeman*, November 28, 1885.

[39] *New York Age*, August 31, November 2, 1889.

[40] *Ibid.*, August 31, 1889, and January 25, 1890.

[41] *Ibid.*, October 5, 12, 19, 1889; Fortune, "The Afro-American League," *A.M.E. Church Review*, VII (July, 1890), 2–6.

[42] *New York Age*, January 25, 1890; the view taken here has followed that presented in Thornbrough, "National Afro-American League," pp. 494–501.

[43] *New York Age*, January 11, March 1, June 14, 1890.

[44] Thornbrough, "National Afro-American League," pp. 499–501.

[45] There is a dispute among historians as to the extent of the Negro protest over failure to pass the Lodge Bill: Vincent DeSantis, "The Republican Party and the Southern Negro," pp. 85–86, has argued that expressions of Negro disappointment were minimal; on the other hand, August Meier, *Negro Thought*, p. 38, has contended that "articulate [Negro] opinion was all but unanimous in support" of the Lodge Bill. For support of the latter position in New York City, see *New York Age*, July 26, 1890. Fortune was upset by the failure of the bill to pass and blamed the Republican party, see *ibid.*, December 20, 1890, and January 10, 17, 1891; Stewart, however, considered the bill a mistake, *ibid.*, March 1, 1890.

[46] *New York Freeman*, June 19, August 28, December 11, 1886; *New York Age*, January 18, June 7, July 5, and September 20, 1890; *New York Times*, October 2, 1890.

[47] *New York Age*, February 23, May 31, July 26, 1890. A year later, though, a law was passed that prohibited life insurance companies from making "any distinction and discrimination between white persons and colored persons . . . as to the premiums or rates charged for policies . . . or in any manner whatever." *Laws of New York, 1891* (Albany, 1891), I, 288; *New York Age*, February 28, April 11, 1891. Discrimination by insurance companies had been a particular grievance of Negroes. *Ibid.*, February 23, 1889; *New York Freeman*, April 30, 1887.

[48] *New York Age*, February 23, July 20, August 31, 1889, and May 17, July 5, 26, 1890; Fortune, "The Republican Party Platform," *A.M.E. Church Review*, IX (October, 1892), 128.

[49] *New York Age*, March 8, 22, July 19, August 2, September 27, October 18, 1890.

[50] *Ibid.*, October 25, November 1, 8, 1890.

[51] Brooklyn *Eagle*, July 28, 1891. See *New York Times*, October 11, 1891 for similar comment.

[52] *New York Age*, August 29, 1891; Cleveland League, *Convention of 1892*, p. 6; Brooklyn *Eagle*, October 12, 1891, and May 18, 1892; Stewart, *Afro-American in Politics*, p. 2.

[53] Brooklyn *Eagle*, February 27, 1896; *New York Times*, June 16, July 4, August 22, 23, 1895.

[54] *New York Times*, June 19, October 19, 1895; *New York Tribune*, June 16, 25, August 14, 1895.

[55] Brooklyn *Eagle*, June 21, 1895, and August 14, 1897; *New York Age*, April 19, July 19, 1906; *New York Times*, June 20, 21, July 3, 1895, and November 17, 1901; *New York Tribune*, April 14, 1901, and February 23, 1903.

[56] Brooklyn *Eagle*, September 5, 1897; *New York Tribune*, July 1, October 16, 1897.

[57] *New York Tribune*, October 21, 27, 1897.

[58] *Ibid.*, October 29, 1898, and August 7, 1900; Brooklyn *Eagle*, January 27, February 10, 1898; *New York Times*, January 26, August 10, 1898; McKay, *Harlem*, p. 125.

[59] *New York Tribune*, September 29, October 20, 29, November 6, 1898; Franklin, *From Slavery to Freedom*, pp. 414–16.

[60] New York *Post*, August 21, 1900; *New York Tribune*, October 29, 1898.

[61] *New York Tribune*, October 20, 22, 24, 27, 1901.

[62] *Ibid.*, September 30, 1903. No Negro newspapers are available for the period 1900–1904.

[63] *New York Age*, January 26, August 31, September 28, October 19, November 2, 9, 1905.

[64] *Ibid.*, September 27, November 8, 22, 29, 1906, and March 7, 1907.

[65] *Ibid.*, September 27, November 8, 22, 29, 1906, and March 7, 1907. See James A. Tinsley, "Roosevelt, Foraker, and the Brownsville Affray," *Journal of Negro History*, XLI (January, 1956), 43–65, for details of Roosevelt's discharge of the Negro soldiers. Tinsley questions both Roosevelt's action and the guilt of the soldiers. For Roosevelt's general attitude toward the Negro, see Scheiner, "President Theodore Roosevelt and the Negro," pp. 169–82.

[66] For Foraker's role in the Brownsville matter, see Tinsley, "Brownsville Affray," pp. 43–65. See Emma Lou Thornbrough, "The Brownsville Episode and the Negro Vote," *Mississippi Valley Historical Review*, XLIV (December, 1957), 483–84, for Negro support of Foraker for the presidency. For the Hughes movement, see *New York Age*, February 6, 1908.

[67] Thornbrough, "Brownsville and the Negro Vote," pp. 481–88.

[68] New York Age, May 7, July 9, August 13, 20, 27, September 17, October 8, 15, 29, 1908.

[69] Ibid., September 1, October 14, December 16, 1909; Crisis, I (December, 1910), 20.

[70] New York Age, October 11, 1890; Crisis, XIII (March, 1917), 223; Meier, Negro Thought, pp. 172–81; Richardson, National Cyclopedia of the Colored Race, p. 447; "Objects, Plan of Organization and Annual Topics of the National Afro-American Council," Rochester, N.Y., September 15, 1898, in Bruce Papers; Thornbrough, "Afro-American League," pp. 501–11; Alexander Walters, My Life and Work (New York, 1917), pp. 102–103.

[71] New York Age, August 3, 10, 1905, and November 1, 1906; New York Times, August 21, 26, 1900, and February 20, June 4, August 4, 1903; New York Tribune, May 20, 1903; Citizens' Protective League, Story of the Riot, pp. 1–2.

[72] Meier, Negro Thought, pp. 181–82; Elliott M. Rudwick, "The Niagara Movement," Journal of Negro History, XLII (July, 1957), 177–91; Thornbrough, "Brownsville Episode and the Negro Vote," p. 476.

[73] Franklin, From Slavery to Freedom, pp. 431–38.

[74] James L. Crouthamel, "The Springfield Race Riot of 1908," Journal of Negro History, XLV (April, 1960), 164–81; Mary White Ovington, "The National Association for the Advancement of Colored People," ibid., IX (April, 1924), 107–16; William English Walling, "The Founding of the NAACP," Crisis, XXXVI (July, 1929), 226; J. Salwyn Schapiro, "Henry Moskowitz: a Social Reformer in Politics," Outlook, CII (October 26, 1912), 446–49; DAB, Supplement II, 689–90.

[75] Crisis, I (November, 1910), 11–12; DAB, XVI, 430–32; XVII, 166–67; XVIII, 96–97; Supplement I, 462–63; Rischin, Promised City, pp. 242–43, 247–48; Meier, Negro Thought, p. 182.

[76] NAACP, Annual Report, 1912 (New York, 1913), 25; Crisis, II (August, 1911), 146; DAB, Supplement II, 622–23.

[77] New York Age, September 2, 1909; December 1, 1910; June 29, 1911; March 21, October 10, November 14, 1912; February 13, April 10, October 16, 1913; August 17, 1918; Crisis, II (August, 1911), 142; III (February, 1912), 158; IV (June, 1912), 64; VI (June, 1913), 71; XI (January, 1916), 117; XVI (June, 1918), 86; New York Tribune, April 14, 1901; New York World, February 23, 1913; Ovington, Half A Man, p. 197; "Troubles of a Black Policeman," Literary Digest, XLIV (January 27, 1912), 177–79.

[78] Jane Addams, "The Progressive Party and the Negro," Crisis, V (November, 1912), 30–31; Arthur S. Link, "The Negro as a Factor in the Campaign of 1912," Journal of Negro History, XXXII (January, 1947), 99; Link, "Theodore Roosevelt in the South in 1912," North Carolina Historical Review, XXIII (July, 1946), 313–24; Link, ed., "Correspondence Relating to the Progressive Party's 'Lily White' Policy in 1912," Journal of Southern History, X (November, 1944), 480–90; George E. Mowry, "The South and the Progressive 'Lily White' Party of 1912," ibid., VI (May, 1940), 237–47.

[79] New York Age, August 15, 29, September 19, 1882.

[80] Ibid., October 24, 1912; Crisis, IV (August, 1912), 181; Du Bois, Dusk of Dawn (New York, 1940), 233–35; Link, "The Negro as a Factor in the Campaign of 1912," pp. 81–99; Link, Wilson:

the Road to the White House (Princeton, 1947), pp. 501–505.

[81] *New York Age,* March 23, June 8, 15, 1911, and July 11, September 12, 19, October 3, 1912; Meier, *Negro Thought,* p. 188; Meier, "The Negro and the Democratic Party, 1875–1915," *Phylon,* XVII (2d quarter, 1956), 185–91. The *Crisis* estimated that Wilson received between 20 and 30 per cent of the New York Negro vote. *Crisis,* V (December, 1912), 59.

[82] Kathleen L. Wolgemuth, "Woodrow Wilson's Appointment Policy and the Negro," *Journal of Southern History,* XXIV (November, 1958), 457–71; Wolgemuth, "Woodrow Wilson and Federal Segregation," *Journal of Negro History,* XLIV (April, 1959), 158–73; Arthur S. Link, *Wilson: the New Freedom* (Princeton, 1956), pp. 243–48. For Negro protests, see *ibid.,* pp. 248–50.

[83] *Tammany Hall vs. Fusion, or Organized Democracy Against Disorganized Aristocracy and Bastard Reform* (New York, 1913), pp. 3–12; *New York Age,* October 16, 1913. The local Democracy also was plagued by intraparty struggles among Negro Democrats between 1911 and 1914, see *ibid.,* September 21, 1911; January 4, December 19, 1912; February 27, 1913; November 19, 26, 1914.

[84] *New York Age,* October 9, 16, 30, November 27, 1913; A. Clayton Powell, Sr., *Against the Tide: an Autobiography* (New York, 1938), p. 56.

[85] *New York Age,* September 4, 18, 25, October 2, 16, 23, 30, November 13, 1913; *Crisis,* XI (April, 1916), 287.

[86] *New York Age,* September 7, 14, 21, October 12, 19, 26, 1916; *Colored American Review,* I (June, 1916), 233; *New York Times,* November 13, 1914; Link, *Wilson: the New Freedom,* pp. 252–53.

[87] *New York Age,* June 1, September 7, November 9, 1916; *Crisis,* XIII (November, 1916), 5–6, 33.

[88] *New York Age,* January 30, April 17, May 29, October 16, 1913; *Crisis,* VI (June, 1913), 71, 144, and XIII (January, 1917), 146; *New York Times,* March 12, 1913.

[89] *New York Age,* July 13, 1916, and February 2, April 20, July 6, 1918.

[90] *Ibid.,* October 8, 1914; March 4, 11, 25, April 1, 1915; January 11, October 25, November 1, 1917; May Childs Nerney, Secretary of the NAACP, "Notice to Members to Protest Birth of a Nation," March 29, 1915, in Bruce Papers.

[91] *New York Age,* October 4, 18, 25, November 1, 1917.

[92] *Ibid.,* March 16, 1918; *Crisis,* XVII (April, 1919), 297; Mayor's Attitude on the Ku Klux Klan, undated memorandum, and John F. Hylan to Joseph McLane, October 26, 1921, Hylan Papers, New York City Municipal Archives.

[93] *New York Age,* September 27, November 15, 1917, and August 2, 30, November 8, 1919; Ralph Bunche, "The Political Status of the Negro," unpublished manuscript prepared for the Carnegie-Myrdal Study of the Negro in America, 7 vols., Schomburg Collection, New York, 1940, V, 1340.

[94] *New York Age,* May 24, 1917, and November 16, 1918; Bardolph, *Negro Vanguard,* p. 134.

[95] *New York Age,* May 24, 31, June 21, 28, 1917, and May 25, July 20, 1918; *Crisis,* XVII (May, 1919), 13–14; Du Bois, "The Black Man in the Revolution of 1914–1918," *ibid.,* XVII (March, 1919), 218–23; Glenn Frank, "The Clash of Color: the Negro in American Democracy," *Century,* XCIX (November, 1919), 89–92; Franklin, *From Slavery to Freedom,* pp. 463–81.

[96] Johnson, *Black Manhattan,* p. 246; Cronon, *Black Moses, passim;*

Spero and Harris, *Black Worker*, p. 387. For discussion of Negro Communist and Socialist groups, see *ibid.*, pp. 386–94.

[97] An example of how Communist hunting groups attempted to lump all Negro protest groups under the Red banner is provided by the report of the Lusk Committee in 1920: Radicals are encouraged "by well-to-do liberals who have taken active part in social uplift organizations, working among the negroes in this State." *Revolutionary Radicalism*, II, 1477. James Weldon Johnson and the *Age*, writing in reply to this and similar charges, asserted that a Negro did not need a Socialist or Communist to tell him of his plight, he knew it. *New York Age*, February 8, August 9, 1919, and January 10, 1920.

[98] Bunche, "Political Status," V, 1340.

[99] *New York Age*, August 2, 1917, and September 18, October 2, 23, 1920; Henry Blumenthal, "Woodrow Wilson and the Race Question," *Journal of Negro History*, XLVIII (January, 1963), 10–15.

[100] *New York Age*, June 19, July 31, September 25, October 16, 23, 1920.

Tables

Table 1

Negro Population of New York City, 1820–1920[a]

YEAR	NEW YORK CITY	MANHATTAN	BROOKLYN
1820	12,647	10,886	1,761
1830	15,983	13,976	2,007
1840	19,204	16,358	2,846
1850	17,880	13,815	4,065
1860	17,580	12,581	4,999
1865	14,804	9,943	4,861
1870	18,760	13,093	5,667
1880	28,815	19,662	9,153
1890	33,888	23,601	10,287
1900	60,666	36,246	18,367
1910	91,709	60,534	22,708
1920	152,407	109,133	31,912

[a] Figures for New York City before 1900 include only Manhattan and Brooklyn. From 1900 to 1920 New York City totals include all five boroughs.

Source: *New York State Census of 1875* (Albany, 1877), p. 151, for 1820 to 1870. *Tenth Census, 1880, Population* (Washington, 1883), I, 417–22; *Eleventh Census, 1890, Population* (Washington, 1895), I, 470–71; *Twelfth Census, 1900, Population* (Washington, 1901), I, 631–32, *Thirteenth Census, 1910, Population* (Washington, 1914), III, 253–58; *Fourteenth Census, 1920, New York State* (Washington, 1923), p. 62.

Table 2

Percentage Growth of Negro Population of New York City in Preceding Decade, 1820–1920[a]

YEAR	NEW YORK CITY	MANHATTAN	BROOKLYN
1830	26.4	36.5	13.9
1840	20.2	17.0	41.8
1850	−6.9	−15.5	30.0
1860	−1.7	−8.8	23.0
1865	−15.8	−20.9	−2.8
1870	26.7	32.7	13.4
1880	53.6	50.2	61.5
1890	17.6	20.0	11.0
1900	79.0	63.6	78.5
1910	51.2	67.4	36.0
1920	66.2	80.3	40.5

[a] See a in table 1. Percentages for 1860 to 1865 and 1865 to 1870 are computed on a five-year basis.
Source: *Ibid.*

Table 3

Population of New York City and Negro Percent of Total, 1820–1920[a]

YEAR	NEW YORK CITY		MANHATTAN		BROOKLYN	
	Total	Negro	Total	Negro	Total	Negro
1820	134,893	9.4	123,706	8.8	11,187	15.7
1830	217,647	7.3	202,589	6.9	20,535	9.7
1840	360,323	5.3	312,710	5.2	47,613	5.9
1850	654,429	2.7	515,547	2.7	138,882	2.8
1860	1,092,791	1.6	813,669	1.5	279,122	1.8
1865	1,037,476	1.4	726,386	1.4	311,090	1.5
1870	1,362,213	1.3	942,292	1.4	419,921	1.3
1880	1,772,962	1.6	1,206,299	1.6	566,663	1.6
1890	2,321,644	1.4	1,515,301	1.5	806,343	1.3
1900	3,437,202	1.8	1,850,093	1.9	1,166,582	1.5
1910	4,766,883	1.9	2,331,542	2.6	1,634,351	1.4
1920	5,620,048	2.7	2,284,103	4.8	2,018,356	1.5

[a] See a in table 1.
Source: *Ibid.*

Table 4

Negro Population of New York State
by Place of Birth, 1870–1920

BIRTHPLACE	NUMBER					
	1870	1880	1890	1900	1910	1920
New England	1,062	1,333	1,399	1,720	2,352	3,253
Middle Atlantic	1,861	3,429	3,339	4,087	5,306	7,148
East North Central	149	238	359	837	1,198	1,979
West North Central	28	67	93	221	478	793
South Atlantic	7,649	13,733	20,667	41,028	57,585	77,859
East South Central	338	409	762	1,558	2,255	4,840
West South Central	160	230	255	384	654	2,109
Mountain	0	66	16	28	164	245
Pacific	5	28	113	153	287	481
New York	38,504	44,639	40,117	44,614	49,750	62,369
Other Native U.S.	1,078	3	1,363	1,050	1,311	5,436
Foreign-Born	1,247	2,673	1,549	3,552	12,851	31,971
Total	52,081	66,848	70,092	99,232	134,191	198,483

Source: *Ninth Census, 1870, Statistics of the Population of the United States* (Washington, 1874), p. 332; *Tenth Census, Population*, I, 488–91; *Eleventh Census, Population*, I, 576–79; *Twelfth Census, Population*, I, 702–705; *Thirteenth Census, Population*, I, 739–42; III, 226; *Fourteenth Census, Population* (Washington, 1922), II, 636–40.

Table 5

Negro Population of New York State
by State of Birth, 1870–1920

BIRTHPLACE	NUMBER					
	1870	1880	1890	1900	1910	1920
Massachusetts	293	391	462	606	917	1,300
Connecticut	516	626	613	727	899	1,128
New Jersey	1,463	1,787	1,799	2,179	2,617	3,537
Pennsylvania	1,398	1,642	1,540	1,908	2,689	3,611
Ohio	86	117	194	470	638	960
Maryland	2,025	2,484	2,440	2,864	3,510	4,272
Virginia	3,458	7,383	12,237	24,118	29,157	31,425
North Carolina	663	1,237	2,244	6,587	10,282	13,326
South Carolina	502	812	1,126	2,724	6,698	13,102
Georgia	290	608	866	1,925	3,792	8,650
Florida	57	153	249	625	1,257	3,657
Kentucky	147	149	326	690	873	1,252
Tennessee	89	109	224	391	648	1,367
Alabama	57	91	135	323	536	1,564
District of Col.	389	680	1,017	1,541	2,080	2,506

Source: *Ibid.*

Table 6

Occupational Categories of the Male Foreign-Born, Negro, and Aggregate Population of New York City, 1890–1920[a]

	1890		1900		1910		1920	
	NUMBER	% OF TOTAL EMPLOYED	NUMBER	% OF TOTAL EMPLOYED	NUMBER	% OF TOTAL EMPLOYED	NUMBER	% OF TOTAL EMPLOYED
AGGREGATE								
Professional	21,367	3.2	60,853	5.5	75,122	5.4	160,058	8.7
Domestic	132,995	20.1	206,215	18.7	141,843	9.9	149,623	8.1
Trade and Transportation	259,829	39.2	406,675	36.8	612,351	43.2	774,482	42.1
Manufacturing	248,779	37.5	419,594	38.2	580,880	40.9	748,183	40.7
FOREIGN-BORN								
Professional	6,841	1.9	19,069	3.4	41,439	5.1	52,241	5.6
Domestic	88,026	25.4	127,900	22.9	92,111	11.4	94,455	10.4
Trade and Transportation	102,642	29.6	155,033	27.8	267,487	33.1	306,217	33.4
Manufacturing	149,008	43.1	249,599	44.8	402,431	49.8	460,494	50.2
NEGRO								
Professional	112	.9	729	2.9	1,526	4.7	3,320	5.9
Domestic	8,118	69.5	16,933	66.5	16,244	50.3	21,144	37.4
Trade and Transportation	2,695	23.1	5,798	22.8	9,797	30.3	19,813	35.1
Manufacturing	755	6.5	1,774	6.9	4,504	13.9	12,067	21.3

[a] Statistics based on New York City and Brooklyn as constituted in 1890 and Greater New York City as constituted in 1900 and 1910 and 1920. Persons employed in agricultural pursuits accounted for less than 1 per cent for each group between 1900 and 1920.

Source: *Eleventh Census, Population,* II, 640, 704; *Twelfth Census, 1900, Special Report of Occupations* (Washington, 1904), pp. 634–40; *Thirteenth Census, Population,* IV, 571–74; *Fourteenth Census, Population,* IV, 1157–62.

Table 7

Occupational Categories of the Female Foreign-Born, Negro, and Aggregate Population of New York City, 1890–1920[a]

	1890		1900		1910		1920	
	NUMBER	% OF TOTAL EMPLOYED	NUMBER	% OF TOTAL EMPLOYED	NUMBER	% OF TOTAL EMPLOYED	NUMBER	% OF TOTAL EMPLOYED
AGGREGATE								
Professional	9,400	4.1	24,422	6.6	45,278	8.5	68,354	9.9
Domestic	108,073	47.5	146,722	39.8	189,619	35.5	156,667	22.7
Trade and Transportation	28,569	12.5	65,318	17.7	131,724	24.7	261,707	37.8
Manufacturing	81,771	35.9	132,535	35.9	166,785	31.3	204,129	29.6
FOREIGN-BORN								
Professional	1,561	1.3	3,583	2.2	10,239	4.0	14,095	5.8
Domestic	77,120	66.7	93,598	56.3	123,552	48.5	87,016	36.2
Trade and Transportation	6,087	5.3	13,120	7.9	26,823	10.6	44,908	18.7
Manufacturing	30,825	26.7	55,841	33.6	94,239	36.9	94,518	39.3
NEGRO								
Professional	78	.9	281	1.7	603	2.3	948	2.3
Domestic	7,455	89.9	14,586	90.5	22,654	86.9	28,937	71.5
Trade and Transportation	25	.3	106	.7	365	1.4	1,464	3.6
Manufacturing	739	8.9	1,138	7.1	2,428	9.4	9,131	22.6

[a] See a in table 6.
Source: Ibid.

Bibliography

MANUSCRIPTS

John E. Bruce Papers, Schomburg Collection.
Citizens' Protective League Papers in Miscellaneous Letters and Papers, Schomburg Collection.
Mayor William J. Gaynor Papers, New York City Municipal Archives.
Mayor John F. Hylan Papers, New York City Municipal Archives.

DOCUMENTS AND REPORTS

African Methodist Episcopal Church. *Minutes of the New York Annual Conference of 1865.* New York, 1865.
Association for the Benefit of Colored Children. *Annual Report, 1878.* New York, 1879.
Association of Day Nurseries of New York City, *Annual Report, 1912.* New York, 1912.
Brooklyn Board of Education. *Proceedings for 1894.* Brooklyn, 1895.
Brooklyn Committee on Urban Conditions Among Negroes. *Report, 1916–1918.* New York, 1917–1919.
Brooklyn Home for Aged Colored People. *Annual Report, 1902.* Brooklyn, 1902.

Brooklyn Urban League for Social Service Among Negroes. *Annual Report, 1919.* New York, 1919.

Charity Organization Society of the City of New York. *Annual Report, 1903–1912.* New York, 1903–1912.

Colored Home. *Annual Report, 1865–1868, 1913.* New York, 1866–1868, 1914.

Colored Orphan Asylum and Association for the Benefit of Colored Children. *Annual Report, 1881, 1885.* New York, 1882, 1886.

Colored Orphan Asylum and Association for the Benefit of Colored Children in New York City. *Annual Report, 1904–1920.* New York, 1904–1920.

Congress of Colored Catholics of the United States. *Proceedings of Three Catholic Afro-American Congresses . . . 1889, 1890, and 1891.* Cincinnati, 1893.

Consumers' League of the City of New York. *Report for 1918.* New York, 1919.

Federation of Churches and Christian Workers in New York City. *Sociological Canvass No. 1.* New York, 1896.

———. *Sociological Canvass No. 2.* New York, 1897.

Free Kindergarten Association for Colored Children. *Annual Report, 1900, 1904, 1905, 1911–1920.* New York, 1900, 1904, 1905, 1911–1920.

Howard Colored Orphan Asylum Society. *Annual Report, 1885.* Brooklyn, 1886.

Mount Olivet Baptist Church. *Mortgage Liquidation Journal.* New York, 1946.

National Association for the Advancement of Colored People. *Annual Report, 1911–1920.* New York, 1912–1921.

National League for the Protection of Colored Women. *Annual Report, 1910–1911.* New York, 1911.

National League on Urban Conditions Among Negroes. *Report, 1910–1917.* New York, 1917.

National Negro Business League. *Report of the Fifth Annual Convention, 1904.* Pensacola, 1904.

———. *Report of the Eleventh Annual Convention, 1910.* Nashville, 1910.

National Urban League. *Annual Report, 1917–1918.* New York, 1918.

New York African Society for Mutual Relief. *Charter and By-laws.* New York, 1921.

New York City Board of Education. *Annual Report, 1865–1897.* New York, 1866–1898.

———. *Annual Report from the Committee on Colored Schools, 1866, 1868.* New York, 1867, 1869.

———. *Directory, 1865–1897.* New York, 1866–1898.

———. *Journal, 1865–1897.* New York, 1866–1898.

New York City Commissioners of Public Charities and Correction. *Annual Report, 1865.* New York, 1866.

New York City Department of Education. *Annual Report, 1898–1920.* New York, 1898–1920.

———. *Journal, 1898–1920.* New York, 1898–1920.

New York City Mission and Tract Society. *Annual Report, 1888, 1890, 1896.* New York, 1889, 1891, 1897.

New York City Police Department. *Annual Report, 1870–1872, 1885–1905.* New York, 1871–1872, 1886–1906.

New York Colored Mission. *Annual Report, 1871–1920.* New York, 1872–1920.

New York Free Kindergarten Association. *Annual Report, 1899–1900.* New York, 1900.

New York Legislature, Joint Committee Investigating Seditious Activities. *Revolutionary Radicalism: Its History, Purpose and Tactics.* 4 vols. Albany, 1920.

New York State Census of 1875. Albany, 1877.

New York State Cleveland League. *Proceedings of the Convention of 1892.* Brooklyn, 1892.

Papers from the Records of the New York City Mission and Tract Society. New York, 1866.

Proceedings and Debates of the Constitutional Convention of the State of New York, 1867–1868. 5 vols. Albany, 1868.

Republican Greeting to 25,000 Free and Loyal Colored Voters of the State of New York, 1887–1888. Albany, 1888.

St. Philip's Parish House. *Annual Report, 1887–1890.* New York, 1888, 1890.

Siloam Presbyterian Church. *Semi-Centennial, May 21 to July 25, 1899.* Brooklyn, 1899.

Society of the Sons of New York. *Second Annual Report, 1886.* New York, 1887.

United States Census. *Eighth Census, 1860, Population*. Washington, 1864.
———. *Ninth Census, 1870, Statistics of the Population of the United States*. Washington, 1874.
———. *Tenth Census, 1880, Population*. Washington, 1883.
———. *Eleventh Census, 1890, Population*. Washington, 1895.
———. *Eleventh Census, 1890, Vital Statistics of New York City and Brooklyn*. Washington, 1894.
———. *Twelfth Census, 1900, Population*. Washington, 1901.
———. *Twelfth Census, 1900, Special Report of Occupations*. Washington, 1904.
———. *Thirteenth Census, 1910, Population*. Washington, 1914.
———. *Fourteenth Census, 1920, New York*. Washington, 1922.
———. *Fourteenth Census, 1920, Population*. Washington, 1922.
———. *Eighteenth Census, 1960, Population of New York, Detailed Characteristics*. Washington, 1961.
United States Department of Labor, Division of Negro Economics. *Negro Migration in 1916–17*. Washington, 1919.
———. *The Negro at Work During the World War and During Reconstruction*. Washington, 1921.
United States Department of Labor, Women's Bureau. *Negro Women in Industry*. Washington, 1920.
White Rose Industrial Association. *Annual Report, 1911*. New York, 1912.

NEWSPAPERS AND PERIODICALS
Brooklyn *Eagle*. 1880–1920.
Charities. 1899–1909.
Colored American Magazine. 1900–1910.
Colored American Review. 1915–1916.
Crisis. 1910–1921.
Crusader. 1921.
Milestones. 1893–1898, 1903–1910.
New York Age. 1887–1892, 1905–1920.
New York Freeman. 1884–1887.
New York Globe. 1883–1884.
New York *Post*. 1880–1920.
New York *Suffragist*. 1880.
New York *Sun*. 1870–1920.

New York Times. 1865–1920.
New York Tribune. 1865–1920.
New York *Weekly Anglo African.* 1865.
New York *World.* 1880–1920.
Survey. 1909–1920.

AUTOBIOGRAPHIES AND MEMOIRS

Du Bois, W. E. B. *Dusk of Dawn.* New York, 1940.

Johnson, James Weldon. *Along This Way.* New York, 1933.

Ovington, Mary White. *The Walls Came Tumbling Down.* New York, 1947.

Powell, A. Clayton, Sr. *Against the Tide: An Autobiography.* New York, 1938.

Ransom, Reverdy C. *The Pilgrimage of Harriet Ransom's Son.* Nashville, 1949.

Steffens, Lincoln. *Autobiography.* New York, 1931.

Walters, Alexander. *My Life and Work.* New York, 1917.

Williamson, Harry A. "Folks in Old New York and Brooklyn." Unpublished paper, Schomburg Collection, 1953.

TRAVEL ACCOUNTS

Archer, William. *Through Afro-America: An English Reading of the Race Problem.* London, 1910.

Berry, C. B. *The Other Side: How it Struck Us.* New York, 1880.

Campbell, Sir George. *White and Black: the Outcome of a Visit to the United States.* London, 1879.

Ferguson, Fergus. *From Glasgow to Missouri and Back.* Glasgow, 1879.

Johnston, Sir Harry H. *The Negro in the World.* London, 1910.

Kirkwood, John. *An Autumn Holiday in the United States and Canada.* Edinburgh, 1887.

Macauley, James. "First Impressions of America and Its People," *The Leisure Hour,* XX (1871), 206.

Money, Edward. *The Truth About America.* London, 1886.

[Rivington, ———— and ———— Harris] [pseud., Two Englishmen]. *Reminiscences of America in 1869.* London, 1870.

Rose, George. *The Great Country; or, Impressions of America.* London, 1868.

Sala, George Augustus. *America Revisited: From the Bay of New York . . . to the Pacific.* 2 vols. London, 1883.

OTHER PUBLISHED PRIMARY SOURCES

Abyssinian Baptist Church. *The Ninety-Fourth Anniversary.* New York, 1902.

Allen, Cleveland G. "Work of the Y.M.C.A. of New York City," *Colored American Magazine,* XIV (May, 1908), 272–77.

Baker, Ray Stannard. "The Negro's Struggle for Survival in the North," *American Magazine,* LXV (March, 1908), 473–85.

Belson, Frederick. *Considerations in the Interests of the Colored People.* Brooklyn, 1868.

Blascoer, Frances. *Colored School Children in New York.* New York, 1915.

Brown, John Smith, Jr. "The New York Branch of the Y.M.C.A.," *Colored American Magazine,* VII (June, 1904), 409–14.

Bulkley, William L. "The Industrial Condition of the Negro in New York City," *Annals of the American Academy of Political and Social Science,* XXVII (June, 1906), 590–96.

———. "The School as a Social Center," *Charities,* XV (October 7, 1905), 76–77.

Carnegie, Andrew. *Gospel of Wealth and Other Timely Essays.* New York, 1901.

Citizens' Protective League. *Story of the Riot.* New York, 1900.

City and Suburban Homes Company. *Negro Housing: A Sound Economic Plan to Solve a Social Problem of the Greatest Importance to Every Citizen.* New York, 1916.

Clarke, James B. "The Negro and the Immigrant in the Two Americas," *Annals of the American Academy of Political and Social Science,* XLIX (September, 1913), 32–37.

Collins, G. L. "The City Within the City," *Outlook,* LXXXIV (September 29, 1906), 274–79.

Cranston, Mary Rankin. "The Housing of the Negro in New York City," *Southern Workman,* XXXI (June, 1902), 327–32.

Daly, Victor R. "The Housing Crisis in New York City," *Crisis,* XXI (December, 1920), 61–62.

Domingo, W. A. "The Tropics in New York," *Survey Graphic,* LIII (March 1, 1925), 648–50.

Du Bois, W. E. B. "The Black Man in the Revolution of 1914–1918," *Crisis,* XVII (March, 1919), 218–23.

Du Bois, W. E. B., ed. *The Negro in Business.* Atlanta, 1899.

———. *The Souls of Black Folk.* 12th ed. Chicago, 1935.

Durham, John Stephens. "The Labor Unions and the Negro," *Atlantic Monthly*, LXXXI (February, 1898), 222–31.

Dyckoff, E. F. "A Negro City in New York," *Outlook*, CVIII (December 23, 1914), 949–54.

Emerson, Edwin, Jr. "The Negro Ghetto," *Harper's Weekly*, XLI (January 9, 1897), 44.

Emerson, Helena Titus. "Children of the Circle: the Work of the New York Free Kindergarten Association for Colored Children," *Charities*, XV (October 7, 1905), 81–83.

Federation of Churches and Christian Organizations in New York City. *The Redemption of Our City*. New York, 1902.

Fortune, T. Thomas. "The Afro-American League," *A.M.E. Church Review*, VII (July, 1890), 2–6.

———. *Black and White: Land, Labor, and Politics in the South.* New York, 1884.

———. "The Democratic Return to Power," *A.M.E. Church Review*, I (January, 1885), 219–21.

———. *The Negro in Politics*. New York, 1886.

———. "The Republican Party Platform," *A.M.E. Church Review*, IX (October, 1892), 126–32.

———. "What Should Be the Negro's Attitude in Politics?" pp. 227–31 in *Twentieth Century Negro Literature*, ed. D. W. Culp. Philadelphia, 1902.

———. "Will the Afro-American Return to Africa?" *A.M.E. Church Review*, VIII (April, 1892), 389.

Frank, Glenn. "The Clash of Color: the Negro in American Democracy," *The Century*, XCIX (November, 1919), 86–92.

Fulton, David Bryant [pseud., Jack Thorne]. *Eagle Clippings*. Brooklyn, 1907.

Griffin, Maude K. "The Hope Day Nursery," *Colored American Magazine*, X (June, 1906), 397–400.

———. "The Negro Church and Its Social Work — St. Mark's," *Charities*, XV (October 7, 1905), 75–76.

Haley, James T., ed. *Afro-American Encyclopaedia; or, the Thoughts, Doings, and Sayings of the Race*. Nashville, 1896.

Hamlin, R. P. "Work of the Y.M.C.A. Among the Young Colored Men of Brooklyn, N.Y.," *Colored American Magazine*, XIV (June, 1908), 337–39.

Hartt, Rollin Lynde. "I'd Like to Show You Harlem," *Independent*, CV (April 2, 1921), 334–35, 357–58.

————. "The Negro Moses and His Campaign to Lead the Black Millions into Their Promised Land," *Independent*, CV (February 26, 1921), 205–206, 218–19.

Haynes, George E. "Conditions Among Negroes in the Cities," *Annals of the American Academy of Political and Social Science*, XLIX (September, 1913), 105–19.

————. "The Negro at Work: A Development of the War and a Problem of Reconstruction," *Review of Reviews*, LIX (August, 1919), 389–93.

————. "Negroes Move North: Their Departure from the South," *Survey*, XL (May 4, 1918), 115–22.

————. "Negroes Move North: Their Arrival in the North," *Survey*, XLI (January 4, 1919), 455–61.

Johnson, Fenton. "Harlem By Day and Night," *Favorite Magazine*, IV (July, 1920), 363–64.

Johnson, James Weldon. "The Making of Harlem," *Survey Graphic*, LIII (March 1, 1925), 635–39.

Kellor, Frances A. "Assisted Emigration from the South: the Women," *Charities*, XV (October 7, 1905), 11–14.

————. *Out of Work: A Study of Unemployment*. rev. ed. New York, 1915.

Kelsey, Carl. "Some Causes of Negro Emigration: the Men," *Charities*, XV (October 7, 1905), 15–17.

Locke, Alain, ed. *The New Negro: An Interpretation*. New York, 1925.

Martin, Charles. "The Harlem Negro," *A.M.E. Zion Quarterly Review*, XXVI (Fourth Quarter, 1916), 1–8.

Miller, Kelly. "The Harvest of Race Prejudice," *Survey Graphic*, LIII (March 1, 1925), 711–12.

"Mission Sketches," *Charities*, XV (October 7, 1905), 59–63.

Mitchel, John Puroy. "The Public Schools of New York," *Crisis*, XIV (July, 1917), 132.

Moton, Robert R. *What the Negro Thinks*. Garden City, N.Y., 1929.

National League on Urban Conditions Among Negroes. "Housing Conditions Among Negroes in Harlem, New York City," *Bulletin*, IV (January, 1915).

————. "Social Service Fellowships for 1917–1918," *Bulletin*, VI (October, 1916).

————. *What you need, Where to find it, How to use what you find.* New York, 1916.

"The Negro in the Cities of the North," *Charities*, XV (October 7, 1905), 1–96.

"The Negro Migration," *New Republic*, VII (July 1, 1916), 213–14.

New York Urban League. "Twenty-Four Hundred Negro Families in Harlem." Unpublished paper, Schomburg Collection, 1927.

Ovington, Mary White. "Fresh Air Work Among Colored Children in New York," *Charities*, XVII (February, 1906), 115–17.

————. "The Gunpowder of Race Antagonism," *American City*, XXI (September, 1919), 248–51.

————. *Half A Man: the Status of the Negro in New York.* New York, 1911.

————. "The Negro Home in New York," *Charities*, XV (October 7, 1905), 25–30.

————. "The Negro in the Trade Unions in New York," *Annals of the American Academy of Political and Social Science*, XXVII (June, 1906), 551–58.

————. "Vacation Days on San Juan Hill — A New York Negro Colony," *Southern Workman*, XXXVIII (November, 1909), 627–34.

————. "The White Brute," *Masses*, V (November, 1915), 17–18.

Parkhurst, Charles H. *Our Fight With Tammany.* New York, 1895.

Phillips, David Graham. "A Walk on Seventh Avenue," *Harper's Weekly*, XXXV (June 20, 1891), 465–66.

Rhodes, E. M. "The Protection of Girls Who Travel: A National Movement," *Colored American Magazine*, XIII (August, 1907), 114–15.

Riis, Jacob A. *A Ten Years' War: An Account of the Battle with the Slum in New York.* New York, 1900.

————. *How the Other Half Lives: Studies Among the Tenements of New York.* New York, 1890.

————. *The Children of the Poor.* New York, 1892.

"St. Mark's Methodist Episcopal Church," *Colored American Magazine*, X (June, 1906), 381–85.

Schapiro, J. Salwyn. "Henry Moskowitz: A Social Reformer in Politics," *Outlook*, CII (October 26, 1912), 446–49.

Scott, Emmett, ed. "Letters of Negro Migrants of 1916–1918," *Journal of Negro History*, IV (July, 1919), 290–340 and (October, 1919), 412–65.

Scottron, Samuel R. "The Industrial and Professional Pursuits of the Colored People of Old New York," *Colored American Magazine*, XIII (October, 1907), 264–67.

"Seven Years of Social Exploration," *Federation*, III (June, 1903), 1–24.

Simmons, Roscoe Conkling. "The Afro-American Realty Company," *Colored American Magazine*, VIII (May, 1905), 264–76.

Speed, J. Gilmer. "The Negro in New York," *Harper's Weekly*, XLIV (December 22, 1900), 1249–50.

Stewart, T. McCants. *The Afro-American in Politics: an Address at a Meeting of Colored Citizens Ratifying the Democratic Ticket, at Everett Hall, October 27, 1891*. Brooklyn, 1891.

"The Superfluous Negro," *New Republic*, VII (June 24, 1916), 187–88.

Tammany Hall vs. Fusion, or Organized Democracy Against Disorganized Aristocracy and Bastard Reform. New York, 1913.

"Troubles of a Black Policeman," *Literary Digest*, XLIV (January 27, 1912), 177–79.

Tucker, Helen A. "Negro Craftsmen in New York," *Southern Workman*, XXXVI (October, 1907), 545–51 and XXXVII (March, 1908), 139–44.

Walling, William English. "The Founding of the NAACP," *Crisis*, XXXVI (July, 1929), 226.

Waring, J. H. N. "Some Causes of Criminality Among Colored People," *Charities*, XV (October 7, 1905), 45–49.

Washington, Booker T. "The Negro and the Labor Unions," *Atlantic Monthly*, CXI (June, 1913), 763.

———. *The Negro in Business*. Boston, 1907.

Wibecau, George E. "New York Negro Clubs," *Souvenir Program of the National Negro Exposition* (July 22, 1915), unpaged.

"Work of the Committee for Improving the Industrial Conditions of Negroes in New York," *Colored American Magazine*, XII (June, 1907), 459–64.

Wright, R. R., Jr. "The Migration of Negroes to the North," *Annals of the American Academy of Political and Social Science*, XXVII (June, 1906), 562–65.

———. "The Negro in Unskilled Labor," *Annals of the American Academy of Political and Social Science,* XLIX (September, 1913), 19–27.

———. "Social Work and the Influence of the Negro Church," *Annals of the American Academy of Political and Social Science,* XXX (November, 1907), 509–21.

SECONDARY SOURCES

Abell, Aaron I. *American Catholicism and Social Action: A Search for Social Justice, 1865–1950.* New York, 1960.

———. *The Urban Impact on American Protestantism, 1865–1900.* Cambridge, 1943.

Andrews, Charles C. *History of the New York African Free School.* New York, 1830.

Bardolph, Richard. *The Negro Vanguard.* Vintage ed. New York, 1961.

Barnes, Charles B. *The Longshoremen.* New York, 1915.

Beard, Charles A. and Mary R. *The Rise of American Civilization.* 2 vols. New York, 1933.

Bloch, Herman D. "Craft Unions and the Negro in Historical Perspective," *Journal of Negro History,* XLIII (January, 1958), 10–33.

———. "The New York City Negro and Occupational Eviction, 1860–1910," *International Review of Social History,* V (Part 1, 1960), 26–38.

Blumenthal, Henry. "Woodrow Wilson and the Race Question," *Journal of Negro History,* XLVIII (January, 1963), 1–21.

Bragg, George F. *History of the Afro-American Group of the Episcopal Church.* Baltimore, 1922.

Bremner, Robert H. *From the Depths: the Discovery of Poverty in the United States.* New York, 1956.

Bunche, Ralph. "The Political Status of the Negro." Unpublished manuscript prepared for the Carnegie-Myrdal Study of the Negro in America, 7 vols., Schomburg Collection, 1940.

Butcher, Margaret Just. *The Negro in American Culture.* New York, 1956.

Carman, Harry J. *The Street Surface Railway Franchises of New York City.* New York, 1919.

Cronon, Edmund D. *Black Moses: the Story of Marcus Garvey*

and the Universal Negro Improvement Association. Madison, 1957.

Crouthamel, James L. "The Springfield Race Riot of 1908," *Journal of Negro History,* XLV (July, 1960), 164–81.

Degler, Cary N. *Out of Our Past: the Forces That Shaped Modern America.* New York, 1959.

DeSantis, Vincent P. *Republicans Face the Southern Question.* Baltimore, 1959.

———. "The Republican Party and the Southern Negro, 1877–1897," *Journal of Negro History,* XLV (April, 1960), 81–86.

Detweiler, Frederick G. *The Negro Press in the United States.* Chicago, 1922.

Dictionary of American Biography. 22 vols. New York, 1928–58.

Donald, Henderson. "The Negro Migration, 1916–1918," *Journal of Negro History,* VI (October, 1921), 383–498.

Du Bois, W. E. B. *Some Notes on the Negroes in New York City.* Atlanta, 1903.

Eaton, Clement. *The Growth of Southern Civilization.* New York, 1961.

Ernst, Robert. "The Economic Status of New York City Negroes, 1850–1863," *Negro History Bulletin,* XII (March, 1949), 131–32, 139–43.

———. *Immigrant Life in New York City, 1825–1863.* New York, 1949.

Essien-Udom, E. U. *Black Nationalism: A Search for an Identity in America.* Chicago, 1962.

Faulkner, Harold U. *The Decline of Laissez Faire, 1898–1917.* New York, 1951.

Fishel, Leslie H. "The Negro in Northern Politics, 1870–1900," *Mississippi Valley Historical Review,* XLII (December, 1955), 466–89.

———. "Northern Prejudice and Negro Suffrage, 1865–1870," *Journal of Negro History,* XXXIX (January, 1954), 8–27.

Fox, Dixon Ryan. "The Negro Vote in Old New York," *Political Science Quarterly,* XXXII (June, 1917), 252–69.

Franklin, Charles L. *The Negro Labor Unionist of New York: Problems and Conditions among Negroes in the Labor Unions in Manhattan with Special Reference to the N.R.A. and Post-N.R.A. Situations.* New York, 1936.

Franklin, John Hope. *From Slavery to Freedom: A History of American Negroes.* rev. ed. New York, 1960.

Frazier, E. Franklin. *Black Bourgeoisie.* Glencoe, Ill., 1957.

————. *The Negro Family in the United States.* Chicago, 1939.

————. *The Negro in the United States.* rev. ed. New York, 1957.

From Cherry Street to Green Pastures: a History of the Colored Orphan Asylum at Riverdale-On-Hudson. New York, 1936.

Garrett, Charles. *The La Guardia Years: Machine and Reform Politics in New York City.* New Brunswick, 1961.

Gibson, Florence E. *The Attitudes of the New York Irish Toward State and National Affairs, 1848–1892.* New York, 1951.

Gordon, Eugene. "The Negro Press," *Annals of the American Academy of Political and Social Science,* CLX (November, 1928), 248–56.

Greater New York Federation of Churches. *The Negro Churches of Manhattan.* New York, 1930.

Handlin, Oscar. *The Newcomers: Negroes and Puerto Ricans in a Changing Metropolis.* Cambridge, 1959.

Haynes, George E. *The Negro at Work in New York: a Study in Economic Progress.* New York, 1912.

Herskovits, Melville. *The Myth of the Negro Past.* New York, 1941.

Higham, John. "Anti-Semitism in the Gilded Age: A Reinterpretation," *Mississippi Valley Historical Review,* XLIII (March, 1957), 559–78.

Hirsch, Leo H., Jr. "The Negro and New York, 1783 to 1865," *Journal of Negro History,* XVI (October, 1931), 382–473.

Hirshon, Stanley P. *Farewell to the Bloody Shirt.* Bloomington, Ind., 1962.

Hofstadter, Richard. *The Age of Reform: From Bryan to F. D. R.* New York, 1955.

Johnson, Charles S. *The Negro in American Civilization: a Study of Negro Life and Race Relations in the Light of Social Research.* New York, 1930.

Johnson, James Weldon. *Black Manhattan.* New York, 1930.

Kennedy, Louise P. *The Negro Peasant Turns Cityward.* New York, 1930.

Kerlin, Robert T. *The Voice of the Negro, 1919.* New York, 1920.

Kessler, Sidney H. "The Organization of Negroes in the Knights of Labor," *Journal of Negro History*, XXXVII (July, 1952), 248–76.

Lincoln, C. Eric. *The Black Muslims in America*. New York, 1961.

Lindsay, Arnett G. "The Economic Condition of the Negroes of New York Prior to 1861," *Journal of Negro History*, VI (April, 1921), 190–99.

Link, Arthur S., ed. "Correspondence Relating to the Progressive Party's 'Lily White' Policy in 1912," *Journal of Southern History*, X (November, 1944), 480–90.

Link, Arthur S. "The Negro as a Factor in the Campaign of 1912," *Journal of Negro History*, XXXII (January, 1947), 81–99.

——. "Theodore Roosevelt and the South in 1912," *North Carolina Historical Review*, XXIII (July, 1946), 313–24.

——. *Wilson: the New Freedom*. Princeton, 1956.

——. *Wilson: the Road to the White House*. Princeton, 1947.

Litwack, Leon F. *North of Slavery: the Negro in the Free States, 1790–1860*. Chicago, 1961.

Locke, Alain. "The Negro's Contribution to American Art and Literature," *Annals of the American Academy of Political and Social Science*, CXL (November, 1928), 234–47.

Logan, Rayford W. *The Negro in American Life and Thought: the Nadir, 1877–1901*. New York, 1954.

Lubove, Roy. *The Progressives and the Slums: Tenement House Reform in New York City, 1890–1917*. Pittsburgh, 1962.

McKay, Claude. *Harlem: Negro Metropolis*. New York, 1940.

Man, Albon P. "Labor Competition and the New York Draft Riots," *Journal of Negro History*, XXXVI (October, 1951), 375–405.

Mandel, Bernard. "Samuel Gompers and the Negro Workers, 1886–1914," *Journal of Negro History*, XL (January, 1955), 34–60.

May, Henry F. *Protestant Churches and Industrial America*. New York, 1949.

Mays, Benjamin E. and Joseph W. Nicholson. *The Negro's Church*. New York, 1933.

Meier, August. "The Negro and the Democratic Party, 1875–1915," *Phylon*, XVII (2d Quarter, 1956), 173–91.

——. *Negro Thought in America, 1880–1915: Racial Ideologies in the Age of Booker T. Washington*. Ann Arbor, 1963.

Morris, John T. "The History and Development of Negro Journalism," *A.M.E. Church Review*, VI (January, 1890), 313.

Mowry, George E. *The Era of Theodore Roosevelt, 1900–1912.* New York, 1958.

——. "The South and the Progressive 'Lily White' Party of 1912," *Journal of Southern History*, VI (May, 1940), 237–47.

Murphy, Paul L. "Sources and Nature of Intolerance in the 1920's," *Journal of American History*, LI (June, 1964), 60–76.

Myrdal, Gunnar. *An American Dilemma: the Negro Problem and Modern Democracy.* 20th anniversary ed. New York, 1962.

National Cyclopedia of American Biography. 54 vols. New York, 1891–1959.

Northrup, Herbert R. *Organized Labor and the Negro.* New York, 1944.

Olson, Edwin. "Negro Slavery in New York, 1626–1827." Unpublished Ph.D. dissertation, New York University, 1938.

Ovington, Mary White. "The National Association for the Advancement of Colored People," *Journal of Negro History*, IX (April, 1924), 107–16.

Palmer, E. Nelson. "A Note on the Development of Negro Lodges in the United States." Unpublished manuscript prepared for the Carnegie-Myrdal Study of the Negro in America, Schomburg Collection, 1940.

Payne, Aaron H. "The Negro in New York Prior to 1860," *Howard Review*, I (June, 1923), 1–64.

Pride, Armistead. "A Register and History of Negro Newspapers in the United States, 1827–1950." Unpublished Ph.D. dissertation, Northwestern University, 1951.

Richardson, Clement, ed. *National Cyclopedia of the Colored Race.* Montgomery, 1917.

Rischin, Moses. *The Promised City: New York's Jews, 1870–1914.* Cambridge, 1963.

Rudwick, Elliott M. "The Niagara Movement," *Journal of Negro History*, XLII (July, 1957), 177–91.

Scheiner, Seth M. "Early Career of T. Thomas Fortune, 1879–1890," *Negro History Bulletin*, XXVII (April, 1964), 170–72.

——. "President Theodore Roosevelt and the Negro, 1901–1908," *Journal of Negro History*, XLVII (July, 1962), 169–82.

Schlesinger, Arthur M. *The Rise of the City.* New York, 1933.

Scott, Emmett J. *Negro Migration During the War*. New York, 1920.

Silberman, Charles E. *Crisis in Black and White*. New York, 1964.

Spencer, Samuel R., Jr. *Booker T. Washington and the Negro's Place in America*. Boston, 1955.

Spero, Sterling D. and Abram I. Harris. *The Black Worker: the Negro and the Labor Movement*. New York, 1931.

Stephenson, Gilbert T. *Race Distinctions in American Law*. New York, 1910.

Thornbrough, Emma Lou. "The Brownsville Episode and the Negro Vote," *Mississippi Valley Historical Review*, XLIV (December, 1957), 469–93.

———. "More Light on Booker T. Washington and the *New York Age*," *Journal of Negro History*, XLIII (January, 1958), 34–49.

———. "The National Afro-American League, 1887–1908," *Journal of Southern History*, XXVII (November, 1961), 494–512.

Tinsley, James A. "Roosevelt, Foraker, and the Brownsville Affray," *Journal of Negro History*, XLI (January, 1956), 43–65.

Van Deusen, John G. "Exodus of 1879," *Journal of Negro History*, XXI (April, 1936), 111–29.

Weaver, Robert C. *The Negro Ghetto*. New York, 1948.

Wesley, Charles H. *Negro Labor in the United States, 1850–1925: a Study in American Economic History*. New York, 1927.

———. "The Negroes of New York in the Emancipation Movement," *Journal of Negro History*, XXIV (January, 1939), 65–103.

———. "Negro Suffrage in the Period of Constitution-Making, 1787–1865," *Journal of Negro History*, XXXII (April, 1947), 143–68.

Who's Who in Colored America. 6 vols. Yonkers, 1927–1950.

Wilson, James Q. *Negro Politics: the Search for Leadership*. Glencoe, Ill., 1960.

Wolgemuth, Kathleen L. "Woodrow Wilson's Appointment Policy and the Negro," *Journal of Southern History*, XXIV (November, 1958), 457–71.

———. "Woodrow Wilson and Federal Segregation," *Journal of Negro History*, XLIV (April, 1959), 158–73.

Woodson, Carter G. *A Century of Negro Migration*. Washington, 1918.

————. *The History of the Negro Church.* 2d ed. Washington, 1921.

Woodward, C. Vann. *The Burden of Southern History.* Vintage ed. New York, 1961.

Woofter, Thomas J. *Negro Problems in Cities.* Garden City, N.Y., 1928.

Index